INTERNATIONAL PUBLISHERS
381 Park Avenue South NEW YORK, N. Y. 10016

The Education of John Reed
Selected Writings

The Education of John Reed

Selected Writings

With an Introductory Essay
by John Stuart

International Publishers
New York

First published by International Publishers, New York, 1955.
This edition is published simultaneously by
International Publishers, New York and
Seven Seas Publishers, Berlin, 1972
ISBN 0-7178-0354-6

CONTENTS

EDITOR'S NOTE

During the ten years between his graduation from Harvard and his untimely death in 1920, John Reed wrote enough to fill several volumes the size of this one. The bulk of his writing expressed his hatred of war and the evils out of which war grew. At the same time what he had to say reflected his profound desire for a future of peace and for a social order in which peace could thrive.

It is these things which have guided the choice of materials for this volume. The selections are representative of Reed's literary output as a reporter, a war correspondent, essayist, and poet. As a journalist, he was with Pancho Villa in Mexico, with striking workers in the United States, on the front lines in Europe during World War I, and in Russia during the revolution. Except for the poetry, grouped separately, the arrangement of selections is more or less chronological, with the year of publication appended. Because *Ten Days That Shook the World* continues in print and is still widely read, only a brief selection from this best known of Reed's works has been included here.

John Stuart's introductory essay on Reed's development and the meaning of his life gives the necessary background for the selections that follow.

INTRODUCTION

The Education of John Reed
By John Stuart

John Reed's life writes itself. Few men who have lived so earnestly, so joyously, and whose eyes consumed so much of the stuff of history, have left a more complete record of themselves. Yet it is not his books that tell his whole story nor his letters and verse. They are there. The poems are facets of his personality; each letter the key to a mood or an incident; each of the articles an incisive impression of what he saw at the moment he saw it and a graph of his opinion as well. They will not, however, delineate the full man. They will not tell why years after his death in 1920 he is etched on the American progressive consciousness, or how he became a spokesman for a new concept of society, a symbol of the writer fused with the man of action, an observer of history and a maker of it.

There are values by which John Reed's life can be assessed. There is the literary value. He was a poet and a great journalist with perhaps no peer among American reporters at the time he wrote. There is the character value. He could not be shattered by the most savage pressures of reaction. Throughout his very brief adult life he was in unceasing rebellion against the unjust. It was not a blind, private rebellion in which the rebel is more often crushed than crushing. He started that way, but he learned that only in solidarity with others could his own strength reach its greatest effectiveness and serve him as the vehicle for his deepest hopes. Reed found his way to the working class and in that hard journey he freed himself of the pestilence of lies and the cruel illusions which have made the same road so perilous for others of his milieu. In shaking hands with the future he accepted

9

the need for fundamental change, for socialism. It was the logic of his experience as an American, the turbulence of his years, that made him a militant crusader for a new society.

John Reed was born in his grandparents' house in Portland, Oregon, on October 20, 1887. It was, he remembered, a lordly mansion modeled on a French chateau, set in a park, with gardens and lawns and tame deer among the trees. His grandfather, Henry Green, had come west in a sailing ship and settled finally in Portland when it was a few years old, a town cut out of the Oregon wilderness. He made his money there and lived lavishly. The Greens were thus among the elite of the community, with the ease and gaiety of people sure of their position and the privileges that came with wealth.

Charles Reed, on the other hand, while he never made the fortune that for a time distinguished his in-laws, was an enterprising business man who had migrated from upstate New York to sell farm equipment and married Margaret Green not long after he was established in Portland.

For Jack and his younger brother it was a boyhood of comfort. It was filled with the imaginative, romantic wandering of a child who loved fantasy, invented witches, giants, and monsters with which he terrified the small boys and girls of the neighborhood and incidentally himself. His mother taught him to read and then he plunged into an orgy of books—everything he could get hold of from Edwin Arnold's *Light of Asia* and Marie Corelli, to Scott, Stevenson, and Sir Thomas Malory. "History," he recalled, "was my passion, kings strutting about and the armored ranks of men-at-arms clashing forward in close ranks against a hail of cloth-yard shafts; but I was equally enamored of Mark Twain, and Bill Nye, and Blackmore's *Lorna Doone*, and Webster's Unabridged Dictionary, and *The Arabian Nights*, and the *Tales of the Round Table*. What I didn't understand, my imagination interpreted. At the age of nine I began to write a Comic History of the

United States—after Bill Nye—and I think it was then that I made up my mind to be a writer."*

He was indifferent toward his schoolwork except when some teacher or subject stirred him and sent him soaring into his private world of Guineveres and Galahads. Moreover, there was too much to do on the outside. The Reed boys had a theater in the attic of their house where they acted their own plays. They built scenic railways in the yard, and log cabins in the woods back of the town, and went on camping trips up the Willamette River. Jack also had a number of schemes for getting adventure and wealth at the same time. He once began to dig a tunnel from his house to school about a mile away. He was going to steal two sheep and hide them in the tunnel, and these two sheep were going to multiply until a large flock had gathered. Then he'd sell them.

"But with all this," he wrote years later, "I wasn't entirely happy. I was often ill. Outside of a few friends, I wasn't a success with the boys. I hadn't strength or fight enough to be good at athletics—except swimming which I have always loved; and I was a good deal of a physical coward. I would sneak out over the back fence to avoid boys who were 'laying' for me, or who I thought were 'laying' for me ... The strange thing was that when I was cornered, and fought, even a licking wasn't a hundredth as bad as I thought it would be."

Between father and son there was a warm and steady affection. The elder Reed was a man of caustic wit, with a fine scorn of the local stuffed shirts, and a political maverick whose beliefs mirrored the newer social consciousness which a host of reformers helped to ripen in the middle class at the turn of the century. As a United States marshal appointed by Theodore Roosevelt, he helped smash the Oregon land fraud ring and later he ran for Congress but lost by a slim margin.

The young son admired his father's fighting qualities, while

* From Reed's autobiographical essay "Almost Thirty" first published in the *New Republic*, April 15 and 29, 1936.

brooding over the fact that he did not completely emulate him in his own relations with the town bullies. Not until after his father died did Reed appreciate how he "poured out his life that we might live like rich men's sons. He and mother always gave us more than we asked, in freedom and understanding as well as material things. And on the day my brother graduated from college, he broke under the terrible effort, and died a few weeks later. It has always seemed to me a bitter irony that he could not have lived to see my little success."

It was at a fashionable preparatory school in Morristown, New Jersey, that Jack began to blossom. He was in fine health and was accepted by the other boys at his own worth. He was impressed by the school's orderly life, by its customs and traditions which he considered so different from what he knew in the raw west. He played football, had a fight or two and stuck it out, and wrote poetry and stories for the school paper. And then there were the perilous adventures of stealing out of school at night to country dances and fussing with the girls and winging his way among the social butterflies. Without trying too hard, he became more self-confident.

In 1906, he entered Harvard. He was desperately lonely during his first year. Despite his sweat to make the freshman crew and win recognition, he felt out of things. Later his loneliness began to disappear. He was elected an editor of two of the college papers, became manager of the musical clubs, captain of the water polo team, and an officer in several undergraduate activities. As song leader of the cheering section, he had what he described as the "supreme blissful sensation of swaying two thousand voices in great crashing choruses during the big football games."

Harvard also found him boisterous and full of pranks, ambitious of place and power. He had a longing to achieve status through his writing. What he wrote for the *Lampoon* and the *Monthly* was not too outstanding among the innumerable things Harvard undergraduates have published. While his verse showed a natural poetic gift, it did not reveal anything original or trenchant. He spent his youthful talent in imitating the successful Victorians. But what he wrote was important to Reed. It is also an index to some of the bitterness he felt toward the Harvard aristocrats. He too was an aristocrat —but from the Oregon hinterland. The Harvard upper gentry appraised him as too much the eager beaver, a little too unconventional to meet the rigid standards of the Back Bay Brahmins. In turn, he was repelled by their cold, cruel stupidity, and the narrowness of their gaudy lives. With his resentment running deep, Jack satirized them in poems and in editorials and poked fun at their foibles.

Reed strongly sensed the rebel tradition in the Harvard community and saw it come to life in his senior year when the students swept the aristocrats from their undergraduate positions. Students criticized the faculty for not educating them, attacked the athletic institutions, and sneered at the sacred private clubs. To Reed this was an insurgency in perfect keeping with the heresy of New England history. What also affected him was what he called "the manifestation of the modern spirit" among a group of students. In a blurred but articulate way the modernists recognized the cleavages that ramified their community. They read and talked about politics and economics as living forces acting on the world, and a few of them formed the Socialist Club with Walter Lippmann as president.

Reed never joined the club, yet he was impressed by what it did and by the freshness and boldness of its members' thinking. The Socialist Club took part in the city elections. It introduced measures into the Massachusetts legislature, blasted the university for not paying its workers a living wage. The faculty was asked for a course in socialism, and prominent radicals were invited to Cambridge to discuss and debate issues of the day. And out of this agitation sprang campus groups such as the Harvard Men's League for Women's Suffrage and a Single Tax Club—an alert undergraduate movement which pierced the college press and pushed forward the radicals in music, painting, poetry, and the theater.

In retrospect after Harvard, Reed saw that "all this made no ostensible difference in the look of Harvard society, and probably the clubmen and the athletes, who represented us to the world, never heard of it. But it made me, and many others, realize there was something going on in the dull outside world more thrilling than college activities, and turned our attention to the writings of men like H. G. Wells and Graham Wallas, wrenching us away from the Oscar Wildean dilettantism that had possessed undergraduate litterateurs for generations."

Reed's sympathies thus began to include the victims of snobbery beyond those in his own sheltered group. As president of the university's Cosmopolitan Club, his contact with students from many nations enlarged his view of the world just as his attraction to the local rebels sharpened his intellectual perception. In thinking of his future he could not, however, make up his mind where exactly he stood in his relations with the rebels and the aristocrats. His drive was in the direction of the serious and he found a comfortable bond between himself and the insurgents. Yet the rewards that went with social position at Cambridge were too tempting and too useful to be tossed away. He hungered for recognition from all sides. In its quest he spilled his boundless energy into college offices, into literary work, athletics—the horseplay that made him different superficially but could not hide his desire to cut his life according to the patterns of his upper class milieu. In his own way, he was re-enacting the conflict in the lives of young, sensitive Americans who needed the kudos of the top crust to make their mark in the world, while their instincts revolted against the cost of its favors. This duality hung onto Reed for some time after he was graduated from Harvard in 1910.

Reed and his generation, of which the Harvard radicals were the academic fragments, grew up in a time of disenchantment. The discovery of corruption, the dissipation of myths that flourished during the seemingly rapturous decades of American development, the disillusionment with doctrines which in the past appeared unassailable brought forth a strong movement of reform and protest.

On its level, the Harvard Socialist Club was one reply to an age in which the lords of the trusts were setting their sights for new areas of conquest abroad. The arrival of a full-blown imperialism had already been announced by the roaring cannon of Manila Bay. The drift to empire was quickly visible in territorial aggrandizement, in the control of other sovereignties by financial manipulation or by direct intervention. For all their pious twaddle the imperialists could not completely hide their ruthlessness, their utter disregard of all morality. The cult of brutal chauvinism infected the press, the pulpits, the classrooms, and fathered all the myths by which a moneyed minority protects itself. The Reverend Josiah Strong preached a mystical racist doctrine which fitted snugly into Captain Alfred Mahan's theories of force and power. Out of all this came the sanctimonious gibberish that the security and progress of the United States depended on giving the light of civilization to barbaric, untutored peoples —a civilization defined in an unprofessorial way by William Sumner of Yale as a world "in which the rule is 'Root, hog, or die' . . . a world in which 'The longest pole knocks down the most persimmons.'"

The insurgent writers and artists, centered in New York, enlisted under their banners wanderers from west of the Hudson who along with them worshiped at many shrines—syndicalism, cubism, anarchism, imagism, feminism. The talk of a vague new freedom enchanted the embattled youth. Some of them, however, took an interest in the I.W.W.* or the Socialist Party. But most of the rebels, Reed among them, who made the pavements of Greenwich Village their tribal grounds, were romanticists whose individualism abhorred

* I.W.W.—Industrial Workers of the World

discipline, and they often crossed lances with the conformists for the sheer fun of it. Nevertheless, they did try to find out what it was that had upset the dreams of an earlier and more hopeful America. They undeniably improved the artistic landscape even if they did not show the way out of monopoly's corruption of cultural life. The philosophy of imperialism, pragmatism, with its disdain of history and its shibboleth that all truth arrives anew with every individual's experience, had a powerful sway over them. In time the cult of the new in the theater, in poetry, in painting and writing became an end in itself.

When American workers to whom some of the dissidents addressed themselves, seemed not to heed or understand their estheticism, they were disillusioned and the very social shams they were supposedly resisting re-emerged in their work. Their efforts at realism became in the end surrealist, their consciousness egocentric. It was a reflection of their distance from working class politics and their failure to understand working class life. Inbreeding led to intellectual sterility, and the constant temptation of the easy dollar won many of the rebels away from their unprofitable rebellion.

In the swirl of this setting, Jack Reed's own educative process was not simple. His romantic impulses had already played him many tricks, and his early writing, especially his poetry, showed how hard he sucked life out of a dim past. But in New York, where he had settled after Harvard and several months of happy-go-lucky wandering in Europe, the present struck him hard. He saw what he had never quite seen before: a city strikingly split into classes and into whose social fabric was woven many patches of peoples and cultures. He threw himself into the city's life, feeling its warmth and its coldness, musing upon its ironic contrasts, and witnessing its endless drama. He tried to press the city to himself with the consuming joy that comes out of new-found love.

"I wandered about the streets," he wrote, "from the soaring imperial towers of downtown, along the East River docks, smelling of spices and the clipper ships of the past, through the swarming East Side—alien towns within towns—where the smoky flare of miles of clamorous push carts made a splendor of shabby streets; coming upon sudden shrill markets, dripping blood and fish scales in the light of torches, the women bawling their wares under the roaring great bridges; thrilling to the ebb and flow of human tides sweeping to work and back, west and east, south and north. I knew Chinatown, and Little Italy, and the quarter of the Syrians; the marionette theater, Sharkey's and McSorley's saloons, the Bowery lodging houses and the places where the tramps gathered; the Haymarket, the German Village, and all the dives of the Tenderloin. I spent one summer night on top of a pier of the Williamburg Bridge; I slept another night in a basket of squid in the Fulton Market, where the red and green and gold sea things glisten in the light of the sputtering arcs. The girls that walk the streets were friends of mine, and the drunken sailors off ships new-come from the world's end, and the Spanish longshoremen down on West Street. . . .

"I knew well the parks, and the streets of palaces, the theaters and hotels; the ugly growth of the city spreading like a disease, the decrepit places whence life was ebbing, and the squares and streets where an old, beautiful leisurely existence was drowned in the mounting roar of the slums. I knew Washington Square, and the artists and writers, the near-Bohemians, the radicals. I went to gangsters' balls at Tammany Hall, on excursions of the Tim Sullivan Association, to Coney Island on hot summer nights. . . . Within a block of my house was all the adventure of the world; within a mile was every foreign country.

"In New York I first loved, and I first wrote of the things I saw, with a fierce joy of creation—and knew at last that I could write. There I got my first perceptions of the life of my time. The city and its people were an open book to me; everything had its story, dramatic, full of ironic tragedy and terrible humor. There I first saw that reality transcended all the fine poetic inventions of fastidiousness and medievalism."

There was little soul scratching in this pragmatist process of learning nor did Reed become the victim of a tormented ego such as afflicted other novices in social discovery. He had little feeling for the value of theory, and he had a cold scorn for the petty doctrinaires "who cling to the skirts of Change." The ideas he encountered had impact upon him only as he could place them in his catalogue of experience. "On the whole," he recalled, "ideas alone didn't mean much to me. I had to see. In my rambles over the city I couldn't help but observe the ugliness of poverty and all its train of evil, the cruel inequality between rich people who had too many motor cars and poor people who didn't have enough to eat. It didn't come to me from books that the workers produced all the world's wealth which went to those who did not earn it."

New York was pushing Reed in a leftward direction but he had to make a living and help his mother. The truth also is that he craved the wealth and reputation that came with literary success. Yet, it was a craving tempered by the fear that success in the fashionable editorial offices would grind him down and warp his talent. After having seen what happened to the popular writers who churned the fattening literary pabulum, he was unhappy over what might happen to him. He was beginning to have qualms about his two souls. For the moment he could ease the clash between them by ribbing the producers of the current literary diet. In lyrics he wrote in 1912 for a Dutch Treat Club musical, he good-naturedly needled the club's writers and artists and the big magazines for which they worked. Of the *Cosmopolitan* he wrote:

> Every month I'm full of spice
> And naughty Robert Chambers makes it nice.
> Some lingerie, a glimpse of stocking.
> Lips unlocking, nothing shocking.
> And Gibson hints at hidden beauty,
> Lovers' booty, tutti frutti.
> Read me once and I'll bet I can
> Refresh the tired business man.

And of the *Outlook* with its pretense at liberalism:

> I'm a moderate reformer
> Just because reform's the thing.
> I've a practical religion
> And my hat is in the ring.
> I'm a catch-as-can uplifter
> With a strong belief in jail.
> It's a policy that gathers in the kale.

Then there was the dart flung at the magazine industry's vaunted freedom of the press:

> It must not be inferred
> That wealth is what we're after.
> We greet that gibe absurd
> With supercilious laughter.
> The criminal and grafter,
> From wickedness deterred,
> Revere the printed word,
> Revere the printed word.

These were gentle gibes at best and they also found their way into several short stories and sketches he wrote about capitalists, the city's night life, the snobs among his friends. The note of irony in them was strong, and they were amusing, but there was not much more. Middle-class values and sentimentalities came in for their usual thumping. He had an itch to defy and to mock the sacrosanct mores of the well-heeled, but there was seemingly no other purpose beyond mockery and defiance. His thinking amounted to contempt for the scrapers and resistance to the outworn. He was intent on sweeping away the long-bearded corpses that blocked the path of the rebels with their impulse for innovation and change—almost any kind of change. And while the business of sweeping kept him bustling, it did not help him grasp what all this spilling of energy meant. Some of his respectable friends thought he was being arrogant deliberately. They hoped he would stop using so many sticks to beat the dog of convention.

When Reed learned that a magazine called *The Masses* was being reorganized and would give the upper gentry a good spanking, he quickly offered his services. A few years earlier, several New York Socialists had founded *The Comrade* to publish "such literary and artistic productions as reflect the soundness of the socialist philosophy ... and to develop the esthetic impulse in the socialist movement." *The Comrade*, however, was an immature, short-lived venture but it had helped foster the idea of proletarian art and Marxist criticism of a sort. *The Masses* was its unappointed successor at a time when the Socialist weekly, *Appeal to Reason*, had nearly half a million paid subscribers with some special issues reaching almost a million readers. *The Masses* excluded from its pages the noisier faddists and attracted enthusiasts in hot pursuit of a new freedom in the arts as well as devoted followers of Marxism. For Reed it was the beginning of a tie as editor and contributor that helped him leaven his thinking and exacted from him his finest work as against the articles he published elsewhere and for which he was paid handsomely. In *The Masses* he felt free to speak his mind.

Reed learned quickest in war, either between classes or between states. His best writing was done amid the clatter of battle in which he was completely immersed and from which he could plead the cause of the side he held dear. He could never be neutral, and being a partisan, he was challenged to muster his full talent.

In the 1913 strike of silk workers in Paterson, New Jersey, he had his first taste of labor in active warfare. The I.W.W. strike leaders had drawn in radical intellectuals from New York, Reed among them. He approached the strike as though it were a lark, but his deepest sympathies were aroused when he saw the terror practiced by the police. More than 2,300 workers had been hauled into the county jail. And like its predecessor at Lawrence, Massachusetts, a year before, the strike in Paterson had shocked the country with its revelation of starvation wages paid by the mill owners. For several weeks Paterson became the focus of Reed's life. He was infuriated by the beatings given the weavers and the talk about labor in Fifth Avenue salons took on a different and sharper meaning.

Reed was arrested while watching the strike and spent four days in jail. Many of the strikers were recent immigrants, and though their English was poor, they managed to convey to him their fears and their hopes and Reed felt the need to give them whatever help they asked. He marveled at their courage, their inventiveness. The mill owners had bedecked Paterson with flags and banners bearing the inscription, "We live under the flag; we fight for this flag; and we will work under this flag." The pickets thrust back: "We wove the flag; we dyed the flag; we won't scab under the flag."

Bill Haywood, the I.W.W. leader, introduced Reed at a strike meeting. Haywood reported how Reed "taught the strikers a song which when sung by 25,000 people made an impression that cannot be realized without hearing such a great crowd give vent to their full voice . . . The sound of 25,000 people shouting 'Boo, boo, boo' was like the blast of Gabriel's trumpet that shook down the walls of Jericho."

Reed quit his job as a sub-editor on the *American Magazine*, and with the strike as the major motif, helped to organize a pageant in the old Madison Square Garden in New York. He rehearsed more than a thousand men and women in Paterson, then led them across the river to Manhattan to act out before an immensely moved audience of twelve thousand the wretchedness of their lives and their bitter struggle against the mill bosses. The pageant was hailed by the Greenwich Village crowd as a grand innovation in the theater. The newspapers spoke of it as though revolution had cracked the gates of the metropolis.

Paterson shook Reed. He learned for himself the things books and talk could not teach. Again he worked primarily through his eyes, letting them break down into particulars the grim Paterson scene. He saw the oppressors and how they squeezed and crushed the life of the workers; and brought home to him in more concrete terms was "the hard knowledge that the manufacturers get all they can out of labor, pay as little as they must, and permit the existence of great masses of the miserable unemployed in order to keep wages down; that the forces of the state are on the side of property against the propertyless."

But if Paterson shook Reed, it did not shake him into making a lasting commitment to the labor movement beyond the episode of the strike itself. When his mother was appalled by what he was doing, he told her, "I am not a Socialist temperamentally any more than I'm an Episcopalian. I know that my business is to interpret and live Life, wherever it may be found—whether in the labor movement or out of it." In Paterson he had plunged joyously into his new role and the novelty of the experience gave him profound satisfaction. It was an exciting incident to be cherished in the course of living an exciting life. But his active responsibility was finished when he decided it was finished. He left for Europe to rest.

After he returned to New York, Reed was asked to cover the revolt of the peons in Mexico against a new set of dictators, the offer coming from the *Metropolitan*, a widely read magazine whose editors were turning the interest in reform into profitable coin. Morris Hillquit, a Socialist leader, wrote for it and George Bernard Shaw and Lincoln Steffens and others with reputations as disturbers of the intellectual peace. For Reed, the Mexican assignment which included a secondary one from the Pulitzer newspaper, the *New York World*, was the big break, an opportunity such as he had not had. He was twenty-six and eager to prove himself and flattered that he had been chosen.

When first he crossed the border, he was seized with a terrible fear of death, of mutilation, of a strange land and strange people whose speech and thought he did not know. But in the heat of battle he discovered that bullets were not very terrifying and his fears soon evaporated. What he wrote from Mexico had a loving ring. Under his amazing descriptive power landscape and men were transformed into a lyrical, vibrant picture. He captured the spirit of the guerrillas, their fighting lives, their miseries. He sang with them, wrote down their ballads and put them into English. They felt his respect for them and gave him theirs in return. This curious foreigner took the same risks they did, shared their burning thirst, their fears, when he could have remained at home without having to live the wretched life of the desert. "That four months," he later recalled before he started out on an even bigger adventure, "of riding hundreds of miles across the blazing plains, sleeping on the ground with the *hombres*, dancing and carousing in looted haciendas all night after an all-day ride, being with them intimately in play, in battle, was perhaps the most satisfactory period of my life. I made good with these wild fighting men, and with myself. I loved them and I loved the life."

At first he did not examine in detail the issues of the struggle and its turbulent history. Nor did he seem to care. The guerrillas were the underdogs; they wanted land; they wanted to rid themselves of the oppressors who had assassinated the liberal provisional president, Madero. That was sufficient reason for Reed to defend them. The Mexicans, moreover, were wonderfully congenial and, he felt, had the same sense of personal liberty so precious to him. He was unconcerned with what the experts said about Pancho Villa, the guerrilla leader with whose troops he rode. In the American press Villa was a natural object of smear, but Reed saw him as a gallant friend of the peasants eager to give them land and schools. Reed considered what he heard from the imperialist agents from up north. They sounded no different from the mill owners in Paterson. They spoke of the guerrillas, in fact of all Mexicans, as though they were beasts to be worked to exhaustion for a pittance.

It was his first encounter with another kind of oppression and another kind of war for freedom; not the relatively simple strike struggle but the more complex one of agrarian revolution in which the fight was against both the internal tyrants and foreign imperialists. At the moment he was there, he did not relate his Mexican experience to the broader issues rending the hemisphere and the world or how these issues were the marks of a violent crisis in which a declining American capitalism was hopelessly involved. Uppermost in Reed's mind was the peasants' land hunger. The great seas of modern life, as he pictured it, were beating around the narrow shores of the Mexican Middle Ages and nothing must hold back the changes that had to come.

On his return home he defended the uprising and showed the harm United States interference would bring to the Mexican revolution. He spoke and wrote against the clamor for intervention. This time, unlike his behavior immediately after the Paterson episode, he recognized that his responsibility was a continuing one. In the *Metropolitan* he wrote that a war on Mexico would end in nothing but tears and disaster. To be sure, he said, "American soldiers will have nothing serious to anticipate in the opposition of the Mexican army. It is the peons and their women, fighting in the streets and at the doors of their houses" that they would have to battle. And what would be changed after American troops left? Nothing. The great estates would be "securely re-established, the foreign interests, stronger than ever, because we supported them, and the Mexican revolution to be fought all over again in the indefinite future." He tried to tell these things in a less blunt way to President Wilson during an interview in the White House arranged by William Jennings Bryan, the Secretary of State. The President seemed sympathetic and defined his policy of non-interference in Mexico. Reed was taken in by the manner, the words, the liberal reputation, and believed Wilson would do the right thing. Although American troops were already in Vera Cruz, Reed saw no reason for not going along with the popular faith in Wilson.

In April, 1914, after he came up from Mexico, he saw more of Wall Street's tyranny. At Ludlow, Col., mine guards aided by the state militia had burned a tent colony of striking miners and their families who had been evicted from their homes. The strike was one of several violent conflicts in Colorado mines which at times assumed the proportions of civil war. The Ludlow outbreak was on a scale larger than that which Reed had witnessed in Paterson. The issues could not be blurred by the mild-mannered operators dominated by the Rockefeller clan or by the newspapers which spoke for them. Reed painstakingly traced the web of intrigue between sheriffs, governor, company-town officials and mine owners— between the state apparatus and big business. And clear to him again was the unbridgeable chasm between two classes. He wrote about the strike with scrupulous attention to details. It was a study as much as it was a colorful report. He hunted for evidence not apparent to the eye, and the whole effort marked his growth as a class-conscious writer not easily satisfied with recording his impressions but who must dig deeper into the play of forces behind them.

There now could be little doubt about Reed's relationship to workers and their struggles. His ties were becoming clearer and he knew better than ever before where he belonged and where he was at ease and most effective. Such drifting as he did from what was more and more his chosen road, was characteristic of a man who had not yet fastened his several interests to a central goal. Some of his Harvard friends had already classed him as an infidel doomed to eternal damnation. And as time went on and his radicalism showed itself to be neither meek nor mild, it seemed to others of his Cambridge friends that he was decidedly dangerous. In their eyes Reed's life was shaping into an outlandish pattern. It might be all right to hold unorthodox beliefs but to act on them and induce others to act made him a public nuisance. More, this intimacy with what they called the "great unwashed" represented a reckless forfeiture of his social rank. Yet, strangely enough, the hostility they felt toward him was often mixed with an attraction for his good spirits, his buoyancy, and his humor. He was a laughing man and his quick mind and fun-loving impulses magnetized even these sneering souls.

Among his former classmates there were also the intellectual snobs. There was Walter Lippmann, who in his middle twenties was already consecrated as one of the pontiffs of liberalism in New York. Reed had regard for Lippmann's talents, but at the same time he was suspicious of the way he sniffed at the world and its people and of his delicately contrived logic. After Reed had returned from Mexico with a shining reputation as a correspondent, Lippmann wrote a piece in *The New Republic* called "Legendary John Reed." In it the snobbery of the liberal intellectuals toward Reed was given the weight of Lippmann's prestige. He laughed at Reed although the piece was carefully stippled with praise. In Walter Lippmann's eyes Reed was only a neophyte in serious political matters. And in patronizing Reed, Lippmann helped create the myth that he was a playboy, that he was unruly, an adventurous, albeit gifted college senior acting the worldly man of affairs.

Reed admitted quickly that in the early days his knowledge of working class theory was crude. But he sought help from others, and he was arriving at Marxism by the pitted route of experience even as Lippmann was discarding his socialist ideas in prim essays. Reed sensed the sham of it. Any lesser man without Reed's instincts might have been shaken by Lippmann's drubbing. But he rejected the Lippmannesque view of the world and of himself, and he would not yield to those of his friends who shook their heads over his imperviousness to their brand of reason.

That was a subtle pressure which Reed withstood. It was nothing, however, compared to the humiliation inflicted upon him by those who pleaded the justness of the imperialist war into which Europe had been plunged in 1914. There was a loss of friends with whom he had to break no matter the pain it cost. There were the economic pressures. There was a shutting of doors that had been wide open to him before. Whatever blows were struck at it, his intransigence emerged livelier and stronger.

When Reed left for Europe in the summer of 1914 to cover

the western front for the *Metropolitan,* he thought he detected in American ruling circles the first faint but ominous signs of partisanship in the war. He knew and he said that it was a traders' war and his estimate was soon confirmed wherever he went in England, France, and Germany. There was none of the spontaneity and idealism which had stirred him in the Mexican revolution. Everything had halted but the engines of destruction. Paris was a sullen and sick city without the *élan* the other correspondents were describing for their home offices. The rich were having a good time, as usual, while most of the Socialist leaders were helping the government send French youth into suffering and slaughter. London was no different except for the more mannerly hypocrisies of the upper classes and their monstrous chatter about the imperial idea. Berlin was the same. It reeked with its own kind of militarist cant. What struck him was that far behind the lines and down among the French, British, and German people there was such little hostile feeling. It was hard for them to explain how they got involved in the terrible butchery, how it had come and what it meant.

Except for the victims, Reed saw nothing with which to identify himself on either side of the belligerents. He was depressed and disgusted by the whole damned business, and because he hated it he found it impossible to write what the *Metropolitan* wanted—color, glory, thunder. He gave them what he had actually seen, and it was not pretty. He would not do a thing to influence his readers away from neutrality.

His tour of Eastern Europe in 1915 was just as oppressive as his trip in the west. If anything the carnage in the Balkans was more frightful, the gloom of disease and death heavier. In Goutchevo, Serbia, he walked over a mountain so thick with dead Austrians and Serbians killed in a desperate charge that sometimes his feet sank through into pits of rotting flesh and crunching bone. Yet it was not the slaughter alone that sickened him. His revulsion came as much from the pretense that all this was a necessary sacrifice to the safekeeping of democracy—the democracy of England's bloody

Lord Kitchener, of France's Poincaré, of Tsar Nicholas. For two hundred miles behind the Russian front he saw the evidences of the horrors inflicted on the Jews. And everywhere officialdom lined its pockets with graft. Whether in Greece or Rumania, Russia or Turkey, the almighty rulers were steeped in a mess of corruption. And among the people on whom the grafters lived there was more interest in bread than in victories.

Again it was hard for Reed to serve up the kind of report for which the *Metropolitan* was eager. Instead, he wrote what he described as impressions of human beings in the stress of war. But the impressions were calculated to show that the war was a colossal imperialist trap in which the U.S. must not be caught. He had good reason for writing this way. The mild partisanship he noticed in the country a year before was now being turned into war fever. Neutrality had been used to camouflage the agreements reached with the British and French imperialists. Now even the camouflage was being removed as officialdom, in colloboration with Wall Street's House of Morgan, consented to additional credits to the Entente countries out of fear that without them they would not be able to pay for war purchases. The war had saved the United States from a severe economic slump, and depression faced it again if London and Paris were cast adrift. The machinery for intervention had, therefore, been set in motion to protect the gigantic Allied mortgages held by American bankers and to expand their world position in the struggle for markets and raw materials. A fine moral flummery was cooked up to justify America's participation.

Except for a small number, the liberals prostituted their talents to glorify the butchery. Gracefully and with all the sickening casuistry that passed for logic, they spelled out the reasons for a successful imperialist war and used them to veil the ruling class aggressions at home. But there was a writer who understood the meaning of this betrayal as well as Reed did. Randolph Bourne had been in Europe on the eve of the war, and when war began to stifle America, his conclusions from what he saw ran almost parallel with Reed's. In their own ways both of them—Reed as a Socialist and Bourne as a disillusioned pragmatist—carried on an anti-war fight, with Bourne writing scalding essays on the cowards. "The intellectuals," Bourne charged, "have identified themselves with the least democratic forces in American life. They have assumed the leadership for war of those very classes whom the American democracy has been immemorially fighting." Bourne insisted: "The war—or American promise: one must choose. One cannot be interested in both. For the effect of the war will be to impoverish American promise. It cannot advance it."

Reed could be cheered by this brave voice, but he could not help despairing that there were not many more. For a time it seemed to him that the war was crushing all he cherished. Woodrow Wilson, to whom Reed and many liberals had rallied in 1916, as the presidential candidate who might be counted on to keep the peace because "Wall Street was against him," had abandoned his pledges in 1917. It turned out that Wilson was not against Wall Street and that, in fact, the Street was not against him. Reed quickly admitted that he had made a grievous blunder, and it was one of the things which weighed on him and added to his despondency brought on by the war and made worse by illness and a momentary rift in his marriage to Louise Bryant. His mother and brother were sending him stinging letters for his anti-war attitude. He was no longer sought after as a writer, although only two or three years before he had been celebrated as a great journalist, compared by the *Metropolitan* with Stephen Crane and Richard Harding Davis, praised by Rudyard Kipling, and called a "genius" by Walter Lippmann. It was easy to ride the wave of success and to profess radicalism when it did not block the way to bread and reputation. This time things were vastly different for him. He was a marked man—the rebel who had gone a little too far and refused to join in the big swim.

He might have found it easier to bear his anguish if, as he

thought, the people he loved, the workers, had asserted themselves and fought the hysteria of which they were the victims. But they seemed to him divided, badly led, bitterly hostile toward each other and blind to their class interest. He remembered them as they were in Paterson and Ludlow, and he wondered what had happened to them since then. Doubts were looming in his mind. Had he in his romantic way imagined more about them than was actually true? He had leaped over the first hurdle and had come to hold the deepest convictions about the class cleavages in capitalist society. It had helped to shape him as a writer. Now there was another hurdle: whether the class in which he placed his faith would reply to the war madness with the strength he knew was in it. He could not be sure.

The truth is that Reed was looking at the war one-sidedly and with eyes befogged by his own gloom. To be sure, he sensed that although the war had done something to everyone and had throttled the political idealism of the earlier rollicking days, things were bound to change, and he could "hardly keep from imagining the splendid and terrible possibilities of the time to come." This whistling in the dark, however, did not dispel his fears. He tried to make himself understand why the Socialists in Europe failed to stop the war and why so many of them were supporting it. He searched for the answer in the history of European socialism, and he concluded that the political bankruptcy of the leadership was the consequence of the unprincipled position of the Second International. The U.S. Socialists recalled their presidential candidate in 1916 who changed to a pro-war attitude. Next year the party convention at St. Louis adopted a strong anti-war resolution.

He did not take into account the increasing number of labor struggles in the country. They were essentially protests against the wartime deterioration in the standard of living, but they often revealed strong anti-war feeling. Moreover, even if the peace forces had not been able to prevent Wall Street from dragging the country into war, the oppressions at home and the growing casualty lists were creating a mood of disillusionment which expressed itself in ever widening sentiment for peace. And most important, Reed failed to estimate the full meaning of international developments hidden at the moment below the surface of European life. A left socialist movement against the war had been begun at Zimmerwald, Switzerland, in 1915. In 1916 this movement was given even greater scope and depth at another conference in the Swiss village of Kienthal. Under Lenin's leadership the meeting had hastened the break between the leaders who supported the war and those who fought it. The Kienthal meeting had registered the leftward shift of Europe's masses.

With his eyes fastened on the immediate scene, Reed did not grasp the significance of these conferences on the course of the war. His doubts were symptomatic of a man who had apparently allied himself with a class but in reality still groped his way on its fringes. Some of the roots of his impatience were imbedded in a highly subjective romanticism. Its positive features kept his mind and heart open to new impulses, to the novelty of experience, the joy of living and dreaming. The negative ones brought dejection when the things which moved him to act did not move workers or moved them too slowly. He had still to conquer the problem of refashioning consciousness by allowing greater assimilation of himself into the working class. He had still to grasp why social ferment was a complex process uneven in results and often contradictory to any individual's most profound wishes.

Despite his low mood, Reed continued fighting "the judicial tyranny, bureaucratic suppression, and industrial barbarism." He could not be indifferent to the tragedy around him or shut himself off to brood over such torment as he felt. "All I know," he said when he was most troubled, "is that my happiness is built on the misery of other people, so that I eat because others go hungry, that I am clothed when other people go almost naked through the frozen cities in winter; and that fact poisons me, disturbs my serenity." Others with the same disquieting feelings could become aloof, proclaim that an epoch without ideals had arrived, or make a cult of pessimism out of their sudden insistence that man was evil. They could even believe that the strength of imperialism was such that nothing and no one could cope with it. Reed was contemptuous of those who surrendered to that attitude. This was a betrayal he fought ceaselessly, for not only did it mean the beheading of the natural opposition but the tragic abandonment of masses of people. Resignation from struggle was but another form of helping the imperialists work their will. He would have none of it.

As the months moved on, fragments of news burst through of intense opposition to the war in Europe. The name of Karl Liebknecht and his anti-war activities in Germany began to appear in the press. Reed's delight was boundless, for it seemed to him to signal the end of the docile mood of Europe's workers and the beginning of the new phase of life he had hoped for in a self-searching piece he wrote in 1917 when he was almost thirty. The essay was the offshoot of his despair which he tried to lighten with a glimpse into the future. Now what he longed to see happen was pressing toward fulfillment. The news from Russia stirred him most. When he was there in 1915 he was struck by the great flow of the country, its vastness. The tsarist government itself commanded no respect. "It is," he wrote, "like a separate nation imposed upon the Russian people." He sensed the country's inner turmoil, but he could not quite answer his own question: "Is there a powerful and destructive fire working in the bowels of Russia, or is it quenched?"

Even when the Tsar was overthrown he still did not believe that a profound change was taking place. A fundamental shift might come, he thought, but for the moment it appeared only as though Russian capitalism had discarded the heavier gear that burdened prosecution of the war. But in a short time the irate Russian rumble had turned into the thunder of revolution, and he was convinced the real thing was happening. And the "real thing," he surmised, "was the long-thwarted rise of the Russian masses . . . and the purpose of it the establishment of a new human society upon the earth." He went off to see it.

Petrograd filled him with fresh vigor. He arrived in the city in September, 1917, shortly after the defeat of General Kornilov's plot against the revolution. The triumph over Kornilov's attempt at a *coup d'état* revealed the shape of forces in the country. Aligned on the counterrevolutionary side were the Mensheviks, the Social Revolutionaries, and the Constitutional Democrats. Reed accurately judged their waning influence. Against them and the perfidious Provisional Government stood the Bolsheviks, with Lenin returned from exile in Switzerland, leading them. Had it not been for them, Kornilov might have taken Petrograd. The Bolsheviks rallied the workers and soldiers to the defense of the city. It was clear to him that "through the tempest of events tumbling over one another . . . the Bolshevik star steadily rises. The Workers' and Soldiers' Soviet which has gained immense power since the Kornilov business, is the real government of Russia again, and the Bolshevik power in the Soviet is growing fast."

Reed wandered over the city, listened to workers, heard the frightened men of the old regime. And how different Petrograd was from the city he had seen during the first visit. "The old town has changed!" he wrote to a friend. "Joy where there was gloom, and gloom where there was joy. We are in the middle of things, and believe me it's thrilling. There is so much dramatic to write about that I don't know where to begin. For color and action and grandeur this makes Mexico look pale." In Smolny, the revolutionary staff headquarters, he asked questions of everyone he could corner, tried to sift the meaning of things as they came pouring in, scribbled endlessly in his notebook. All that he witnessed confirmed him in his belief that he was at the center of a supreme turning point in history, in at the start of the socialist era which, in Lenin's words, had already wrenched "the first hundred million people of this earth from the clutches of imperialist war and the imperialist world." Wherever Reed went, to the front, to meetings, along the streets of Petrograd, he felt the vitality, the great gladness that came with the release from the bondage of the past. The people had clambered out of the pit of despair and were showing what creative genius lay in them now that they had the power to rule themselves. He could understand the rapture of the worker who looked across Petrograd and then burst out to him: "All mine now! My Petrograd."

When Lenin spoke in Smolny to the Second Congress of Soviets on the night of Thursday, November 8, 1917, quietly uttering the electrifying words: "We shall now proceed to construct the Socialist order!" Reed leaped up with the rest roaring their approval. "Suddenly, by common impulse," he later recorded, "we found ourselves on our feet, mumbling together into the smooth lifting unison of the *Internationale*. A grizzled old soldier was sobbing like a child ... The immense sound rolled through the hall, burst windows and doors and seared into the quiet sky ... And when it was over, as we stood there in a kind of awkward hush, some one in the back of the room shouted, 'Comrades! Let us remember those who died for liberty!' So we began to sing the Funeral March, that slow, melancholy and yet triumphant chant, so Russian and so moving ... For this [for the people's happiness] did they lie there in their cold Brotherhood Grave on Mars Field; for this thousands and tens of thousands had died in the prisons, in exile, in Siberian mines ..."

During the revolution Reed found the answers to what had been gnawing at his heart. No longer was there any question in his mind about workers. Once aroused, the Russian working class fought hard, tapping reserves of strength in its ally, the poor peasantry. When others fled from the logic of the next step, the workers stood firm; neither the pretenses of liberalism nor momentary defeats could keep them from the road to their complete emancipation.

The revolution was the kind of school in which John Reed

could learn quickly. It taught him convincingly "that in the last analysis the property-owning class is loyal only to its own property. That the property-owning class will never readily compromise with the working class. That the masses of workers are not only capable of great dreams but have in them the power to make dreams come true." This had been the core of his inner conflict and now it no longer stabbed at him. Paterson, Mexico, Ludlow, the war itself, prepared him for the revolution, and in Petrograd and Moscow he knew what to look for and how to look at it, and thus knitted together were the loose threads of the years past. It was a hard but steady growth.

He could no longer content himself with the mere recording of impressions, however lyrically he expressed them. More than ever before he sought the interconnection between things, the continuous process of shift and change. The difference between most of his earlier writing and that on the revolution was the difference between the close sympathizer and the participant. In Mexico he had shared the life of the guerrillas to satisfy his quest for experience and to lend dramatic color to his reports. His identification was limited to the work in hand and by the very character of the uprising itself. But in Russia his identification with the revolution was complete and lasting, for not only had he finally come to know that the militant labor movement was the anchor of his life, but he knew that here was the revolution that had opened a new future to all oppressed. His writing thus gained an emotional charge and an intellectual dimension beyond a skilled use of words in a rhythmically constructed sentence. There was now an acute sense of history, a deeper appreciation of theory. What he wrote about the Russian Revolution in *Ten Days That Shook The World,* with its extraordinary weaving of significant detail into a triumphal theme, was a measure of the great leap forward he had made.

Ten Days was the first major account in America of the revolution's universal impact. Reed had mastered its broad fundamentals, although he was not familiar with the complex politics which characterized the revolution from the beginning of 1917. He was not, for example, familiar with the proceedings of the Sixth Congress of the Bolshevik Party in late July and early August, held in secret because of the Provisional Government's campaign of terror against it. But the Congress was of decisive importance. It headed the Bolsheviks toward the final struggle against the Kerensky government and the war-mad bourgeoisie whom Kerensky represented. Lenin, hunted by the police, had been forced into hiding, and Stalin, in Lenin's absence, spoke at the Congress in behalf of Lenin and the Central Committee of the Bolshevik Party. He made the two major reports on both the political situation and the tactics of the Bolsheviks. This Congress took up the struggle against the capitulators within the party and defeated their attempt to turn it aside from the path of socialist revolution.

These were some of the critical events Reed did not know, and he was therefore ignorant of Stalin's role and of his close collaboration with Lenin. And because Reed also depended on others for information on the decisions and discussions of the Bolshevik leadership, he erred in reporting what transpired at the meetings of the Central Committee, especially at the time of the decision in October to launch the final struggle for power. Yet, for all its serious shortcomings, *Ten Days* was a unique document. It became in its time a force for socialism by rousing others in the same way Reed had been roused. It helped to break the cordon of censorship thrown around Russia by a bitterly hostile imperialist world, and it compelled its many readers to think hard on the great historic event of their time.

Reed came back to the United States in April, 1918. He had tried to hasten his return in order to appear at the trial of *The Masses* editors, with whom he had been indicted for "conspiring" to interfere in the recruiting of military personnel and to promote insubordination in the armed forces. But the government's case was so patently flimsy the jury could not reach a decision, and the day before Reed arrived in New York part of the indictment was voided, although the first charge remained.

The country was in the grip of wartime hysteria, and the authorities gave Reed no peace. His papers were confiscated as soon as he landed. The big magazines and dailies were completely shut to him. Here by wide acknowledgment was a great American journalist, an eyewitness to the greatest story of the time, but not an editor outside the tiny radical press would give him an inch of space. He could have all the front pages he wanted if he would platitudinize, burn Moscow by the hour, but he was not to kindle a healthy curiosity in the Russian Revolution by telling its story where millions could read it. The conspiracy to foster myths, to perpetuate ignorance and hate, was well in the making and Reed, as a writer, was among the first to feel its deadly hand.

But he spoke at dozens of meetings in the East and across to the Middle West. Wherever he went, the halls were packed with eager audiences—and the police. At a meeting in Brooklyn, a hundred policemen surrounded him; in Philadelphia, he was assaulted by a police lieutenant who then proceeded to arrest him for inciting to riot; the day after he spoke in the Bronx he was picked up and charged with sedition. It was a wearying business, but Reed seemed tireless and audiences quickly caught his good cheer and his enthusiasm. He showed them that what they read as news about Russia was less than clever humbug. He explained at length the operation of the Soviets. He denounced the interventionists, and again and again reminded his listeners that although the first working class state was ringed round with vast hatred, no power could destroy it.

Reed was under no illusion that his words were making any decisive difference in a country overcome with fear. But for all the oppressive atmosphere his was no longer one of the lonely voices. The new brutal measures taken to crush opposition betokened that opposition was growing. He took satisfaction in the strong fight still carried on by the left-wing Socialists and the I.W.W. They were being joined by others in the labor movement. Raids, beatings, hot tar and feathers seemed to drive home the nature of the war to more and more Americans, and if what he had to say revealed the war's true face, he would continue saying it no matter what it cost. He had already been cursed and threatened, and one newspaper demanded that he be lynched forthwith. But from the other side there came hundreds of letters from men and women imprisoned in the struggle for civil rights, from those who heard him at meetings or read his articles—all grateful for the fight he was making. One letter was from Gene Debs. "You write differently," he told him, "than anyone else and your style is most appealing to me. There is something that breathes and throbs in all you say." The letter was one Reed cherished just as he cherished the man who never flinched from fighting against the imperialist war.

Reed had become one of the best-known figures of the left in the United States. His reputation was all the more exasperating to his enemies because not only were his gifts as a writer so apparent, but he was from an old American family and a Harvard alumnus to boot. He spoiled for them the myth that anyone who pleaded for friendship with the Russians must himself surely be foreign born. His acquaintances of the Harvard Club were also annoyed that he seemed so confident and calm. Although outwardly he was unchanged and remained gay and sunny, he had also become tougher and more disciplined. In court, during the second *Masses* trial, he told of the horrors he had seen in Europe as a war correspondent, and how he had been disgusted by the New York society columns with their stories of festive war parties. The judge kept hammering at him, not letting him explain why he was opposed to the war except in terms that would have sent him to prison. The jury again disagreed.

If in all this turmoil there was an occasional moment of grief for Reed, it was that he had no time for poetry. He had always thought of himself as a poet and the rich cadences of his prose, the power of his images, derived from his poetic skill. And now there was hardly a moment to spare for it. He yielded to his political commitments but not without the hope that some day in the future he would be able to return to poetry. Most of his poetry was written when he was younger and under the influence of conventional forms into which he fitted conventional themes. Without doubt, had he been able to give it time, it would have reflected his newer consciousness. As it stood, it had genuine poetic feeling, a music and technical facility that were undeniable. Yet on the whole it hinged on sensation and merely glimpsed life, for in the past he had thought of poetry as a world apart from everything else. It thus happened that his verse often lapsed into the mystical and the platitudinous. But in "America, 1918," a long poem he began in revolutionary Petrograd and finished in New York, he displayed a fresher approach. The poem was autobiographical with the seeming purpose of re-arranging his feelings, his impressions, to a new pattern. He spoke of his boyhood in the wide West:

> The blue thunderous Pacific, blaring sunsets,
> Black smoking forests on surf-beaten headlands,
> Lost beaches, camp-fires, wail of hunting cougars . . .
> By the rolling range, and the flat sunsmitten desert,
> Night with coyotes yapping, domed with burst of stars,
> The gray herd moving eastward, towering dust,
> Ropes whistling in slow coils, hats flapping, yells . . .
> By the miles of yellow wheat rippling in the Chinook,
> Orchards forever endless, deep in blooming,
> Green-golden orange-groves and snow peaks looming
> over . . .
> By raw audacious cities sprung from nothing,
> Brawling and bragging in their careless youth . . .
> I know thee, America!

He continued with a song of his schooling at Harvard and the excitement and adventure of New York:

By proud New York and its man-piled Matterhorns,
The hard blue sky overhead and the west wind blowing,
Steam-plumes waving from sun-glittering pinnacles,
And deep streets shaking to the million-river—

Manhattan, zoned with ships, the cruel
Youngest of all the world's great towns,
Thy bodice bright with many a jewel,
Imperially crowned with crowns . . .

Who that hath known thee but shall burn
In exile till he come again
To do thy bitter will, O stern
Moon of the tides of men!

And then:

Dear and familiar and ever-new to me is the city
As the body of my lover . . .
All sounds—harsh clatter of the Elevated, rumble of the sub-
    way,
Tapping of policemen's clubs on midnight pavements,
Hand-organs plaintive and monotonous, squawking motor
    horns,
Gatling crepitation of airy riveters,
Muffled detonations deep down underground,
Flat bawling of newsboys, quick-clamoring ambulance gongs,
Deep nervous tooting from the evening harbor,
And the profound shuffling thunder of myriad feet . . .

The steeple-jack swaying at the top of the Woolworth flag-
    pole,
Charity workers driving hard bargains for the degradation
    of the poor,
Worn-out snarling street-car conductors, sentimental
    prize-fighters,
White wings scouring the roaring traffic ways, foul-
    mouthed truck-drivers,
Spanish longshoremen heaving up freight-mountains, hollow-
    eyed silk workers,

Structural steel workers, catching hot rivets on high-up
    spidery girders,
Sand-hogs in hissing air-locks under the North River, sweat-
    ing subway muckers, hard-rock men blasting beneath
    Broadway,
Ward-leaders with uptilted cigars, planning mysterious
    underground battles for power . . .

Thus the poem rolled on. Judged by Reed's convictions it
was not a successful piece of work. The poem as a whole
lacked the quality of struggle. It was unconsciously chau-
vinistic in a few of its lines and it was quite removed,
for all his intentions, from the actual America of 1918. But
for what he had to say, the old masters he followed in the
past were not entirely useful. He needed to borrow the
method, the strength and spirit of the Whitman tradition.
And because he was unpracticed in it, the poem suffered
from overcataloguing as though he were trying to pile under
an enlarging glass the thirty-odd tumbling years of his life.
What did come through was Reed's deep love of country,
his faith in the untold possibilities before it. He was beginning to rethink in newer poetic terms much of his experience
and if he had had the leisure, he might have been able in
time to fuse his beliefs into a poetry as vital as his prose.

The vision which had captured his imagination and his ener-
gies was the vision of socialism. More than once, after Reed
had come back from Russia, he was called a foreign agent.
No one knew better than he how hollow was the accusation.
In the Russian Revolution and in socialism he recognized the
fulfillment of ideals and the practicability of dreams he had
held in common with innumerable Americans long before
November, 1917. He was, if anything, the agent of an in-
vincible idea which could never be circumscribed and which
belonged to no people or country except as it belonged to all
the oppressed of the earth.
    But between the idea and its realization there was a wide

gap and how this gap could be closed was exactly what he had learned. It was this that his enemies feared most about him. And his enemies were not only those from an opponent class but within the dominant leadership of the American Socialist Party itself. Its policies had proved bankrupt—as bankrupt as the policies pursued by the majority of Socialist leaders in Europe during the war and after, when a wave of revolution swept over several countries. The American leadership had become steeped in bureaucracy. It had diluted and distorted Marxism beyond recognition.

Reed, therefore, wanted a new leadership in the party built around its left wing which in years past had tried but failed to depose the opportunists. More, he and others wanted a party rooted solidly among class-conscious workers and in Marxism. He had hoped, when the battle within the party became intense, that it could be saved from the deadly leadership and converted into a militant force. This proved impossible and Reed helped to establish what later became the Communist Party of the United States.

It was work that required immersion in Marxism and despite the whirl of activities he plunged into it. In articles he wrote, he tried to get at the reasons for the particular way in which the American Federation of Labor had developed. He then went on to survey the history of the American Socialist movement and why as a party it had lost its militancy. And finally he made an attempt at analyzing the state in its relation to American working class struggles.

The articles and such other theoretical writing as he did showed crudities which were as much the evidence of his own inexperience with theory as they were of a movement that had not yet found itself and in which non-Marxist influences were strong. But the special stamp of this writing was his effort to find those features of American history and the labor movement that had handicapped the unfolding of a truly Marxist party of the American working class. Up until the time he had begun this examination—although he came prepared with a unique range of experience—his political knowledge was empirical and chaotic. It made for an impetuousness not lessened by the anarchic society in which he moved and by the conflict between what he willed and what he saw actually happening. By digging into the past without losing the focal point of the present, he separated from the confusion of experience those elements in American life that would give sustenance to a new militant party. His recent experiences had helped him enormously in confronting this task which, without knowing it, he had long evaded and which had also evaded him until he began using Marxism with the utmost seriousness. He was a pioneer in the exact sense that he tried to pierce the musty thinking on the question of how the promise of American life could be fulfilled.

When he returned to Russia in the fall of 1919, what he saw in Moscow reaffirmed for him the heroism of the Russians. In the two years since he had left, civil war had broken out and foreign intervention had added its own terrible devastation. Yet the mood he immediately detected was spirited and hopeful. The Soviets were building as rapidly as possible. The signs of progress were visible everywhere—in new schools, improved social facilities, and in the initiative shown by workers in industry. Reed took a room in the city, cooked his own meals, and made trips to factories and into the countryside. From time to time he called on Lenin. Again he was struck by the genius of the man, his viselike logic, the brilliance of his insight, and his great intellectual audacity.

While he was away, A. Mitchell Palmer, President Wilson's Attorney General, began a series of raids on the meeting halls and offices of Communists and Socialists. Five thousand of them were arrested and Reed, as a Communist leader, was indicted in Chicago in absentia. He sought immediately to return home. In the second attempt he made to get through the anti-Soviet blockade, he was arrested by the Finnish police. Washington refused to intervene to obtain his release or to help him get back to New York. "I asked the

43

American minister here," he wrote his wife from his cell in Abo, "for a passport home. He did not reply—as he has refused to answer all communications from me. But he told a Finnish government official that he could on no circumstances give me a passport." Seemingly, this was the only way the press could maintain the outrageous falsehood that he was evading trial. When at last he was freed by the Finnish authorities, he had no alternative but to return to Moscow.

The eleven weeks spent in solitary confinement had undermined his health, and although he had not fully recovered, he began to help with the preparations for the Second Congress of the Communist International. The meeting opened in July, 1920, with Reed a member of the International's executive committee. Throughout the hectic days of the International's meetings, Reed was obviously not well. He seemed tireless and his old gaiety of heart, his vitality and humor hid the fact that he was really exhausted and quite sick. But he would not refuse a request that he and others attend the Congress of Oriental Nations in Baku.

Back in Moscow he found that his wife had just arrived. They spent several days together, visiting Lenin and other Soviet leaders, roaming through the art galleries, and attending the ballet. He talked of writing another book, of getting back home to stand trial, and of his future work in the American Communist movement. And then he fell ill. At first it seemed as though he only had influenza, but later the disease was diagnosed as typhus. The doctors in attendance tried to save him, but their skill was of no avail, handicapped as they were by the lack of drugs in a blockaded country. On Sunday, October 17, 1920, three days before his thirty-third birthday, John Reed died.

The body, watched over by an honor guard of Red Army men, lay in state for a week in Moscow's trade union center. Thousands of Russians came to pay tribute to the American who so well understood their struggles. And back home in a dozen cities in a time of terror and oppression there were tears of grief poured deep out of the heart for the young leader who had fought so magnificently for the class that had adopted him. Even the newspapers which had showered venom on the living Reed praised him. The lion was dead and the jackals could now howl their relief.

In his lifetime, John Reed watched a world wither and crumble in the blast of war. He was among the first to cross the frontier to socialism, and after he crossed it, he gained in maturity and his partisanship in its cause became irrevocable. In his passionate faith in a future without war and poverty, he found the full dignity of man and, in socialism, the road to full freedom. The road was not easy to discover and harder yet to travel. But struggle steeled him, made him a relentless foe of imperialism.

His biography does not end with his death. The years since his passing have magnified his pioneer work in drawing closer the American and Soviet peoples in enduring ties of friendship and understanding. John Reed lives as a luminous symbol of peace, of a patriotism that demands one's country play a full and honorable role in the progressive history of mankind.

War in Paterson

There's war in Paterson, New Jersey. But it's a curious kind of war. All the violence is the work of one side—the mill owners. Their servants, the police, club unresisting men and women and ride down law-abiding crowds on horseback. Their paid mercenaries, the armed detectives, shoot and kill innocent people. Their newspapers, the Paterson *Press* and the Paterson *Call,* publish incendiary and crime-inciting appeals to mob violence against the strike leaders. Their tool, Recorder Carroll, deals out heavy sentences to peaceful pickets that the police net gathers up. They control absolutely the police, the press, the courts.

Opposing them are about twenty-five thousand striking silk workers, of whom perhaps ten thousand are active, and their weapon is the picket line. Let me tell you what I saw in Paterson and then you will say which side of this struggle is "anarchistic" and "contrary to American ideals."

At six o'clock in the morning a light rain was falling. Slate-gray and cold, the streets of Paterson were deserted. But soon came the cops—twenty of them—strolling along with their nightsticks under their arms. We went ahead of them toward the mill district. Now we began to see workmen going in the same direction, coat collars turned up, hands in their pockets. We came into a long street, one side of which was lined with silk mills, the other side with the wooden tenement houses. In every doorway, at every window of the houses clustered men and women, laughing and chatting as if after breakfast on a holiday. There seemed no sense of expectancy, no strain or feeling of fear. The sidewalks were almost empty, only over in front of the mills a few couples—

there couldn't have been more than fifty—marched slowly up and down, dripping with the rain. Some were men, with here and there a man and woman together, or two young boys. As the warmer light of full day came the people drifted out of their houses and began to pace back and forth, gathering in little knots on the corners. They were quick with gesticulating hands, and low-voiced conversation. They looked often toward the corners of side streets.

Suddenly appeared a policeman, swinging his club. "Ah-h-h!" said the crowd softly.

Six men had taken shelter from the rain under the canopy of a saloon. "Come on! Get out of that!" yelled the policeman, advancing. The men quietly obeyed. "Get off this street! Go on home, now! Don't be standing here!" They gave way before him in silence, drifting back again when he turned away. Other policemen materialized, hustling, cursing, brutal, ineffectual. No one answered back. Nervous, bleary-eyed, unshaven, these officers were worn out with nine weeks incessant strike duty.

On the mill side of the street the picket line had grown to about four hundred. Several policemen shouldered roughly among them, looking for trouble. A workman appeared, with a tin pail, escorted by two detectives. "Boo! Boo!" shouted a few scattered voices. Two Italian boys leaned against the mill fence and shouted a merry Irish threat, "Scab! Come outa here I knock your head off!" A policeman grabbed the boys roughly by the shoulder. "Get to hell out of here!" he cried, jerking and pushing them violently to the corner, where he kicked them. Not a voice, not a movement from the crowd.

A little further along the street we saw a young woman with an umbrella, who had been picketing, suddenly confronted by a big policeman.

"What the hell are *you* doing here?" he roared. "God damn you, you go home!" and he jammed his club against her mouth. "I *no* go home!" she shrilled passionately, with blazing eyes. "You big stiff!"

Silently, steadfastly, solidly the picket line grew. In groups or in couples the strikers patrolled the sidewalk. There was no more laughing. They looked on with eyes full of hate. These were fiery Italians, and the police were the same brutal thugs that had beaten them and insulted them for nine weeks. I wondered how long they could stand it.

It began to rain heavily. I asked a man's permission to stand on the porch of his house. There was a policeman standing in front of it. His name, I afterwards discovered, was McCormack. I had to walk around him to mount the steps.

Suddenly he turned round, and shot at the owner: "Do all them fellows live in that house?" The man indicated the three other strikers and himself, and shook his head at me.

"Then you get to hell off of there!" said the cop, pointing his club at me.

"I have the permission of this gentleman to stand here," I said. "He owns this house."

"Never mind! Do what I tell you! Come off of there, and come off damn quick!"

"I'll do nothing of the sort."

With that he leaped up the steps, seized my arm, and violently jerked me to the sidewalk. Another cop took my arm and they gave me a shove.

"Now you get to hell off this street!" said Officer McCormack.

"I won't get off this street or any other street. If I'm breaking any law, you arrest me!"

Officer McCormack was dreadfully troubled by my request. He didn't want to arrest me, and said so with a great deal of profanity.

"I've *got* your number," said I sweetly. "Now will you tell me your name?"

"Yes," he bellowed, "an' I got *your* number! I'll arrest you." He took me by the arm and marched me up the street.

He was sorry he *had* arrested me. There was no charge he could lodge against me. I hadn't been doing anything. He felt he must make me say something that could be construed as a violation of the law. To which end he God-damned me harshly, loading me with abuse and obscenity, and threatened me with his night stick, saying, "You big - - lug, I'd like to beat the hell out of you with this club."

I returned airy persiflage to his threats.

Other officers came to the rescue, two of them, and supplied fresh epithets. I soon found them repeating themselves, however, and told them so. "I had to come all the way to Paterson to put one over on a cop!" I said. Eureka! They had at last found a crime! When I was arraigned in the Recorder's Court that remark of mine was the charge against me!

Ushered into the patrol wagon, I was driven with much clanging of gongs along the picket line. Our passage was greeted with "Boos" and ironical cheers, and enthusiastic waving. At headquarters I was interrogated and lodged in the lockup. My cell was about four feet wide by seven feet long, at least a foot higher than a standing man's head, and it contained an iron bunk hung from the side-wall with chains, and an open toilet of disgusting dirtiness in the corner. A crowd of pickets had been jammed into the same lockup only three days before, *eight or nine in a cell,* and kept there without food or water for *twenty-two hours!* Among them a young girl of seventeen, who had led a procession right up to the police sergeant's nose and defied him to arrest them. In spite of the horrible discomfort, fatigue and thirst, these prisoners had *never let up cheering and singing* for a day and a night!

In about an hour the outside door clanged open, and in came about forty pickets in charge of the police, joking and laughing among themselves. They were hustled into the cells, two in each. Then pandemonium broke loose! With one accord the heavy iron beds were lifted and slammed thunderingly against the metal walls. It was like a cannon battery in action.

"Hooray for I.W.W.!" screamed a voice. And unanimously answered all the voices as one, "Hooray!"

"Hooray for Chief Bums!" (Chief of Police Bimson).

"Boo-o-o-!" roared forty pairs of lungs—a great boom of echoing sound that had more of hate in it than anything I ever heard.

"To hell with Mayor McBride!"

"Boo-o-o-!" It was an awful voice in that reverberant iron room, full of menace.

"Hooray for Haywood!* One big Union! Hooray for strike! To hell with the police! Boo-o-o-o! Boo-o-o-o! Hooray!"

"Music! Music!" cried the Italians. Whereupon one voice went "Plunk-plunk! Plunk-plunk!" like a guitar, and another, a rich tenor, burst into the first verse of the Italian-English song, written and composed by one of the strikers to be sung at the strike meetings. He came to the chorus:

> Do you like Miss Flynn?**
> (Chorus) Yes! Yes! Yes! Yes!
> Do you like Mayor McBride?
> (Chorus) No! No! NO! NO!!!
> Hooray for I.W.W.!
> Hooray! Hooray!! Hooray!!!

"*Bis! Bis!*" shouted everybody, clapping hands, banging the beds up and down. An officer came in and attempted to quell the noise. He was met with "Boos" and jeers. Some one called for water. The policeman filled a tin cup and brought it to the cell door. A hand reached out swiftly and slapped it out of his fingers on the floor. "Scab! Thug!" they yelled. The policeman retreated. The noise continued.

---

* William D. ("Big Bill") Haywood, leader of the Western Federation of Miners, one of the founders of the Industrial Workers of the World, and a leader of many American labor struggles. In later years he joined the Communist Party.—*Ed.*

** Elizabeth Gurley Flynn, at the time a leading member of the I.W.W. Later active in labor defense, and a leader of the Communist Party.—*Ed.*

The time approached for the opening of the Recorder's Court, but word had evidently been brought that there was no more room in the county jail, for suddenly the police appeared and began to open the cell doors. And so the strikers passed out, cheering wildly. I could hear them outside, marching back to the picket line with the mob which had waited for them at the jail gates.

And then I was taken before the court of Recorder Carroll. Mr. Carroll has the intelligent, cruel, merciless face of the ordinary police court magistrate. But he is worse than most police court magistrates. He sentences beggars to *six months' imprisonment* in the county jail without a chance to answer back. He also sends little children there, where they mingle with dopefiends, and tramps, and men with running sores upon their bodies—to the county jail, where the air is foul and insufficient to breathe, and the food is full of dead vermin, and grown men become insane.

Mr. Carroll read the charge against me. I was permitted to tell my story. Officer McCormack recited a clever *mélange* of lies that I am sure he himself could never have concocted. "John Reed," said the Recorder. "Twenty days." That was all.

And so it was that I went up to the county jail. In the outer office I was questioned again, searched for concealed weapons, and my money and valuables taken away. Then the great barred door swung open and I went down some steps into a vast room lined with three tiers of cells. About eighty prisoners strolled around, talked, smoked, and ate the food sent in to them by those outside. Of this eighty almost half were strikers. They were in their street clothes, held in prison under 500 dollar bail to await the action of the Grand Jury. Surrounded by a dense crowd of short, dark-faced men, Big Bill Haywood towered in the center of the room. His big hand made simple gestures as he explained something to them. His massive, rugged face, seamed and scarred like a mountain, and as calm, radiated strength. These strikers, one of many desperate little armies in the vanguard of the battleline of labor, quickened and strengthened by Bill Haywood's face and voice, looked up at him lovingly, eloquently. Faces deadened and dulled with grinding routine in the sunless mills glowed with hope and understanding. Faces scarred and bruised from policemen's clubs grinned eagerly at the thought of going back on the picket line. And there were other faces, too–lined and sunken with the slow starvation of a nine weeks' poverty–shadowed with the sight of so much suffering, or the hopeless brutality of the police. But not one showed discouragement; not one a sign of faltering or of fear. As one little Italian said to me, with blazing eyes: "We all one big Union. I.W.W.–the word is pierced in the heart of the people!"

"Yes! Yes! right! I.W.W.! One big Union"–they murmured with soft, eager voices, crowding around.

I shook hands with Haywood.

"Boys," said Haywood, indicating me, "this man wants to *know* things. You tell him everything–"

They crowded around me, shaking my hand, smiling, welcoming me. "Too bad you get in jail," they said, sympathetically. "We tell you everything. You ask. We tell you. Yes. Yes. You good feller."

And they did. Most of them were still weak and exhausted from their terrible night before in the lockup. Some had been lined up against a wall, as they marched to and fro in front of the mills, and herded to jail on the charge of "unlawful assemblage!" Others had been clubbed into the patrol wagon on the charge of "rioting," as they stood at the track, on their way home from picketing, waiting for a train to pass! They were being held for the Grand Jury that indicted Haywood and Gurley Flynn. *Four of these jurymen were silk manufacturers, another the head of the local Edison company–which Haywood tried to organize for a strike–and not one a workingman!*

"We not take bail," said another, shaking his head. "We stay here. Fill up the damn jail. Pretty soon no more room. Pretty soon can't arrest no more pickets!"

It was visitors' day. I went to the door to speak with a friend. Outside the reception room was full of women and children, carrying packages, and pasteboard boxes, and pails full of dainties and little comforts lovingly prepared, which meant hungry and ragged wives and babies, so that the men might be comfortable in jail. The place was full of the sound of moaning; tears ran down their work-roughened faces; the children looked up at their fathers' unshaven faces through the bars and tried to reach them with their hands. . . .

The keeper ordered me to the "convicted room," where I was pushed into a bath and compelled to put on regulation prison clothes. I shan't attempt to describe the horrors I saw in that room. Suffice it to say that forty-odd men lounged about a long corridor lined on one side with cells; that the only ventilation and light came from one small skylight up a funnel-shaped airshaft; that one man had syphilitic sores on his legs and was treated by the prison doctor with sugar-pills for "nervousness"; that a seventeen-year-old boy *who had never been sentenced* had remained in that corridor without ever seeing the sun for over *nine months*; that a cocaine fiend was getting his "dope" regularly from the inside, and that the background of this and much more was the monotonous and terrible shouting of a man who had lost his mind in that hell-hole and who walked among us.

There were about fourteen strikers in the "convicted" room—Italians, Lithuanians, Poles, Jews, one Frenchman and one "free-born" Englishman! That Englishman was a peach. He was the only Anglo-Saxon striker in prison except the leaders—and perhaps the only one who *had been* there for picketing. He had been sentenced for insulting a mill owner who came out of his mill and ordered him off the sidewalk. "Wait till I get out," he said to me. "If them damned English-speaking workers don't go on picket *I'll* put the curse o' Cromwell on 'em!"

Then there was a Pole—an aristocratic, sensitive chap, a member of the local strike committee, a born fighter. He was reading Bob Ingersoll's lectures, translating them to the others. Patting the book, he said with a slow smile: "Now I don't care if I stay in here one year. . . ."

With laughter, the strikers told me how the combined clergy of the city of Paterson had attempted from their pulpits to persuade them back to work—back to wage-slavery and the tender mercies of the mill owners on grounds of religion! They told me of that disgraceful and ridiculous conference between the clergy and the strike committee, with the clergy in the part of Judas. It was hard to believe that until I saw in the paper the sermon delivered the previous day at the Presbyterian Church by the Reverend William A. Littell. He had the impudence to flay the strike leaders and advise workmen to be respectful and obedient to their employers—to tell them that the saloons were the cause of their unhappiness—to proclaim the horrible depravity of Sabbath-breaking workmen and more rot of the same sort. And this while living men were fighting for their very existence and singing gloriously of the Brotherhood of Man! . . .

Then there was the strikebreaker. He was a fat man, with sunken, flabby cheeks, jailed by some mistake of the Recorder. So completely did the strikers ostracize him—rising and moving away when he sat by them, refusing to speak to him, absolutely ignoring his presence—that he was in a pitiable condition of loneliness.

"I've learned my lesson," he moaned. "I ain't never goin' to scab on workingmen no more!"

One young Italian came up to me with a newspaper and pointed to three items in turn. One was "American Federation of Labor hopes to break the strike next week," another, "Victor Berger says 'I am a member of the A. F. of L., and I have no love for the I.W.W. in Paterson,'" and the third, "Newark Socialists refuse to help the Paterson strikers."

"I no understand," he told me, looking up at me appealingly. "You tell me. I Socialist—I belong union—I strike with I.W.W. Socialist, he say, 'Workmen of the world, unite!' A. F. of L., he say, 'All workmen join together.' Both these organizations, he say, 'I am for the working class.' All right,

I say, I am the working class. I unite, I strike. Then he say, 'No! You *cannot* strike.' What that? I no understand. You explain me."

But I could not explain. All I could say was that a good share of the Socialist Party and the American Federation of Labor have forgotten all about the class struggle, and seem to be playing a little game with capitalistic rules, called "Button, button, who's got the vote!"

When it came time for me to go out I said good-bye to all those gentle, alert, brave men, ennobled by something greater than themselves. *They* were the strike—not Bill Haywood, not Gurley Flynn, not any other individual. And if they should lose all their leaders other leaders would arise from the ranks, even as *they* rose, and the strike would go on! Think of it! Twelve years they have been losing strikes—twelve solid years of disappointments and incalculable suffering. They must not lose again! They cannot lose!

And as I passed out through the front room they crowded around me again, patting my sleeve and my hand, friendly, warm-hearted, trusting, eloquent. Haywood had gone out on bail.

"You go out," they said softly. "That's nice. Glad you go out. Pretty soon we go out. Then we go back on picket line."

1913

Insurgent Mexico

At Yermo there is nothing but leagues and leagues of sandy desert, sparsely covered with scrubby mesquite and dwarf cactus, stretching away on the west to jagged, tawny mountains, and on the east to a quivering skyline of plain. A battered watertank, with too little dirty alkali water, a demolished railway station shot to pieces by Orozco's cannon two years before, and a switch track compose the town. There is no water to speak of for forty miles. There is no grass for animals. For three months in the spring bitter, parching winds drive the yellow dust across it.

Along the single track in the middle of the desert lay ten enormous trains, pillars of fire by night and of black smoke by day, stretching back northward farther than the eye could reach. Around them, in the chaparral, camped nine thousand men without shelter, each man's horse tied to the mesquite beside him, where hung his one serape and red strips of drying meat. From fifty cars horses and mules were being unloaded. Covered with sweat and dust, a ragged trooper plunged into a cattle-car among the flying hoofs, swung himself upon a horse's back, and jabbed his spurs deep in, with a yell. Then came a terrific drumming of frightened animals, and suddenly a horse shot violently from the open door, usually backward, and the car belched flying masses of horses and mules. Picking themselves up, they fled in terror, snorting through wide nostrils at the smell of the open. Then the wide, watchful circle of troopers turned *vaqueros* lifted the great coils of their lassoes through the choking dust, and the running animals swirled round and round upon one another in panic. Officers, orderlies, generals with their staffs, sol-

57

diers with halters, hunting for their mounts, galloped and ran past in inextricable confusion. Bucking mules were being harnessed to the caissons. Troopers who had arrived on the last trains wandered about looking for their brigades. Way ahead some men were shooting at a rabbit. From the tops of the boxcars and the flatcars, where they were camped by the hundreds, the *soldaderas* and their half-naked swarms of children looked down, screaming shrill advice and asking everybody in general if they had happened to see Juan Moneros, or Jesus Hernandez, or whatever the name of their man happened to be.... One man trailing a rifle wandered along shouting that he had nothing to eat for two days and he couldn't find his woman who made his *tortillas* for him, and he opined that she had deserted him to go with some——of another brigade.... The women on the roofs of the cars said, *"Válgame Dios!"* and shrugged their shoulders; then they dropped him down some three-days-old *tortillas*, and asked him for the love he bore Our Lady of Guadalupe, to lend them a cigarette. A clamorous, dirty throng stormed the engine of our train, screaming for water. When the engineer stood them off with a revolver, telling them there was plenty of water in the water train, they broke away and aimlessly scattered, while a fresh throng took their places. Around the twelve immense tank-cars, a fighting mass of men and animals struggled for a place at the little faucets ceaselessly pouring. Above the place a mighty cloud of dust, seven miles long and a mile wide, towered up into the still, hot air, and, with the black smoke of the engines, struck wonder and terror into the Federal outposts fifty miles away on the mountains back of Mapimi.

When Villa* left Chihuahua for Torreon, he closed the telegraph wires to the north, stopped train service to Juarez, and forbade on pain of death that anyone should carry or send news of his departure to the United States. His object

* Francisco (Pancho) Villa, a guerrilla leader in the peasant revolt against the despotic rule of President Porfirio Diaz.—*Ed*.

was to take the Federals* by surprise, and it worked beautifully. No one, not even Villa's staff, knew when he would
leave Chihuahua; the army had delayed there so long that
we all believed it would delay another two weeks. And then
Saturday morning we woke to find the telegraph and railways cut, and three huge trains, carrying the Brigada Gon-
zalez-Ortega, already gone. The Zaragosa left the next day,
and Villa's own troops the following morning. Moving with
the swiftness that always characterizes him, Villa had his
entire army concentrated at Yermo the day afterward, without the Federals knowing that he had left Chihuahua.

There was a mob around the portable field telegraph that
had been rigged up in the ruined station. Inside, the instru-
ment was clicking. Soldiers and officers indiscriminately
choked up the windows and the door, and every once in a
while the operator would shout something in Spanish and a
perfect roar of laughter would go up. It seemed that the telegraph had accidentally tapped a wire that had not been destroyed by the Federals–a wire that connected with the Federal military wire from Mapimi to Torreon.

"Listen!" cried the operator. "Colonel Argmedo in command of the *cabecillos colorados*** in Mapimi is telegraphing
to General Velasco in Torreon. He says that he sees smoke
and a big dust cloud to the north, and thinks that some rebel
troops are moving south from Escalon!"

Night came, with a cloudy sky and a rising wind that began to lift the dust. Among the miles and miles of trains, the
fires of the *soldaderas* flared from the tops of the freight cars.
Out into the desert so far that finally they were mere pin-
points of flame stretched the innumerable campfires of the
army, half obscured by the thick billowing dust. The storm
completely concealed us from Federal watchers. "Even
God," remarked Major Leyva, "even God is on the side of
Francisco Villa!" . . .

* Mexican government conscripts.–*Ed.*
** The irregular troops of the Mexican Army.–*Ed.*

Out in that dust storm, on a flatcar immediately ahead of ours, some soldiers lay around their fires with their heads in their women's laps, singing *The Cockroach,* which tells in hundreds of satirical verses what the Constitutionalists* would do when they capture Juarez and Chihuahua from Mercado and Orozco.

Above the wind one was aware of the immense sullen murmur of the host, and occasionally some sentry challenged in a falsetto howl: *"Quién vive?"* And the answer: *"Chiapas!" "Qué gente?" "Chaco!"* ... Through the night sounded the eerie whistle of the ten locomotives at intervals as they signaled back and forth to one another.

At dawn next morning General Torribio Ortega came to the car for breakfast–a lean, dark Mexican, who is called "The Honorable" and "The Most Brave" by the soldiers. He is by far the most simple-hearted and disinterested soldier in Mexico. He never kills his prisoners. He has refused to take a cent from the Revolution beyond his meager salary. Villa respects and trusts him perhaps beyond all his generals. Ortega was a poor man, a cowboy. He sat there, with his elbows on the table, forgetting his breakfast, his big eyes flashing, smiling his gentle, crooked smile, and told us why he was fighting.

"I am not an educated man," he said. "But I know that to fight is the last thing for any people. Only when things get too bad to stand, eh? And, if we are going to kill our brothers, something fine must come out of it, eh? You in the United States do not know what we have seen, we Mexicans! We have looked on at the robbing of our people, the simple, poor people, for thirty-five years, eh? We have seen the *rurales* and the soldiers of Porfirio Diaz shoot down our brothers and our fathers and justice denied to them. We have seen our little fields taken away from us, and all of us sold

* Volunteer Mexican fighters pledged to defend the constitution and progress in the country.–*Ed.*

into slavery, eh? We have longed for our homes and for schools to teach us, and they have laughed at us. All we have ever wanted was to be let alone to live and to work and to make our country great, and we are tired—tired and sick of being cheated. . . ."

Outside in the dust, that whirled along under a sky of driving clouds, long lines of soldiers on horseback stood in the obscurity, while their officers passed along in front, peering closely at cartridge belts and rifles. . . .

Across the desert westward toward the distant mountains rode strings of cavalry, the first to the front. About a thousand went, in ten different lines, diverging like wheel spokes; the jingle of their spurs ringing, their red-white-and-green flags floating straight out, crossed bandoliers gleaming dully, rifles flopping across their saddles, heavy, high sombreros and many-colored blankets.

Behind each company plodded ten or twelve women on foot, carrying cooking utensils on their heads and backs, and perhaps a pack mule loaded with sacks of corn. And as they passed the cars they shouted back to their friends on the trains. . . .

Villa himself stood leaning against a car, hands in his pockets. He wore an old slouch hat, a dirty shirt without a collar, and a badly frayed and shiny brown suit. All over the dusty plain in front of him men and horses had sprung up like magic. There was an immense confusion of saddling and bridling—a cracked blowing of tin bugles. The Brigada Zaragosa was getting ready to leave camp—a flanking column of two thousand men who were to ride southeast and attack Tlahualilo and Sacramento. Villa, it seemed, had just arrived at Yermo. He had stopped off Monday night at Camargo to attend the wedding of a *compadre*. His face was drawn into lines of fatigue.

"*Carramba!*" he was saying with a grin. "We started dancing Monday evening, danced all night, all the next day, and last night, too! What a *baile!* And what *muchachas!* The girls of Camargo and Santa Rosalia are the most beautiful in Mexico! I am worn out—*rendido!* It was harder work than twenty battles...."

Then he listened to the report of some staff officer who dashed up on horseback, gave a concise order without hesitating, and the officer rode off. He told Señor Calzado, general manager of the railroad, in what order the trains should proceed south. He indicated to Señor Uro, the quartermaster-general, what supplies should be distributed from the troop trains. To Señor Munoz, director of the telegraph, he gave the name of a Federal captain surrounded by Urbina's men a week before and killed with all his men in the hills near La Cadena, and ordered him to tap the Federal wire and send a message to General Velasco in Torreon purporting to be a report from this captain from Conejos, and asking for orders ... He seemed to know and order everything....

In a great circle, ready for action, the artillery was parked, with caissons open and mules corralled in the center. Colonel Servin, commander of the guns, sat perched high up on an immense bay horse, a ridiculous tiny figure, not more than five feet tall. He was waving his hand and shouting a greeting across to General Angeles, Carranza's* Secretary of War— a tall, gaunt man, bareheaded in a brown sweater, with a war map of Mexico hanging from his shoulder; who straddled a small burro. In the thick dust clouds, sweating men labored. The five American artillery men had squatted down in the lee of a cannon, smoking. They hailed me with a shout:

"Say, bo! What in hell did we get into this mess for? Nothing to eat since last night—work twelve hours—say, take our pictures, will you?"

Late in the afternoon the Brigada Zaragosa rode away over the desert, and another night came down.

The wind rose steadily in the darkness, growing colder and colder. Looking up at the sky, which had been ablaze with polished stars, I saw that all was dark with cloud. Through

* Venustiano Carranza, leader of the revolutionary forces and president of Mexico.—*Ed.*

the roaring whirls of dust a thousand thin lines of sparks from the fires streamed southward. The coaling of the engines' fireboxes made sudden glares along the miles of trains. At first we thought we heard the sound of big guns in the distance. But all at once, unexpectedly, the sky split dazzlingly open from horizon to horizon, thunder fell like a blow, and the rain came level and thick as a flood. For a moment the human hum of the army was silenced. All the fires disappeared at once. And then came a vast shout of anger and laughter and discomfiture from the soldiers out on the plain, and the most amazing wail of misery from the women that I have ever heard. The two sounds only lasted a minute. The men wrapped themselves in their serapes and sank down in the shelter of the chaparral; and the hundreds of women and children exposed to the cold and the rain on the flatcars and the tops of the boxcars silently and with Indian stoicism settled down to wait for dawn. . . .

The water train pulled out first. I rode on the cowcatcher of the engine, which was already occupied by the permanent home of two women and five children. They had built a little fire of mesquite twigs on the narrow iron platform, and were baking *tortillas* there; over their heads, against the windy roar of the boiler, fluttered a little line of wash. . . .

It was a brilliant day, hot sunshine alternating with big white clouds. In two thick columns, one on each side of the train, the army was already moving south. As far as the eye could reach, a mighty double cloud of dust floated over them; and little straggling groups of mounted men jogged along, with every now and then a big Mexican flag. Between slowly moved the trains; the pillars of black smoke from their engines, at regular intervals, growing smaller, until over the northern horizon only a dirty mist appeared.

I went down into the caboose to get a drink of water, and there I found the conductor of the train lying in his bunk reading the Bible. He was so interested and amused that he didn't notice me for a minute. When he did he cried delightedly: *"Oiga,* I have found a great story about a chap called Samson who was *muy hombre*–a good deal of a man–and his woman. She was a Spaniard, I guess, from the mean trick she played on him. He started out being a good Revolutionist, a Maderista,* and she made him a *pelón!"*

Pelón means literally "cropped head," and is the slang term for a Federal soldier, because the Federal army is largely recruited from the prisons.

Our advance guard, with a telegraph field operator, had gone on to Conejos the night before, and they met the train in great excitement. The first blood of the campaign had been spilt; a few *colorados* scouting northward from Bermejillo had been surprised and killed just behind the shoulder of the big mountain which lies to the east. The telegrapher also had news. He had again tapped the Federal wire, and sent to the Federal commander in Torreon, signing the dead captain's name and asking for orders, since a large force of rebels seemed to be approaching from the north. General Velasco replied that the captain should hold Conejos and throw out outposts to the north, to try and discover how large the force was. At the same time the telegrapher had heard a message from Argumedo, in command at Mapimi, saying that the entire north of Mexico was coming down on Torreon, together with the Gringo army!

Conejos was just like Yermo, except that there was no water tank. A thousand men, with white-bearded old General Rosalio Hernandez riding ahead, went out almost at once, and the repair train followed them a few miles to a place where the Federals had burned two railroad bridges a few months before. Out beyond the last little bivouac of the immense army spread around us, the desert slept silently in the heat waves. There was no wind. The men gathered with their women on the flatcars, guitars came out, and all night hundreds of singing voices came from the trains.

* A follower of Francisco Madero, Mexican liberal leader and president of the country from 1911 until his assassination in 1913.–*Ed.*

The next morning I went to see Villa in his car. This was a red caboose with chintz curtains on the windows, the famous little caboose which Villa has used in all his journeys since the fall of Juarez. It was divided by partitions into two rooms—the kitchen and the general's bedroom. This tiny room, ten by twenty feet, was the heart of the Constitutionalist army. There were held all the councils of war, and there was scarcely room enough for the fifteen generals who met there. In these councils the vital immediate questions of the campaign were discussed, the generals decided what was to be done—and then Villa gave his orders to suit himself. It was painted a dirty gray. On the walls were tacked photographs of Carranza and a picture of Villa himself. Two double-width wooden bunks folded up against the wall, in one of which Villa and General Angeles slept, and in the other José Rodriguez and Doctor Raschbaum, Villa's personal physician. That was all. . . .

"*Qué desea, amigo?* (What do you want?)" said Villa, sitting on the end of the bunk in blue underclothes. The troopers who lounged around the place lazily made way for me.

"I want a horse, *mi General.*"

"*Ca-r-r-r-r-ai-i*, our friend here wants a horse!" grinned Villa sarcastically amid a burst of laughter from the others. "Why, you correspondents will be wanting an automobile next! *Oiga*, señor reporter, do you know that about a thousand men in my army have no horses? Here's the train. What do you want a horse for?"

"So I can ride with the advance."

"No," he smiled. "There are too many *balazos*—too many bullets flying in the advance. . . ."

He was hurrying into his clothes as he talked, and gulping coffee from the side of a dirty tin coffee pot. Somebody handed him his gold-handled sword.

"No!" he said contemptuously. "This is to be a fight, not a parade. Give me my rifle!"

He stood at the door of his caboose for a moment, thoughtfully looking at the long lines of mounted men, picturesque in their crossed cartridge belts and varied equipment. Then he gave a few quick orders and mounted his big stallion.

"Vámonos!" cried Villa. The bugles brayed and a subdued, clicking ringing sounded as the companies wheeled and trotted southward in the dust. . . .

And so the army disappeared. During the day we thought we heard cannonading from the southwest, where Urbina was reported to be coming down from the mountains to attack Mapimi. And late in the afternoon news came of the capture of Bermejillo, and a courier from Benavides said that he had taken Tlahualilo.

We were in a fever of impatience to be off. About sundown Señor Calzado remarked that the repair train would leave in an hour, so I grabbed a blanket and walked a mile up the line of trains to it.

The first car of the repair train was a steel-encased flatcar, upon which was mounted the famous Constitutionalist cannon *"El Niño,"* with an open caisson full of shells behind it. Behind that was an armored car full of soldiers, then a car of steel rails, and four loaded with railroad ties. The engine came next, the engineer and fireman hung with cartridge belts, their rifles handy. Then followed two or three boxcars full of soldiers and their women. It was a dangerous business. A large force of Federals were known to be in Mapimi, and the country swarmed with their outposts. Our army was already far ahead, except for five hundred men who guarded the trains at Conejos. If the enemy could capture or wreck the repair train the army would be cut off without water, food, or ammunition. In the darkness we moved out. I sat upon the breech of *"El Niño,"* chatting with Captain Diaz, the commander of the gun, as he oiled the breech lock of his beloved cannon and curled his vertical mustachios. In the armored recess behind the gun, where the captain slept, I heard a curious, subdued rustling noise.

"What's that?"

"Eh?" cried he nervously. "Oh, nothing, nothing!"

Just then there emerged a young Indian girl with a bottle in her hand. She couldn't have been more than seventeen, very lovely. The captain shot a glance at me, and suddenly whirled around.

"What are you doing here?" he cried furiously to her. "Why are you coming out here?"

"I thought you said you wanted a drink," she began.

I perceived that I was one too many, and excused myself. They hardly noticed me. But as I was climbing over the back of the car I couldn't help stopping and listening. They had gone back to the recess, and she was weeping.

"Didn't I tell you," stormed the captain, "not to show yourself when there are strangers here? I will not have every man in Mexico looking at you. . . ."

I stood on the roof of the rocking steel car as we nosed slowly along. Lying on their bellies on the extreme front platform, two men with lanterns examined each foot of the track for wires that might mean mines planted under us. Beneath my feet the soldiers and their women were having dinner around fires built on the floor. Smoke and laughter poured out of the loopholes. There were other fires aft, brown-faced, ragged people squatting at them, on the car tops. Overhead the sky blazed stars, without a cloud. It was cold. After an hour of riding we came to a piece of broken track. The train stopped with a jar, the engine whistled, and a score of torches and lanterns jerked past. Men came running. A fire sprang up in the brush, and then another. Soldiers of the train guard straggled by, dragging their rifles, and formed impenetrable walls around the fires. Iron tools clanged, and the "Wai-hoy!" of men shoving rails off the flatcar. A Chinese dragon of workmen passed with a rail on their shoulders, then others with ties. Four hundred men swarmed upon the broken spot, working with extraordinary energy and good humor, until the shouts of gangs setting rails and ties, and the rattle of sledges on spikes, made a continuous roar. It was an old destruction, probably a year old, made when the same Constitutionalists were retreating north in the face of Mercado's Federal army, and we had it all fixed in an hour. Then on again. Sometimes it was a bridge burned out, sometimes a hundred yards of track twisted into grape vines by a chain and a backing engine. We advanced slowly. At one big bridge that it would take two hours to prepare, I built by myself a little fire in order to get warm. Calzado came past, and hailed me. "We've got a hand-car up ahead," he said, "and we're going along down and seeing the dead men. Want to come?"

"What dead men?"

"Why, this morning an outpost of eighty *rurales* was sent scouting north from Bermejillo. We heard about it over the wire and informed Benavides on the left. He sent a troop to take them in the rear, and drove them north in a running fight for fifteen miles until they smashed up against our main body and not one got out alive. They're scattered along the whole way just where they fell."

In a moment we were speeding south on the handcar. At our right hand and our left rode two shadowy figures on horseback—cavalry guards, with rifles ready under their arms. Soon the flares and fires of the train were left behind, and we were enveloped and smothered in the vast silence of the desert.

"Yes," said Calzado, "the *rurales* are brave. They are *muy hombres*. *Rurales* are the best fighters Diaz and Huerta ever had. They never desert to the Revolution. They always remain loyal to the established government. Because they are police."

It was bitter cold. None of us talked much.

"We go ahead of the train at night," said the soldier at my left, "so that if there are any dynamite bombs underneath–"

"We could discover them and dig them out and put water in them, *carramba!*" said another sarcastically. The rest laughed. I began to think of that, and it made me shiver. The dead silence of the desert seemed an expectant hush. One couldn't see ten feet from the track.

68

"Oiga!" shouted one of the horsemen. "It was just here that one lay." The brakes ground and we tumbled off and down the steep embankment, our lantern jerking ahead. Something lay huddled around the foot of a telegraph pole—something infinitely small and shabby, like a pile of old clothes. The *rural* was upon his back, twisted sideways from his hips. He had been stripped of everything of value by the thrifty rebels—shoes, hat, underclothing. They had left him his ragged jacket with the tarnished silver braid, because there were seven bullet holes in it; and his trousers, soaked in blood. He had evidently been much bigger when alive—the dead shrink so. A wild red beard made the pallor of his face grotesque, until you noticed that under it and the dirt, and the long lines of sweat of his terrible fight and hard riding, his mouth was gently and serenely open as if he slept. His brains had been blown out.

"Carrai!" said one guard. "There was a shot for the dirty goat! Right through the head!"

The others laughed. "Why, you don't think they shot him there in the fight, do you, *pendejo?"* cried his companion. "No, they *always* go around and make sure afterward—"

"Hurry up! I've found the other," shouted a voice off in the darkness.

We could reconstruct this man's last struggle. He had dropped off his horse, wounded—for there was blood on the ground—into a little dry arroyo. We could even see where his horse had stood while he pumped shells into his Mauser with feverish hands, and blazed away, first to the rear, where the pursuers came running with Indian yells, and then at the hundreds and hundreds of bloodthirsty horsemen pouring down from the north, with the demon Pancho Villa at their head. He must have fought a long time, perhaps until they ringed him around with living flame—for we found hundreds of empty cartridges. And then, when the last shot was spent, he made a dash eastward, hit at every step; hid for a moment under the little railroad bridge, and ran out upon the open desert, where he fell. There were twenty bullet holes in him.

They had stripped him of all save his underclothes. He lay sprawled in an attitude of desperate action, muscles tense, one fist clenched and spread across the dust as if he were dealing a blow; the fiercest exultant grin on his face. Strong, savage, until one looked closer and saw the subtle touch of weakness that death stamps on life—the delicate expression of idiocy over it all. They had shot him through the head three times—how exasperated they must have been!

Crawling south through the cold night once more . . . A few miles and then a bridge dynamited, or a strip of track wrecked. The stop, the dancing torches, the great bonfires leaping up from the desert, and the four hundred wild men pouring furiously out and falling upon their work . . . Villa had given orders to hurry. . . .

We had taken Bermejillo the afternoon before—the army breaking into a furious gallop five kilometers north of the town and pouring through it at top speed, driving the unprepared garrison in a rout southward—a running fight that lasted five miles, as far as the Hacienda of Santa Clara—and killing a hundred and six *colorados*. Within a few hours afterward Urbina came in sight above Mapimi, and the eight hundred *colorados* there, informed of the astonishing news that the entire Constitutionalist army was flanking them on their right, evacuated the place, and fled hotly to Torreon. All over the country the astounded Federals were falling back in a panic upon the city.

Late in the afternoon a dumpy little train came down the narrow-gauge track from the direction of Mapimi, and from it proceeded the loud strains of a string orchestra of ten pieces playing *"Recuerdos* of Durango"—to which I had so often *baile'd* with the Tropa. The roofs, doors, and windows were packed with Mexicans, singing and beating time with their heels, as they fired their rifles in a sort of salute upon entering the town. At the station this curious equipage drew up, and from it proceeded—who but Patricio, General Urbina's fighting stage-driver at whose side I had so often ridden and danced! He threw his arms around me yelling: "Juanito! Here is Juanito, *mi General!*"* In a minute we were asking and answering each other a million questions. Did I have the photographs I took of him? Was I going to the battle of Torreon? Did he know where Don Petronilo was? And Pablo Seanes? And Raphaelito? And right in the midst of it somebody shouted, "Viva Urbina!" and the old general himself stood at the top of the steps—the lion-hearted hero of Durango. He was lame, and leaned upon two soldiers. He held a rifle in his hand—an old, discarded Springfield, with the sights filed down—and wore a double cartridge belt around his waist. For a moment he remained there, absolutely expressionless, his small, hard eyes boring into me. I thought he did not recognize me, when all at once his harsh, sudden voice shot out: "That's not the camera you had! Where's the other one?"

I was about to reply when he interrupted: "I know. You left it behind you in La Cadena. Did you run very fast?"

"Yes, *mi General.*"

"And you've come to Torreon to run again?"

"When I began to run from La Cadena," I remarked, nettled, "Don Petronilo and the troops were already a mile away."

He didn't answer, but came haltingly down the steps of the car, while a roar of laughter went up from the soldiers. Coming up to me, he put a hand over my shoulder and gave me a little tap on the back. "I'm glad to see you, *compañero*," he said. . . .

Across the desert the wounded had begun to straggle in from the battle of Tlahualilo to the hospital train, which lay far up near the front of the line of trains. On the flat barren plain, as far as I could see, there were only three living things in sight: a limping, hatless man, with his hand tied up in bloody cloth; another staggering beside his staggering horse;

* Before joining Villa's forces in their march on Torreon, Reed had been with General Urbina's troops when they were pushed out of La Cadena.—*Ed.*

71

and a mule mounted by two bandaged figures far behind them. And in the still hot night we could hear from our car groans and screams. . . .

Late Sunday morning we were again on *"El Niño"* at the head of the repair train, moving slowly down the track abreast of the army. *"El Chavalito,"* another cannon mounted on a flatcar, was coupled behind, then came two armored cars, and the workcars. This time there were no women. The army wore a different air, winding along in two immense serpents each side of us—there was little laughter or shouting. We were close now, only eighteen miles from Gomez Palacio, and no one knew what the Federals planned to do. It seemed incredible that they would let us get so close without making one stand. Immediately south of Bermejillo we entered a new land. To the desert succeeded fields bordered with irrigation ditches, along which grew immense green alamos, towering pillars of freshness after the baked desolation we had just passed through. Here were cotton fields, the white tufts unpicked and rotting on their stalks; cornfields with sparse green blades just showing. Along the big ditches flowed swift, deep water in the shade. Birds sang, and the barren western mountains marched steadily nearer as we went south. . . .

At Santa Clara the massed columns of the army halted and began to defile to left and right, thin lines of troops jogging out under the checkered sun and shade of the great trees, until six thousand men were spread in one single front, to the right over fields and through ditches, beyond the last cultivated field, across the desert to the very base of the mountains; to the left over the roll of the flat world. The bugles blared faintly and near, and the army moved forward in a mighty line across the whole country. Above them lifted a five-mile-wide golden dust-glory. Flags flapped. In the center, level with them, came the cannon car, and beside that Villa rode with his staff. At the little villages along the way the big-hatted, white-bloused *pacíficos* stood in silent wonder, watching this strange host pass. An old man drove his goats homeward. The foaming wave of troopers broke upon him, yelling with pure mischief, and all the goats ran in different directions. A mile of army shouted with laughter—the dust rolled up from their thousand hoofs, and they passed. At the village of Brittingham the great line halted, while Villa and his staff galloped up to the peons watching from their little mound.

"*Oye!*" said Villa. "Have any troops passed through here lately?"

"*Si señor!*" answered several men at once. "Some of Don Carlo Argumedo's *gente* went by yesterday pretty fast."

"Hum," Villa meditated. "Have you seen that bandit Pancho Villa around here?"

"No, señor!" they chorused.

"Well, he's the fellow I'm looking for. If I catch that *diablo* it will go hard with him!"

"We wish you all success!" cried the *pacificos,* politely.

"You never saw him, did you?"

"No. God forbid!" they said fervently.

"Well!" grinned Villa. "In the future when people ask if you know him you will have to admit that shameful fact! I am Pancho Villa!" And with that he spurred away, and all the army followed. . . .

Such had been the surprise of the Federals, and they had fled in such a hurry, that for many miles the railroad was intact. But toward afternoon we began to find little bridges burned and still smoking, and the telegraph poles cut down with an axe—badly and hastily done bits of destruction that were easily repaired. But the army had got far ahead, and by nightfall, about eight miles from Gomez Palacio, we reached the place where eight solid miles of torn-up track began. There was no food on our train. We had only a blanket apiece; and it was cold. In the flare of torches and fires, the repair gang fell upon their work. Shouts and hammering steel, and the thud of falling ties. . . . It was a black night, with a few dim stars. We had settled down around one fire, talking and drowsing, when suddenly a new sound smote the air—a sound heavier than hammers, and deeper than the wind. It shocked—and was still. Then came a steady roll, as of distant drums, and then shock! shock! The hammers fell, voices were silent, we were frozen. Somewhere ahead, out of sight, in the darkness—so still it was that the air carried every sound—Villa and the army had flung themselves upon Gomez Palacio, and the battle had begun. It deepened steadily and slowly, until the booffs of cannon fell echoing upon each other, and the rifle fire rippled like steel rain.

"Andale!" screamed a hoarse voice from the roof of the cannon-car. "What are you doing? Get at that track! Pancho Villa is waiting for the trains!"

And, with a yell, four hundred raging maniacs flung themselves upon the break. . . .

I remember how we besought the colonel in command to let us go to the front. He would not. Orders were strict that no one should leave the trains. We pled with him, offered him money, almost got on our knees to him. Finally he relented a little.

"At three o'clock," he said, "I'll give you the sign and countersign and let you go."

We curled miserably about a little fire of our own, trying to sleep, trying at least to get warm. Around us and ahead the flares and the men danced along the ruined track; and every hour or so the train would creep forward a hundred feet and stop again. It was not hard to repair—the rails were intact. A wrecker had been hitched to the right-hand rail and the ties twisted, splintered, torn from their bed. Always the monotonous and disturbing furious sound of battle filtered out of the blackness ahead. It was so tiresome, so much the *same*, that sound; and yet I could not sleep. . . .

About midnight one of our outposts galloped from the rear of the trains to report that a large body of horsemen had been challenged coming from the north, who said they were Urbina's *gente* from Mapimi. The colonel didn't know of any

74

body of troops that were to pass at that time of night. In a minute everything was a fury of preparation. Twenty-five armed and mounted men galloped like mad to the rear, with orders to stop the newcomers for fifteen minutes—if they were Constitutionalists, by order of the colonel; if not, by holding them off as long as possible. The workmen were hurried back to the train and given their rifles. The fires were put out, the flares—all but ten—extinguished. Our guard of two hundred slipped silently into the thick brush, loading their rifles as they went. On either side of the track the colonel and five of his men took up their posts, unarmed, with torches held high over their heads. And then, out of the thick blackness, the head of the column appeared. It was made up of different men from the well-clothed, well-equipped, well-fed soldiers of Villa's army. These were ragged, gaunt people, wrapped in faded, tattered serapes, without shoes on their feet, crowned with the heavy, picturesque sombreros of the back-country. Lasso ropes hung coiled at their saddles. Their mounts were the lean, hard, half-savage ponies of the Durango mountains. They rode sullenly, contemptuous of us. They neither knew the countersign nor cared to know it. And as they rode, whole files sang the monotonous, extemporaneous balladas that the peons compose and sing to themselves as they guard the cattle at night on the great upland plains of the north.

And suddenly, as I stood at the head of the line of flares, a passing horse was jerked to his haunches, and a voice I knew cried "Hey, Meester!" the enfolding serape was cast high in the air, the man fell from his horse, and in a moment I was clasped in the arms of Isidro Amaya. Behind him burst forth a chorus of shouts: "*Qué tal!* Meester! O Juanito, how glad we are to see you! Where have you been? They said you were killed in La Cadena! Did you run fast from the *colorados? Mucho susto*, eh?" They threw themselves to the ground, clustering around, fifty men reaching at once to pat me on the back; all my dearest friends in Mexico—the *compañeros* of La Tropa and the Cadena!

The long file of men, blocked in the darkness, raised a chorus of shouts: "Move on! *Vámonos!* What's the matter? Hurry up! We can't stay here all night!" And the others yelled back: "Here's meester! Here's the Gringo we were telling you about who danced the *jota* in La Zarca! Who was in La Cadena!" And then the others crowded forward too.

There were twelve hundred of them. Silently, sullenly, eagerly, sniffing the battle ahead, they defiled between the double line of high-held torches. And every tenth man I had known before. As they passed the colonel shouted to them: "What is the countersign? Turn your hats up in front! Do you know the countersign?" Hoarsely, exasperatedly, he bawled at them. Serenely and insolently they rode by, without paying the least attention to him. "To hell with the countersign!" they hooted, laughing at him. "We don't need any countersign! They'll know well enough which side we're on when we begin to fight!"...

The steady noise of battle filled all the night. Ahead torches danced, rails clanged, sledges drummed on the spikes, the men of the repair gang shouted in the frenzy of their toil. It was after twelve. Since the trains had reached the beginning of the torn track we had made half a mile. Now and then a straggler from the main body came down the line of trains, shuffled into the light with his heavy mauser awry across his shoulders, and faded into the darkness toward the debauch of sound in the direction of Gomez Palacio. The soldiers of our guard, squatting about their little fires in the fields, relaxed their tense expectancy; three of them were singing a little marching song, which began:

> I don't want to be a Porfirista,
> I don't want to be an Orozquista,
> But I want to be a volunteer in the army Maderista!

Curious and excited, we hurried up and down the trains, asking people what they knew, what they thought. I had never heard a real killing-sound before, and it made me

76

frantic with curiosity and nervousness. We were like dogs in a yard when a dogfight is going on outside. Finally the spell snapped and I found myself desperately tired. I fell into a dead sleep on a little ledge under the lip of the cannon, where the laborers tossed their wrenches and sledge-hammers and crowbars when the train moved forward a hundred feet, and piled on themselves with shouts and horseplay.

In the coldness of before dawn I woke with the colonel's hand on my shoulder.

"You can go now," he said. "The sign is 'Zaragosa' and the countersign 'Guerrero.' Our soldiers will be recognized by their hats pinned up in front. May you go well!"

It was bitter cold. We threw our blankets around us, serape fashion, and trudged down past the fury of the repair gang as they hammered at it under the leaping flares—past the five armed men slouching around their fire on the frontier of the dark.

"Are you off to the battle, *compañeros?*" cried one of the gang. "Look out for the bullets!" At that they all laughed. The sentries cried, *"Adios!* Don't kill them all! Leave a few *pelónes* for us!"

Beyond the last torch, where the torn track was wrenched and tumbled about on the uprooted roadbed, a shadowy figure waited for us.

"Vámonos together," he said, peering at us. "In the dark three are an army." We stumbled along over the broken track, silently, just able to make him out with our eyes. He was a little dumpy soldier with a rifle and a half-empty cartridge belt over his breast. He said that he had just brought a wounded man from the front to the hospital train and was on his way back.

"Feel this," he said, holding out his arm. It was drenched. We could see nothing.

"Blood," he continued unemotionally. "His blood. He was my *compadre* in the Brigada Gonzales-Ortega. We went in this night down there and so many, so many—We were cut in half."

It was the first we had heard, or thought, of wounded men. All of a sudden we heard the battle. It had been going on steadily all the time, but we had forgotten—the sound was so monstrous, so monotonous. Far rifle fire came like the ripping of strong canvas, the cannon shocked like pile drivers. We were only six miles away now.

Out of the darkness loomed a little knot of men—four of them—carrying something heavy and inert in a blanket slung between. Our guide threw up his rifle and challenged, and his answer was a retching groan from the blanket.

"*Oiga, compadre,*" lisped one of the bearers huskily. "Where, for the love of the Virgin, is the hospital train?"

"About a league—"

"*Válgame Dios!* How can we—"

"Water! Have you any water?"

They stood with the blanket taut between them, and something fell from it, drip, drip, drip, on the ties.

That awful voice within screamed once, "To drink!" and fell away to a shuddering moan. We handed our canteens to the bearers—and silently, bestially, they drained them. The wounded man they forgot. Then, sullen, they pitched on. . . .

Others appeared, singly, or in little groups. They were simply vague shapes staggering in the night, like drunkards, like men incredibly tired. One dragged between two walkers, his arms around their shoulders. A mere boy reeled along with the limp body of his father on his back. A horse passed with his nose to the ground, two bodies flopping sideways across the saddle, and a man walking behind and beating the horse on the rump, cursing shrilly. He passed, and we could hear his falsetto fading dissonantly in the distance. Some groaned, with the ugly, deadened groan of uttermost pain; one man, slouched in the saddle of a mule, screamed mechanically every time the mule took a step. . . .

Soon we were near the battle. In the east, across the vast level country, a faint gray light appeared. The noble alamo trees, towering thickly in massy lines along the ditches to the

78

west, burst into showers of bird song. It was getting warm, and there came the tranquil smell of earth and grass and growing corn—a calm summer dawn. Into this the noise of battle broke like something insane. The hysterical chatter of rifle fire, that seemed to carry a continuous undertone of screaming—although when you listened for it it was gone. The nervous, deadly stab—stab—stab—stab of the machine guns, like some gigantic woodpecker. The cannon booming like great bells, and the whistle of their shells. Boom—Pi-i-i-e-e-a-uuu! And that most terrible of all the sound of war, shrapnel exploding. Crash—Whee-e-eaaa!!

The great hot sun swam up in the east through a faint smoke from the fertile land, and over the eastern barrens the heat waves began to wiggle. It caught the startlingly green tops of the lofty alamos fringing the ditch that paralleled the railroad on our right. The trees ended there, and beyond, the whole rampart of bare mountains, piled range on range, grew rosy. We were now in scorched desert again, thickly covered with dusty mesquite. Except for another line of alamos straggling across from east to west, close to the city, there were no trees in all the plain but two or three scattered ones to the right. So close we were, barely two miles from Gomez Palacio, that we could look down the torn track right into the town. We could see the black round water tank, and back of that the roundhouse, and across the track from them both the low adobe walls of the Brittingham Corral. The smoke-stacks and buildings and trees of La Esperanza soap factory rose clear and still, like a little city, to the left. Almost directly to the right of the railroad track, it seemed, the stark, stony peak of the Cerro de la Pila mounted steeply to the stone reservoir that crowned it, and sloped off westward in a series of smaller peaks, a spiny ridge a mile long. Most of Gomez lay behind the shoulder of the Cerro, and at its western end the villas and gardens of Lerdo made a vivid patch of green in the desert. The great brown mountains on the west made a mighty sweep around behind the two cities, and then fell away south again in folds on folds of gaunt desolation. And directly south from Gomez, stretched along the base of this range, lay Torreon, the richest city of northern Mexico.

The shooting never ceased, but it seemed to be subdued to a subordinate place in a fantastic and disordered world. Up the track in the hot morning light straggled a river of wounded men, shattered, bleeding, bound up in rotting and bloody bandages, inconceivably weary. They passed us, and one even fell and lay motionless nearby in the dust—and we didn't care. Soldiers with their cartridges gone wandered aimlessly out of the chaparral, dragging their rifles, and plunged into the brush again on the other side of the railroad, black with powder, streaked with sweat, their eyes vacantly on the ground. The thin, subtle dust rose in lazy clouds at every footstep, and hung there, parching throat and eyes. A little company of horsemen jogged out of the thicket and drew up on the track, looking toward town. One man got down from his saddle and squatted beside us.

"It was terrible," he said suddenly. "*Carramba!* We went in there last night on foot. They were inside the water tank, with holes cut in the iron for rifles. We had to walk up and poke our guns through the holes and we killed them all—a death trap! And then the Corral! They had two sets of loopholes, one for the men kneeling down and the other for the men standing up. Three thousand *rurales* in there—and they had five machine guns to sweep the road. And the roundhouse, with three rows of trenches outside and subterranean passages so they could crawl under and shoot us in the back. . . . Our bombs wouldn't work, and what could we do with rifles? *Madre de Dios!* But we were so quick—we took them by surprise. We captured the roundhouse and the water tank. And then this morning thousands came—thousands—reinforcements from Torreon—and their artillery—they drove us back again. They walked up to the water tank and poked their rifles through the holes and killed all of us—the sons of the devils!"

We could see the place as he spoke and hear the hellish

80

roar and shriek, and yet no one moved, and there wasn't a sign of the shooting—not even smoke, except when a shrapnel shell burst yelling down in the first row of trees a mile ahead and vomited a puff of white. The cracking rip of rifle fire and the staccato machine guns and even the hammering cannon didn't reveal themselves at all. The flat, dusty plain, the trees and chimneys of Gomez, and the stony hill, lay quietly in the heat. From the alamos off to the right came the careless song of birds. One had the impression that his senses were lying. It was an incredible dream, through which the grotesque procession of wounded filtered like ghosts in the dust. . . .

We returned along the winding path through the mesquite, crossed the torn-up track, and struck out across the dusty plain southeastward. Looking back along the railroad I could see smoke and the round front of the first train miles away; and in front of it throngs of active little dots swarming on the right of way, distorted like things seen in a wavy mirror. We strode along in a haze of thin dust. The giant mesquite dwindled until it scarcely reached to our knees. To the right the tall hills and the chimneys of the town swam tranquilly in the hot sun; rifle fire had almost ceased for the moment, and only dazzling bursts of thick white smoke marked our occasional shells along the ridge. We could see our drab guns rocking down the plain, spreading along the first line of alamos, where the searching fingers of the enemy's shrapnel probed continually. Little bodies of horsemen moved here and there over the desert, and stragglers on foot, trailing their rifles.

An old peon, stooped with age and dressed in rags, crouched in the low shrub gathering mesquite twigs.

"Say, friend," we asked him, "is there any way we can get in close to see the fighting?"

He straightened up and stared at us.

"If you had been here as long as I have," said he, "you wouldn't care about seeing the fighting. *Carramba!* I have seen them take Torreon seven times in three years. Sometimes they attack from Gomez Palacio and sometimes from the mountains. But it is always the same—war. There is something interesting in it for the young, but for us old people, we are tired of war." He paused and stared out over the plain. "Do you see this dry ditch? Well, if you will get down in it and follow along it will lead you into the town." And then, as an afterthought, he added curiously, "What party do you belong to?"

"The Constitutionalists."

"So. First it was the Maderistas, and then the Orozquistas, and now the—what did you call them? I am very old, and I have not long to live; but this war—it seems to me that all it accomplishes is to let us go hungry. Go with God, señores." And he bent again to his slow task, while we descended into the arroyo. It was a disused irrigation ditch running a little south of west, its bottom covered with dusty weeds, and the end of its straight length hidden from us by a sort of mirage that looked like a glaring pool of water. Stooped a little, so as to be hidden from the outside, we walked along, it seemed, for hours, the cracked bottom and dusty sides of the ditch reflecting the fierce heat upon us until we were faint with it. Once horsemen passed quite near on our right, their big iron spurs ringing; we crouched down until they passed, for we didn't want to take any chances. Down in the ditch the artillery fire sounded very faint and far away, but once I cautiously lifted my head above the bank and discovered that we were very near the first line of trees. Shells were bursting along it, and I could even see the belch of furious haze hurling out from the mouths of the cannon, and feel the surf of sound waves hit me like a blow when they fired. We were a good quarter of a mile in front of our artillery, and evidently making for the water tank on the very edge of the town. As we stooped again the shells passed overhead and whined sharply and suddenly across the arc of sky and were cut off abruptly until the sudden echoless booff! of their explosion. There ahead, where the railroad trestle of the main line crossed the arroyo, huddled a little pile of bodies—evidently left from the first attack. . . .

Under the shadow of the trestle four men sat playing cards. They played listlessly, without talking, their eyes red with lack of sleep. The heat was frightful. Occasionally a stray bullet came by screaming, "Where—is-s-s-z—ye!" This strange company took our appearance as a matter of course. The sharpshooter doubled up out of range and carefully put another cartridge clip in his rifle.

"You haven't got another drop of water in that canteen, have you?" he asked. "*Aido!* we haven't eaten or drunk since yesterday!" He guzzled the water, furtively watching the card players lest they, too, should be thirsty. "They say that we are to attack the water tank and the Corral again when the artillery is in position to support us. Chi-*hua*hua *hombre!* but it was *duro* in the night! They slaughtered us in the streets there. . . ." He wiped his mouth on the back of his hand and began firing again. We lay beside him and looked over. We were about two hundred yards from the deadly water tank. Across the track and the wide street beyond lay the brown mud walls of the Brittingham Corral, innocent looking enough now, with only black dots to show the double line of loopholes.

"There are the machine guns," said our friend. "See them, those slim barrels peeping over the edge?" We couldn't make them out. Water tank, Corral, and town lay sleeping in the heat. Dust hovered still in the air, making a thin haze. About fifty yards in front of us was a shallow exposed ditch, evidently once a Federal trench, for the dirt had been piled on our side. Two hundred drab, dusty soldiers lay in it now—the Constitutionalist infantry. They were sprawled on the ground, in all the attitudes of weariness; some sleeping on their backs, facing up to the hot sun; others wearily transferring the dirt with their scooped hands from rear to front. Before them they had piled up irregular heaps of rocks. . . .

Of a sudden the artillery in our rear boomed all together, and over our heads a dozen shells screamed toward the Cerro.

"That is the signal," said the man at our side. He clambered down into the ditch and kicked the sleeper. "Come on," he yelled. "Wake up. We're going to attack the *pelones*." The snorer groaned and opened his eyes slowly. He yawned and picked up his rifle without a word. The card players began to squabble about their winnings. A violent dispute broke out as to who owned the pack of cards. Grumbling and still arguing, they stumbled out and followed the sharpshooter up over the edge of the ditch.

Rifle fire rang along the edge of the trench in front. The sleepers flopped over on their stomachs behind their little shelters—their elbows worked vigorously pumping the guns. The hollow steel water tank resounded to the rain of thumping bullets; chips of adobe flew from the wall of the Corral. Instantly the wall bristled with shining barrels and two awoke crackling with hidden vicious firing. Bullets roofed the heavens with whistling steel—drummed the smoking dust up until a yellow curtain of whirling cloud veiled us from the house and the tank. We could see our friend running low along the ground, the sleepy man following, standing erect, still rubbing his eyes. Behind strung out the gamblers, squabbling yet. Somewhere in the rear a bugle blew. The sharpshooter running in front stopped suddenly, swaying, as if he had run against a solid wall. His left leg doubled under him and he sank crazily to one knee in the exposed flat, whipping up his rifle with a yell.

"— — the dirty monkeys!" he screamed, firing rapidly into the dust. "I'll show the —! The cropped heads! The jailbirds!" He shook his head impatiently, like a dog with a hurt ear. Blood drops flew from it. Bellowing with rage, he shot the rest of his clip, and then slumped to the ground and thrashed to and fro for a minute. The others passed him with scarcely a look. Now the trench was boiling with men scrambling to their feet, like worms when you turn over a log. The rifle fire rattled shrilly. From behind us came running feet, and men in sandals, with blankets over their shoulders, came falling and slipping down the ditch, and scrambling up the other side—hundreds of them, it seemed. . . .

They almost hid from us the front, but through the dust and spaces between running legs we could see the soldiers in the trench leap their barricade like a breaking wave. And then the impenetrable dust shut down and the fierce stabbing needle of the machine guns sewed the mighty jumble of sound together. A glimpse through a rift in the cloud torn by a sudden hot gust of wind—we could see the first brown line of men reeling altogether like drunkards, and the machine guns over the wall spitting sharp, dull red in the sunshine. Then a man came running back out of it, the sweat streaming down his face, without a gun. He ran fast, half sliding, down into our ditch and up the other side. Other dim forms loomed up in the dust ahead.

"What is it? How is it going?" I cried.

He answered nothing, but ran on. Suddenly and terribly the monstrous crash and scream of shrapnel burst from the turmoil ahead. The enemy's artillery! Mechanically I listened for our guns. Except for an occasional boom they were silent. Our homemade shells were failing again. Two more shrapnel shells. Out of the dust cloud men came running back—singly, in pairs, in groups, a stampeding mob. They fell over us, around us—drowned us in a human flood, shouting, "To the alamos! To the trains! The Federals are coming!" We struggled up among them and ran, too, straight up the railroad track. . . . Behind us roared the shells searching in the dust, and the tearing musketry. And then we noticed that all the wide roadway ahead was filled with galloping horsemen, yelling shrill Indian cries and waving their rifles—the main column! We stood to one side as they whirled past, about five hundred of them—watched them stoop in their saddles and begin to shoot. The drumming of their horses' hoofs was like thunder.

"Better not go in there! It's too hot!" cried one of the infantry with a grin.

"Well, I'll bet I'm hotter," answered a horseman, and we

all laughed. We walked tranquilly back along the railroad track, while the firing behind wound up to a continuous roar. A group of peons—*pacíficos*—in tall sombreros, blankets, and white cotton blouses, stood along here with folded arms, looking down the track toward town.

"Look out there, friends," joshed a soldier. "Don't stand there. You'll get hit."

The peons looked at each other and grinned feebly. "But, señor," said one, "this is where we always stand when there is a battle. . . ."

I was dead tired, reeling from lack of sleep and food and the terrible heat of the sun. About a half-mile out I looked back and saw the enemy's shrapnel poking into the line of trees more frequently than ever. They seemed to have thoroughly got the range. And just then I saw the gray line of guns, limbered to their mules, begin to crawl out from the trees toward the rear at four or five different points. Our artillery had been shelled out of their positions . . . I threw myself down to rest in the shade of a big mesquite bush.

Almost immediately a change seemed to come in the sound of the rifle fire, as if half of it had been suddenly cut off. At the same time twenty bugles shrilled. Rising, I noticed a line of running horsemen fleeing up the track, shouting something. More followed, galloping at the place where the railroad passed beyond the trees on its way into town. The cavalry had been repulsed. All at once the whole plain squirmed with men, mounted and on foot, all running rearward. One man threw away his blanket, another his rifle. They thickened over the hot desert, stamping up the dust, until the flat was crowded with them. Right in front of me a horseman burst out of the brush, shouting, "The Federals are coming! To the trains! They are right behind!" The entire Constitutionalist army was routed! I caught up my blanket and took to my heels. A little way farther on I came upon a cannon abandoned in the desert, traces cut, mules gone. Underfoot were guns, cartridge belts and dozens of serapes. It was a rout. Coming to an open space, I saw ahead a large crowd of fleeing soldiers, without rifles. Suddenly three men on horseback swept across in front of them, waving their arms and yelling. "Go back!" they cried. "They aren't coming out! Go back, for the love of God!" Two I didn't recognize. The other was Villa.

About a mile back the flight was stopped. I met the soldiers coming back, with the relieved expression of men who have feared an unknown danger and been suddenly set free from it. That was always Villa's power—he could explain things to the great mass of ordinary people in a way that they immediately understood. The Federals, as usual, had failed to take advantage of their opportunity to inflict a lasting defeat upon the Constitutionalists. Perhaps they feared an ambush like the one Villa had arranged at Mapula, when the victorious Federals sallied out to pursue Villa's fleeing army after the first attack on Chihuahua, and were repulsed with heavy slaughter. Anyway, they did not come out. The men came straggling back, hunting in the mesquite for their guns and blankets, and for other people's guns and blankets. You could hear them shouting and joking all over the plain. . . .

"O Juan," cried one man to another, "I always told you I could beat you running!"

"But you didn't, *compadre*. I was a hundred meters ahead, flying through the air like a cannon ball! . . ."

The truth was that after riding twelve hours the day before, fighting all night, and all morning in the blazing sun, under the frightful strain of charging an entrenched force in the face of artillery and machine guns, without food, water, or sleep, the army's nerves had suddenly given way. But from the time that they returned after the flight the ultimate result was never in doubt. The psychological crisis was past. . . .

1914

The Traders' War

The Austro-Serbian conflict is a mere bagatelle—as if Hoboken should declare war on Coney Island—but all the civilization of Europe is drawn in.

The real war, of which this sudden outburst of death and destruction is only an incident, began long ago. It has been raging for tens of years, but its battles have been so little advertised that they have been hardly noted. It is a clash of traders.

It is well to remember that the German empire began as a business agreement. Bismarck's first victory was the *Zollverein*, a tariff agreement between a score of petty German principalities. This commercial league was solidified into a powerful state by military victories. It is small wonder that German businessmen believe that their trade development depends on force.

"Ohne Armee, kein Deutschland" ["Without an army, no Germany"] is not only the motto of the Kaiser and the military caste. The success of the militarist propaganda of the Navy League and other such jingo organizations depends on the fact that nine Germans out of ten read history that way. . . .

After the Franco-Prussian war of 1870 came the *"Gründerzeit"* (the "foundation period"). Everything German leaped forward in a stupendous impulse of growth.

The withdrawal of the German mercantile marine from the sea has reminded us of the world-wide importance of their transportation services. All these great German fleets of ocean liners and merchantmen have sprung into being since 1870. In steel manufacture, in textile work, in mining and trading, in every branch of modern industrial and commercial life, and also in population, German development has been equally amazing.

But geographically all fields for development were closed.

In the days when there had been no army and no united Germany, the English and French had grabbed all the earth and the fullness thereof. . . .

England and France met German development with distrust and false sentiments of peace. "We do not intend to grab any more territory. The peace of Europe demands the maintenance of the status quo."

With these words scarcely cold on her lips, Great Britain took South Africa. And pretended to endless surprise and grief that the Germans did not applaud this closing of another market.

In 1909, King Edward—a great friend of peace—after long secret conferences, announced the *Entente Cordiale,* whereby France promised to back up England in absorbing Egypt, and England pledged to support France in her Morocco adventure.

The news of this underhand "gentleman's agreement" caused a storm. The Kaiser, in wild indignation, shouted that "Nothing can happen in Europe without my consent."

The peace-lovers of London and Paris agreed that this threat of war was very rude. But they were getting what they wanted without dirtying their hands in blood, so they consented to a Diplomatic Conference at Algeciras. France solemnly promised *not* to annex Morocco, and above all pledged herself to maintain "the Open Door." Everyone was to have an equal commercial chance. The storm blew over. . . .

One example out of a thousand of how the French observed their pledge to maintain an Open Door in Morocco is furnished by the method of buying cloth to uniform the Moorish Army.

In accordance with the "Act of Algeciras," which required that all contracts should be put up at international auction, it was announced that the Sultan had decided on a large order of khaki to make uniforms for his soldiers. "Specifications" would be published on a certain day—in accordance with the law—and the cloth manufacturers of the world were invited to be present.

The "specifications" demanded that the cloth should be delivered in three months and that it should be of a certain width—three yards, as I remember. "But," protested the representatives of a German firm, "there are no looms in the world of that width. It would take months to build them." But it developed that a far-seeing—or forewarned—manufacturer of Lyons had installed the necessary machines a few months before. He got the contract.

The Ambassador at Tangier has had to hire extra clerks to forward to Berlin the complaints of German merchants protesting against the impossibleness of France's "Open Door."...

Perhaps the most exasperating thing of all has been the row over the Baghdad Railroad. A group of German capitalists secured a franchise for a railroad to open up Asia Minor by way of Baghdad and the Persian Gulf. It was an undeveloped country which offered just the kind of commercial outlet they needed.

The scheme was blocked by England on the pretext that such a railroad might be used by the Kaiser to send his army halfway round the world to steal India. But the Germans understood very well that the English merchants and shipowners did not want to have their monopoly of Indian trade threatened.

Even when they scored this big commercial victory—the blocking of the Baghdad Railroad—the English diplomats protested their love of peace and their pure-hearted desire to preserve the status quo. It was at this juncture that a deputy in the Reichstag said, "The status quo is an aggression."

The situation in short is this. German capitalists want more profits. English and French capitalists want it all. This war of commerce has gone on for years....

No one can have a more utter abhorrence of militarism than I. No one can wish more heartily that the shame of it may be erased from our century. "It is neither by parliamentary oratory nor the votes of majorities that the great questions of the day can be solved but by blood and iron"—"*durch Blut und Eisen*"—these words of Bismarck are the motto of the Reaction. Nothing stands more squarely in the path of democratic progress.

And no recent words have seemed to me so ludicrously condescending as the Kaiser's speech to "his" people when he said that in this supreme crisis he freely forgave all those who had ever opposed him. I am ashamed that in this day in a civilized country anyone can speak such archaic nonsense.

But worse than the "personal government" of the Kaiser, worse even than the brutalizing ideals he boasts of standing for, is the raw hypocrisy of his armed foes, who shout for a peace which their greed has rendered impossible.

More nauseating than the crackbrained bombast of the Kaiser is the editorial chorus in America which pretends to believe—would have us believe—that the White and Spotless Knight of Modern Democracy is marching against the Unspeakably Vile Monster of Medieval Militarism.

What has democracy to do in an alliance with Nicholas, the tsar? Is it liberalism which is marching from the Petersburg of Father Gapon,* from the Odessa of pogroms? Are our editors naïve enough to believe this?

No. There is a falling out among commercial rivals. One side has observed the polite forms of diplomacy and has talked of "peace"—relying the while on the eminently pacific navy of Great Britain and the army of France and on the millions of semi-serfs whom they have bribed the Tsar of All the Russias (and The Hague) to scourge forward against

---

* A Russian priest who became a police agent. He led workers to present a petition to the tsar at the St. Petersburg Winter Palace, January 22, 1905, only to have them shot down by troops.—*Ed.*

the Germans. On the other side there has been rudeness—and the hideous Gospel of Blood and Iron.

We, who are Socialists, must hope—we may even expect—that out of the horror of bloodshed and dire destruction will come far-reaching social changes—and a long step forward towards our goal of peace among men.

But we must not be duped by this editorial buncombe about Liberalism going forth to Holy War against Tyranny.

This is not Our War.

1914

With the Allies

At the height of the great European war, the cataclysm of western civilization, Geneva glitters like Monte Carlo at the height of the season—Geneva, mother of the Red Cross; hostess of humanitarian congresses for the civilizing of warfare. It has come at last, what all the world dreaded, with the bombarding of open towns, the massacre of noncombatants, murder and mutilation of the wounded—the sack and burning of Louvain—and in Geneva are gathered the gaiety and frivolity of Europe. Germans, English, French dine together, dance together, and throng the gambling-table of the *Kursaal* at night, or crowd to see the latest naughty revue from Paris. At night the lights along the lake are a string of jewels. Red-coated orchestras play the lightest, merriest music, drowned in the laughing chatter of extravagant women and men in evening dress—English, French, German. The gay streets are patrolled by the fantastic girls of the Parisian boulevards. Nobody has any money; everyone is a trifle shabby. But all mention of the greatest war in the world's history is considered distinctly bad taste. Except for the Swiss mobilization orders posted on the walls, the companies of young soldiers drilling in the fields among the ungathered harvests, the silent throngs of French and German reservists in front of their consulates, war is a remote, an incredible thing. The papers speak of it, and every train brings piles of blatant, shrieking French and German journals. Everybody reads the papers; for a few minutes they discuss the news—"Do you think the Germans will actually get to Paris?" "Will that end the war?" "They actually wanted me to serve my military service, the brutes!"—and then the talk veers round to women and the theater and the latest place to dine. You take your *apéritif* and look out across the sunlit lake toward the mighty barrier of snow peaks, with the white little towns at their foot, and wonder if it isn't time to go to lunch. . . .

We took what was said to be the last train for Paris. The Germans, which was our name for a curious, alien race absolutely unconnected with those nice people in Berlin and Munich, were reported within thirty kilometers. It was even doubtful if our train would ever arrive. At Cernadon we pulled into the station beside ten third-class carriages which rocked with singing and cheering. Every door and window was decorated with masses of green vines and the branches of trees; and through the leaves stared hundreds of young faces and waving arms. They were the youth and the young blood of France, the Class of 1914, bound for the military centers to undergo a training that should stamp out all their impulses and ideas, and turn them into infinitesimal parts of an obedient machine to hurl against the youth of Germany, who had been treated the same way. *"Vive la France!"* they shouted. "We'll cut the Kaiser's mustaches! We want Alsace-Lorraine!" Ten different choruses in as many different stages of the *Marseillaise,* others singing the *Sambre et Meuse,* a hundred various renditions of the latest Paris music-hall songs roared in tremendous cacophony, a glorious hymn of youth out of school and out on a gigantic lark. On the sides of the cars they had chalked lascivious caricatures of Prussians in humiliating postures before a conquering French soldier. *"Mort aux Pruscos!* This train express for Berlin! Guides may be obtained here for Germans desiring to tour France!"

Later I saw regiments of veterans who had seen service in Algeria and in Belgium. Their cars were not decorated. They neither cheered nor sang, although they were going to the front. They went with that curious, detached professional air of a man going to work in a silk mill in the morning. Beasts, they wisely spent their spare time eating, drinking, and sleep-

94

ing, and for the rest obeyed their officers. That was what the Class of 1914 would become. It was not a pleasant thought.

We hitched the ten cars on behind our train, and the cheering and singing floated to us as we went on. It was late. We began to notice that every station was thronged with silent, gray-clad people, mostly women. Every crossroads was packed with them. They leaned from the windows of the houses fronting the railway, anxious-faced, weeping, waving their handkerchiefs—sisters, mothers and lovers of the Class of 1914. It began to rain toward dark, but still they stood there in the open—had been standing for hours, probably—silent, gray in the rain and gathering darkness, to see for the last time their boys on their way to fight the Germans for reasons they did not know, at the order of that superior intelligence, the Government.

At Bourg, where the line from the eastern frontier joins the railway to Lyons, we left the train for dinner, and found ourselves in a crowd of soldiers hurrying here and there, and many women dressed in the white costume of Red Cross nurses. A train pulled in slowly from the direction of Belfort. As it slowed up there came from it the appalling stench of iodoform. Men with wounded arms and hands and heads leaned out of the windows and bellowed for cigarettes. "Where are you from?" I asked one of them. "Beyond in Alsace," he answered. And the soldiers on the platform shouted: "They are from Alsace! Have we got Strasbourg yet?" "I don't know," said one of the wounded. "In the trenches one knows nothing. But there are no more Germans in France." *"Eh bien, mon ami,"* cried another, "they are within thirty kilometers of Paris!" "Do you hear that, *mes enfants?*" "That's not true," said another man with his head all wrapped up in a bloody bandage. "We killed too many of them. How many, then, are there of these damned *Pruscos?*"

"Ah, well, *je m'en fous!* I am going home to my country and eat eggs and drink wine and the damned war can go to the devil."

The train whistled, and the long line of carriages glided away south, a vista of waving, bandaged arms. At the end were two flatcars, their floors covered with straw; as they passed we could see by the feeble light the long rows of the desperately wounded lying on their backs, and there came to us a low buzzing hum of groaning. . . .

We drew close to Paris. Soldiers thickened along the roads. At the edge of every little patch of woods cavalry horses stood hitched, and the smoke of the men's breakfasts rose from the trees. Off yonder, on a low rise of ground, a company of soldiers with their coats off were digging a trench, their high-swung spades catching the sunlight. Here a swarm of men leveled a wood with swinging axes. There they piled cobblestones in carts, furniture and tree trunks across the road in a rude barricade at the entrance of some village. Train after train of soldiers, carrying long gray guns on flat-cars, passed us. We were now within the fortifications of the entrenched camp of Paris.

I remember how we saw the first British Tommy. Our train made a long stop in the middle of a bridge over a great river. On the parapet of the bridge, not twenty feet from us, sat a British soldier, fishing. His line was fastened to the tip of his bayonet, his cap was a little on one side of his head, and he whistled "It's a Long Way to Tipperary" as he gazed contentedly off toward the west. Hearing our English greeting, he came politely over and began to retail his adventures.

"O yuss, I been retreatin' with the others all the wye from Belgium; we'd a bit of a mix-up around Monss wye, an' I seen the Irish Guards cut to bits in Viviers Woods. My chum got took by the Prussies at a plyce I think they call it Cat-teau. They took the britches off him, an'—"

Just in the middle of this thrilling story another soldier came up.

"I sye," he said respectfully, "we ain't got no news down here whatever. Could you tell me, sir—do you know whether the Russians has entered Berlin?"

"Garn!" responded the other in great disgust. "Why, they 'aven't even crossed the Pyrenees yet!"

"What's the name of this place?" I asked.

"I don't rightly know, sir," answered Tommy. "We ain't been here but a week. It tykes a time to learn 'ow to sye it. These Frenchie nymes is all alike. . . ."

Our engine whistled, and we went on.

We came into Paris when the German advance was only thirty kilometers away. It was a beautiful September morning, with just a hint of crispness in the air—the kind of day when Paris returns from the country, and the streets of the city sparkle most of all the year. We emerged from the station into a city of the dead. Long vistas of empty streets—no omnibuses, no trucks, no streetcars—all the shops with their shutters down and literally covered with flags. Every window displayed five flags: French, Belgian, Russian, Serbian, and English. It was almost noon; yet along the Grands Boulevards, where it is said that one can sit on the *terrasse* of a café for an hour and see the whole world pass, scarcely a human being could be seen. Not a person was visible the whole length of the Rue de la Paix. The thunder of omnibuses, the roar of motor horns, shouting of street venders, and tramping of horses' hoofs that once made this the noisiest corner in the world were still. It was as if the city had decked itself out for some vast rejoicing, and then had sickened. For a deathlike silence was over everything, in which the hoofs of my cab horse echoed loudly. The newsboys were forbidden to cry their papers. They held them up mutely. "We will be arrested if we tell you how close the German army is to Paris, but you may read the whole thing here for five centimes." So we would buy, and cast our eye over the latest official communiqué, which said: "The strategic retreat of the Allies continues with great success. . . ."

Paris for the first time in its history failed to express any emotion. We've all heard a good deal about the calm stoicism of the Parisians when the city was in danger—of the stern courage with which they faced the siege. But the truth is that with two millions of the youth of France fighting a losing battle against the German hordes pouring down from the north, Paris, the heart and soul of France, remained tranquil, ignorant, apathetic. As the enemy approached, far from facing them, Paris emptied itself toward the south and west. Almost two million people left the city. The splendid and luxurious hotels, the palaces of the rich were offered to the Red Cross under the excuse of patriotism, but really so that the Red Cross flag would save them from German destruction. On the shutters of the closed shops were posted notices saying: "The proprietor and all the clerks have joined the army. *Vive la France!*" And yet when, after the Battle of the Marne, the population poured back into the city, these same shops reopened, and the proprietor and his clerks shamelessly reappeared; even some of the great hotels and houses were withdrawn from the Red Cross when all danger seemed past.

Regularly, day after day, a German airplane appeared out of the north, flying low over the roofs of the city, dropping a bomb here and there on innocuous streets, and a sheaf of proclamations summoning the Parisians to surrender, as the Germans were at the gates of the city. It always came at about four o'clock in the afternoon, and at that time all Paris was on the streets. One became cognizant of its presence by the sound of a terrific fusillade that followed along beneath the airplane and rolled away over the city. The population took to their roofs with a variety of firearms of the most fantastic description, and blazed away. The waiter serving you at the café dropped your drink with a crash, ran in and seized his gun, and emerged again on the street to bang away at the sky. A surging wave of small boys running and people on bicycles followed the course of the machine along the streets to see where the next bomb would fall. At the cafés the waiters adopted the custom of asking you to pay as soon as they brought your *apéritif*, because they said that all the customers ran away after the airplane without paying. The German airplanes were the diversion of Paris for a long time, and everyone was disappointed when they did not come.

Meanwhile the only stores that did a rushing business were those which advertised: *Complete mourning in six hours.* Each day the number of people in black on the streets increased. At the Mairies hundreds of anxious women stood in line all day long asking for news of their men. That was the only real emotion that one could see anywhere about the war. No lists of wounded or dead were published. You asked for a certain man. If he were well, there was no information. If dead, the fact was briefly stated, and within twenty-four hours you received the little tin identification tag with which every soldier was equipped on going into battle.

At night Paris was the most changed. The cafés closed at eight o'clock and the restaurants at nine. There were no theaters except an occasional moving picture show. The brilliant flood of lights from the cafés, the great golden arcs in the boulevards, the graceful necklace of lamps that traced the curves of the river and the bridges, the white brilliance of the Champs Elysées—all were dark. At half past nine the streets were absolutely deserted. But the great white beams of five searchlights played above the roofs of Paris, sweeping the sky for the long-expected airship attack. And through the dark streets the swinging tramp of regiments under my window, coming from unknown posts, and bound no one, not even themselves, knew whither.

This morning the drums were beating for the Guignol show; we paid our two sous and sat behind a deliriously delighted mob of very small children while Papa Guignol wrestled with the Devil, and his son outwitted the Gendarme. Some of the little children wore *crêpe* bands on their left arm—and they were perfectly delighted with the performance. The sunlight fell in checkers through the leaves. Looking up through a gap in the trees we saw an airplane, very high, glinting in the sun like a metallic bird. And as we strolled down toward the gate of the Gardens there came from outside a blare of trumpets and the rolling of drums. Everyone heard it. A regiment was passing, dusty, limping, the faces of the men unshaven and lined with dirt—a regiment from the front. It swung along stiffly, the tread of sore-footed men, its slanting bayonets swinging in unison. I stood thirty feet away, yet the smell was ghastly. It was the same smell that one gets in a Bowery lodginghouse on a winter's night when the heat of the stove begins to thaw bodies foul with disease and grime, and clothes crawling with vermin. The trumpets blew proudly, and the Thirtieth Regiment of the Line of the French Army shuffled swinging past between crowded sidewalks. No one made a sound. We looked on curiously, dully, at these unfamiliar beings clothed in uniforms, smelling of the slums, fresh from the glories of the battlefields, yet who were so absolutely unconnected with the Guignol show of the Luxembourg Gardens. . . .

Wraiths of mist were wreathing the top of the white tower of the Calais lighthouse when we left the restaurant and sauntered out into the Rue Royale after dinner. The Rue Royale is the Broadway of Calais. Streetcars clanged along, the shops and moving picture shows were open, and past the crowd waiting at the corner store for London papers by the last boat from Folkstone strolled a laughing, chattering stream of people—bourgeoisie of the good town of Calais: soldiers, sailors, fishermen, and their girls.

From the end of the pier we could follow with our eyes the blinding funnel of the enormous searchlight that lay straight and unmoving out across the Channel until it met at the center the white focus of the English light from Dover, just where a long gray British warship slipped north from the dark into the dark again.

In the Place d'Armes they were taking down the trestles and booths of the weekly market, with laughter and shouting, by the light of torches. We wandered along a silent cobbled street between ancient gray houses and found two drunken sailors, who conducted us to a Maison de Société, where there was an all-night café, music and girls. The place was full of sailors, with a sprinkling of soldiers. In twenty different keys and times they were roaring the *Marseillaise,* punctuated with shouts of *Vive la France!* We treated, and the crowd welcomed us like brothers. It appeared that the sailors belonged to the crews of three submarines which were to leave at five o'clock in the morning for the North Sea to do battle with the Germans; the soldiers, who had been wounded, were now convalescent, and were to rejoin their regiments the next day somewhere up on the vast battleline of the Aisne.

Toward morning, long after the sailors had gone, we drank champagne to the glory of the French arms with the three soldiers and two of the girls; and my socialist friend wanted to discover what was the real feeling back of the *Marseillaise* and the shouts of *Vive la France!* which made men so joyously go to their death.

"Why do you fight?" he asked.

"Because France is attacked by the Germans."

"But the Germans think that they are attacked, too."

"Yes, I know that," said one. "There have been some German prisoners in Calais. They are very good fellows."

"But perhaps they were attacked? Perhaps they were right?"

"It is possible," said the Frenchman.

"But if they were attacked, then why are you fighting?"

"Because," answered the other, "we were attacked, too."

"Besides," added a second, "we were called to the colors to fight for the *patrie.*"

My socialist friend embarked on a discussion of war. He said that the people did not profit by war; that the advance of the working class absolutely ceased with war; that it destroyed the best blood of the race; that it checked civilization, and hurled the poor back into the misery from which they had so long struggled to emerge. The three soldiers listened to this with the most profound interest.

"It is true," they said; "war is a terrible thing."

A grizzled man of about forty leaned forward earnestly and remarked:

"Monsieur is absolutely right. I have seen my comrades fall about me now for seven years. My best friend was killed at Charleroi, and, by God, I will avenge him on these *sacrés Pruscos!* Just wait until I get back on the firing line. I know war," he added, shaking his head proudly. "I have been six years in the Colonies. Look: here is a picture of me in the middle of my native troops in Indochina, where we have built up a fine native army to put down uprisings."

Another, a slight fellow with a charming face, said eagerly: "Yes, I am a socialist."

"Ah!" said my friend, "now at last we have something. Why are you fighting?"

"I am fighting," answered the other, with the air of one repeating a lesson, "to destroy Prussian despotism and set the working class free."

"But the Prussian working class is fighting to destroy Russian despotism."

"Yes, that is very true. They have told me that."

"But what will you get out of destroying Prussian militarism?"

"We will get freedom from Prussian militarism...."

"After this war," said the third, "there will be no more war."

"No more war," repeated the other two.

"Let's order another bottle of champagne," said the man from Indochina. "Tomorrow we are going back to our comrades. This time we give no quarter. The Germans have been killing our wounded, and two can play at that game...."

I asked the women what they thought of the war.

"The French and English are noble," said one. "The Germans are all *cochons! Vive la France!*"

"But what do you get out of it, this war you are cheering?"

"I? Nothing! Why should I get anything out of it? But it is good for me. There are many more soldiers and sailors in Calais than ever before."

I still retain the magnificent picture of my friend exchanging clothes with one of the French soldiers and strutting about the room with martial gestures, saying that he felt he would make a fine soldier! And after that we went home through the silent streets of Calais singing, until a patrol of suspicious military men informed us that Calais was under martial law, and that the war made it impossible to allow singing on the streets. . . .

Two weeks after the terrible battle of the Marne we went to Esternay to see the battlefield. Between Esternay and Sezanne the fiercest fighting took place. There the entire front of Von Bülow's army smashed into the French right wing and fought ceaselessly for three days; continuing a rearguard battle as it retreated northward again.

In the café at Esternay where we had lunch there were several French officers, and the French commandant of the place looked over our passports and courteously directed us to the battlefield. In Esternay itself there was a hole in a wall where a shell had struck. It had been plastered up again and two weeks more of sun and rain would so obliterate the newness that one would never know that there had been any shell. The chief indication of war was that eggs and milk were still hard to get. And then there were flies—thousands and thousands of flies—which had come to light upon the dead and would be gone with the cold weather. . . .

We passed the railway track, and walked along the Sezanne road. Regularly every three feet on the south side of the road was a little single trench where the German riflemen had held off the French infantry under a hail of shrapnel from the French guns. The French infantry had come down and across and up the meadow under cover of their artillery, and had taken the trenches at the point of the bayonet. The slaughter here had been frightful. For three days the French guns had rained death on that sloping meadow and in the woods beyond. We could see their effect upon the barns and outbuildings of a chateau that stood at the crossing of the roads, which had been utterly destroyed by the cannon and still sent up thin smoke and the stench of burned animals.

But already along the length of the battlefield a man driving a plow shouted to his oxen; already many scars of the shells lay under the brown furrow, nor could one tell where they had been. Even in the valley where the French infantry had reformed again and again under the awful fire, and where wisps of straw and a few tin cans were all that remained to show where an army had camped, new pale violet crocuses stood up from the exuberant earth like lamps in the shade.

We continued along the side road up the hill, apple trees loaded with fruit on one side, and on the other lush narrow meadows at the edge of the forest, to Chatillon, a village which had been exposed to the full flame of battle. There it was that the Germans had made their first desperate stand, and on retreating had burned and sacked the village. Shell fire had done the rest. Directly before us, fronting the crossroads, stood the gaunt empty walls of the village's combined store, café, and hotel; and in both directions stretched a ghastly vista of roofless houses with the stain of fire on their gaping door lintels. Only the village church and the schoolhouse remained intact—the latter, according to the schoolmaster, because three French soldiers in the attic had kept off the Germans through holes in the tiles. We imagined the horror of those terrible days—how the simple villagers, overcome by the blasting flame of war, had been slaughtered in the streets or had fled in terror from their homes, never to return. But the schoolmaster informed us that three days after the battle all the inhabitants had come back and were staying with their friends in the neighborhood until things could be rebuilt. Even the most complete and intentional destruction, and all the concentrated fire of all the French artillery, had not been able to obliterate this one small village. . . .

In the crisp, golden afternoon we went singing along the white road to Sezanne. A French officer warned us not to go into the woods, because soldiers were searching for a few miserable half-starved Germans who had hidden there after the battle; and from the heart of the forest we heard, indeed, two rifle shots. All the time, immeasurably distant in the north, sounded the troubling thunder of the cannon, where sleepless, wretched men mechanically killed each other near Rheims. We stood for a time listening to it and looking out over the yellow, rolling plains of Champigny, the same now as when Attila the Hun had been there more than a thousand years ago.

Here in the fields were long flat mounds of yellow earth—traces of quicklime about their edges—where the dead had been dragged by the leg and buried; Germans and French together. One long mound bore a wooden cross hung with flowers, on which was inscribed: "Here lie forty-three Frenchmen of the 73rd Regiment of the Line."

1914

The Colorado War

HERRINGTON *(Attorney for the Colorado Fuel and Iron Company)*: Just what is meant by "social freedom" I do not know. Do you understand what the witness meant by "social freedom," Mr. Welborn?

MR. WELBORN *(President of the Colorado Fuel and Iron Company)*: I do not.

From the testimony before the United States Congressional Investigating Committee.

I got into Trinidad about ten days after the massacre at Ludlow. Strolling up and down the main street, talking in little groups on the corners, lounging in and out of strike headquarters, were hundreds of big, strong-faced miners in their Sunday best. They sauntered along quietly, good-naturedly, hailing one another across the street in foreign tongues like a crowd of farmers come in for the country fair. The noticeable thing was there were no women. The women didn't come out of their cellars for several days later. . . .

It was a bright, sunny day. Stores and moving picture shows were open, streetcars and automobiles and ranchers on horseback went by. Policemen stood twirling their clubs on the corners just as if three nights before a lawless mob with rifles had not tramped the streets and prepared for a desperate house-to-house battle with the militia. Towering over the town to the east rose the great snow-covered rock of Fisher's Peak; to the north and west began the steep foothills, rocky and covered with scrub pines, in whose canyons lay the feudal coal towns, occupied by armed detectives with machine guns and searchlights.

A man came bursting into strike headquarters and said: "Three scab-herders coming down the street. Don't know whether they're coming here or—" The strikers all tried to get out of the door at once. On the sidewalks I saw that the moving crowd had stopped—frozen—and that all eyes were in one direction. The life of the town was suddenly paralyzed. In the hush the clatter of a passing horse sounded unnaturally loud.

Three militiamen were hurrying toward the station. They walked in the middle of the street, with their eyes on the ground, joking nervously and loudly. They walked between two lines of men on the sidewalks—two lines of hate. The strikers spoke no word; they never even hissed. They just looked, stiffening like hunting dogs, and as the soldiers passed they closed up silently, instinctively, behind them. The town held its breath. The streetcars stopped running. You couldn't hear anything but the silent tramping of a thousand feet and the shrill voices of the militiamen. Then the train came along and they boarded it. We straggled back. The town sprang to life again.

At the Trades Assembly Hall, where they fed the women and children, school had just let out. The children were singing one of the strike songs:

There's a fight in Colorado for to set the miners free.
From the tyrants and the money-kings and all the powers
    that be;
They have trampled on the freedom that was meant for
    you and me,
        But Right is marching on.

        Cheer, boys cheer the cause of Union,
        The Colorado Miners' Union;
        Glory, glory to our Union;
        Our cause is marching on.

On the school blackboard someone had written: "If a pious hypocrite goes slumming for Christ in New York and goes gunning for miners in Colorado, where does the uplift come in? If he endeavors to suppress white slaves in New York while fostering conditions favorable to the traffic elsewhere, does it buy him anything in 'the Sweet Bye and Bye?'"

I asked who wrote that, and they told me a Trinidad doctor who had no connection with the union. That is the extraordinary thing about this strike: that nine out of ten business and professional men in the coal district towns are violent strike sympathizers. After Ludlow, doctors, ministers, hack drivers, drug store clerks, and farmers joined the fighting strikers with guns in their hands. Their women organized the Federal Labor Alliance even among women whose husbands are not union men, to provide food and clothing and medical attendance for workers on strike. They are the kind of people who usually form Law and Order Leagues in times like these; who consider themselves better than laborers, and think that their interests lie with the employers. Many Trinidad shopkeepers had been ruined by the strike. A very respectable little woman, the wife of a clergyman, said to me: "I don't see why they ever made a truce until they had shot every mine guard and militiaman, and blown up all the mines with dynamite." That was indicative, for this class is the most self-satisfied. . . .

There is nothing revolutionary about this strike. The strikers are neither socialists, anarchists nor syndicalists. They do not want to confiscate the mines nor destroy the wage system; industrial democracy means nothing to them. They consider the boss almost a god. Humble, patient, and easily handled, they had reached a desperation of misery in which they did not know what to do. They had come to America eager for the things that the Statue of Liberty in New York harbor seemed to promise them. They came from countries where law is almost divine, and here, they thought, was a better law. They wanted to obey the laws. But the first thing they discovered was that the boss, in whom they trusted, insolently broke the laws.

To them the union was the first promise of happiness and of freedom to live their own lives. It told them that if they would combine and stand together they could force the boss to pay them enough to live on, and make it safe for them to work. And in the union they discovered all at once thousands of fellow workers who had been through the fight themselves, and were now ready to help them. This flood of human sympathy was an absolutely new thing to the Colorado strikers. As one Mexican said to me: "We go out despairing and there comes a river of friendship from our brothers that we never knew!"

A large part of those who are striking today were brought in as strikebreakers in the great walkout in 1903. Now in that year more than seventy per cent of the miners in southern Colorado were English speaking: Americans, English, Scotch, and Welsh. Their demands were practically the same as the present ones. Before that, every ten years, back to 1884, there had been similar strikes. Militia and imported mine guards wantonly murdered, imprisoned and deported out of the state hundreds of miners. Two years before the 1903 strike, six thousand men were blacklisted and beaten out of the mines, in defiance of the state law, because they belonged to the union. In spite of the eight hour law, no man worked less than ten hours, and when the miners went out Adjutant General Sherman Bell of the militia suspended the right of *habeas corpus*, remarking: "To hell with the Constitution!" After the strike was broken ten thousand men found themselves blacklisted, for the operators made a careful study of people most patient under oppression, and deliberately imported foreigners to fill the mines, carefully massing in each mine men of many different languages, who would not be able to organize. They policed their camps with armed guards, who had the right of trial and sentence for any crime.

Now, in order to understand the strike, the geography of the southern Colorado district is important. Two railroads run directly south from Denver to Trinidad. To the east stretches a vast, flat plain, far over the borders of Kansas.

Westward lie the foothills of the Rocky Mountains, running (roughly) north and south, and beyond them are the magnificent snow peaks of the Sangre de Cristo range. It is in the canyons between these foothills that most of the mines lie, and around these mines are feudal towns—the houses of the workmen, the stores, saloons, mine buildings, schools, post offices—all on private property, all fortified and patrolled as if in a state of war.

Three big coal companies—the Colorado Fuel and Iron Company, the Rocky Mountain Fuel Company, and the Victor American Fuel Company—produce sixty-eight per cent of all the coal in the state, and have advertised that they represent ninety-five per cent of the output. They naturally also control the prices and the policy of all the other coal companies in the state. Of these, the Colorado Fuel and Iron Company produces forty per cent of all the coal mined there, and of the Colorado Fuel and Iron Company Mr. Rockefeller owns forty per cent of the stock. Mr. Rockefeller absolutely controls the policy of the coal mining industry of Colorado. He said on the stand that he trusted absolutely in the knowledge and ability of the officers of the Colorado Fuel and Iron Company. He testified that he knew nothing of the conditions under which his miners worked, and that he left all to President Welborn and Chairman Bowers. They in turn testified that they knew nothing of the conditions under which the miners worked, but that they left all that to their subordinates. They did not even know how much stock Mr. Rockefeller held. And yet these men dared to go on the witness stand and say that the miners had no grievances, but were "a happy family!"

There has been a good deal of talk about the high wages paid to miners. As a matter of fact, most department store clerks get more. A coal miner, a man who actually digs the coal, was paid so much a ton for the pure coal dug, separated from impurities, loaded on cars and pushed out of the mine. The operators give glowing accounts of miners making 5 dollars a day. But the average number of working days a year in Colorado was 191, and the average gross wage of a coal digger was 2.12 dollars a day. In many places it was much lower. Men with a "pull" with the company made high wages; others have been known to work eight days without making money enough to pay for their blasting powder. For they must buy that themselves. They had to pay one dollar a month for doctor fees, and in some places for a broken leg or arm 10 dollars more. Anyway, the doctor only visited the mine every two weeks or so, and if you wanted him any other time you had to pay for an extra visit.

Many of these mine towns were incorporated towns. The mayor of the town was the mine superintendent. The school board was composed of company officials. The only store in town was the company store. All the houses were company houses, rented by the company to the miners. There was no tax on property, and all the property belonged to the mining company. . . .

According to the State Labor Commissioner, from 1901 up to 1910 the number of people killed in coal mines in Colorado, as compared with the rest of the United States all together, was 2 to 1; from 1910 up to the present time it is 3⅓ to 1. It was conclusively shown that the coal companies refused to take any precautions for the safety of their employees until they were forced to by law, and that even after that they refused to obey the recommendations of the State Mine Inspector. . . .

The coroner of Las Animas County is the head of an undertaking establishment officially employed by the coal companies, in which at least two coal company officials owned shares not long ago. His juries in these great accidents consisted of company employees chosen by the mine superintendents. In five years of unprecedented disaster, only one coroner's verdict in Las Animas County laid the blame on the company. You see, these verdicts were particularly valuable to the operators, because they disposed of the danger of damage suits. There haven't been any damage suits in that county for ten years.

This is a slight indication of the way in which the coal companies control politics in Las Animas and Huerfano counties. District attorneys, sheriffs, county commissioners, and judges were practically appointed in the offices of the Colorado Fuel and Iron Company. The people could not secure a delegate to the convention to nominate a justice of the peace without telephoning to Denver and asking permission of Cass Herrington, political manager for the Colorado Coal and Iron Company. . . .

After the 1903 strike the United Mine Workers had been wiped out of the country. In 1911 they re-established a branch office in Trinidad. From that time on there were rumors of a strike, and it is only from that time that the mine operators began partially to obey the laws. But most of the abuses were not corrected, and the miners realized at last that in order to secure any permanent justice from their employers they must be able to bargain with them collectively.

The United Mine Workers did everything they could to avoid the strike. They appealed to Governor Ammons to call a meeting of the operators to confer with them concerning the demands of the men; the company officials refused to meet them, and have so refused ever since. Then a convention of operators and employees was called at Trinidad, and an appeal was made to the employers to meet their men and listen to their grievances. For answer, the operators began to prepare for war. They set in motion their powerful machine for breaking strikes—a merciless engine refined by thirty years of successful industrial struggle. Gunmen were imported from Texas, New Mexico, West Virginia, and Michigan—strikebreakers and guards who had had long experience in labor troubles, soldiers of fortune, army deserters and ex-policemen. W. F. Reno, chief detective for the Colorado Fuel and Iron Company, recruited in the basement of a Denver hotel. To those that could shoot he gave rifles and ammunition and sent them down to the mines. The notorious Baldwin-Felts Detective Agency of strikebreakers was engaged, and many of their men, under bond for murder in other states, were made deputy sheriffs in the southern counties. Anywhere from twelve to twenty machine guns were shipped to the mines and put at their disposal. . . .

At the convention in Trinidad, September 16, delegates from all the mines in the district unanimously voted to call a strike on September 22. They demanded recognition of the union, a ten per cent advance in wages, an eight-hour day, pay for all "dead work," check weighmen, the right to trade at any store they pleased and to choose their own boarding place and doctor, enforcement of the Colorado mining laws, and the abolition of the guard system. . . .

The United Mine Workers announced that they would establish tent colonies to take care of the strikers, and, in the face of open menaces by the mine officials and the guards that they would repeat the slaughter and deportation of the 1903 strike, the miners began to arm themselves. . . .

There was a blizzard of snow and sleet on September 23. It was bitter cold. Early in the morning the guards made the rounds of the mines, asking the people whether or not they were going to work. When they answered no they were told to get out. At Tabasco guards came into the houses and threw women and children out into the snow, dumping their furniture and their clothes on the wet ground. At Tercio the workmen were given an hour to leave town; their furniture was thrown out into the street and they were followed out of the mine by guards, abusing them and threatening them with rifles. For fifty miles the mouths of canyons belched groups of men, and women with babies in their arms, and children trudging in the snow. Some had wagons, and long trains of broken-down hacks and carriages, piled high with the possessions of many families, straggled along the many roads toward the open plain.

At Pryor the company had offered special inducements for miners to build and own their own houses on the company grounds. They were ejected from these, and the women told by the mine guards to "Get to hell out or we'll burn you out!"

In West Virginia the operators had given strikers four days to leave. In Colorado it was twenty-four hours. Nobody was prepared. They were driven ruthlessly down the canyon without their clothes or furniture, and when wagons were sent back for their property, in many places, as at Primero, they were not allowed to get it.

And the tents had not arrived. Out on the cold plain, with the snow and sleet falling, huddled hundreds of refugees: men, women, and children, at the places where their leaders told them to gather. Still the tents did not come. Some of them remained for two days without shelter, digging holes in the ground and burrowing into them like animals, with nothing to eat or drink. There was a frantic raid on the tent stores in Denver, and along the base of the foothills for fifty miles the tent colonies began to rise, white in the white snow. It was like the migration of a race. Out of 13,000 miners at work in Colorado before the strike, 11,000 were out. The colonies were planted strategically at the mouths of the canyons leading up to the mines, to watch the roads by which strikebreakers might be brought in. Besides the big Ludlow colony, there were others at Starkville, Gray Creek, Suffield, Aguilar, Walsenburg, Forbes, and five or six other places.

Mother Jones* was up and down the district all this time, making speeches, encouraging the strikers to protect themselves, taking care of children, helping fix up tents, and nursing sick people. The operators in the meanwhile were shouting for the militia. They said that violence would soon break out and that Mother Jones was a dangerous agitator and ought to be deported from the state. Governor Ammons replied that if the local authorities could not handle the strike, the militia would certainly be sent, but that it would not on any account be used to allow the operators to import strikebreakers nor to intimidate miners.

---

* Mary ("Mother") Jones, a well-known figure in several labor battles, especially among the miners in West Virginia and Colorado.– *Ed.*

"I intend," he said, "to put an end to the inflammatory statements of Mother Jones. I will see that she is held in such a way that she cannot talk to the entire country as a prisoner. She will not be allowed to advertise strike conditions outside of the state with the extravagant language she has been using in the coal regions."

Emma F. Langdon, state secretary of the Socialist Party, announced publicly: "If they harm one gray hair on Mother Jones' head, I shall issue a call for the good women of Colorado to organize themselves and march on the city of Trinidad, if necessary, to free her."

From that day to this not a single word has been heard of the Socialist Party of Colorado, although shortly afterward, Mother Jones was imprisoned and held incommunicado for nine weeks in Trinidad.

The first step was to make deputy sheriffs of all these mine guards and detectives. The superintendents of the mines phoned the sheriff how many deputies they needed, and the sheriff sent blank commissions by mail. Union officials asked Sheriff Grisham to deputize a few strikers. He replied: "I never arm both factions. . . ."

Sheriff Jeff Farr reported that strikers had mounted a hill 500 feet high, overlooking Oakview mine, and fired a thousand shots into the buildings. But the newspapermen who investigated found only three bullet holes, and those horizontal. Then a Greek striker got into a personal altercation with Camp Marshal Bob Lee, of Segundo, a notorious killer once connected with the Jesse James outlaws—and the Greek shot first. Everywhere the mine guards were trying to make trouble. At Sopris they dynamited a company house and tried to blame it on the strikers; but, unfortunately, a man in the plot gave it away. It was expensive for the coal companies—this maintenance of an army. They wanted the militia to do their dirty work at the expense of the state. And also, the strikers' tent colonies interfered seriously with the importation of workmen to run their mines.

The largest of these colonies was at Ludlow, lying at the

crossing of the two roads leading to Berwin and Tabasco on one hand and Hastings and Delagua on the other. There were more than twelve hundred people there, divided into twenty-one nationalities, undergoing the marvelous experience of learning that all men are alike. When they had been living together for two weeks, the petty race prejudices and misunderstandings that had been fostered between them by the coal companies for so many years began to break down. Americans began to find out that Slavs and Italians and Poles were as kind-hearted, as cheerful, as loving and as brave as they were. The women called upon one another, boasting about their babies and their men, bringing one another little delicacies when they were sick. The men played cards and baseball together. . . .

"I never did have much use for foreigners before I went to Ludlow," said a little woman. "But they're just like us, only they can't speak the language."

"Sure," answered another. "I used to think Greeks were just common, ignorant, dirty people. But in Ludlow the Greeks were certainly perfect gentlemen. You can't ever say anything bad to me about a Greek now."

Everybody began to learn everybody else's language. And at night there would be a dance in the Big Tent, the Italians supplying the music, and all nations dancing together. It was a true welding of peoples. These exhausted, beaten, hard-working people had never before *had time* to know one another. . . .

It is almost impossible to believe that this peaceful colony was threatened with destruction by the mine guards. They were not utter villains. They were only hardened characters acting under orders. And orders were that the Ludlow colony must be wiped out. It stood in the way of Mr. Rockefeller's profits. When workingmen began to understand one another as well as that, the end of exploitation and blood money forever was in sight. Ludlow colony had been established about a week when the gunmen began to threaten they would come down the canyon and annihilate the inhabitants.

All the visiting, the playing of games and the dances stopped. The colony was in an abject state of terror. There was no organization, no leaders. Seventeen guns and pistols of various kinds had been procured, and very little ammunition. With these, the men of the colony stood guard over their women and children all the long, cold nights, and from the hill above Hastings a searchlight played ceaselessly on the tents. . . .

All through the last week in September streams of people poured out of the canyons into the tent colonies, bringing stories of how they had been thrown out of their houses into the snow and their furniture broken, and the men beaten up and driven down the road at the point of a rifle; and all that week strikers going to get their mail in the mining town post offices were beaten and shot at and refused the right to travel on the country roads. Word came that the colonists at Aguilar were in terror of their lives and were arming to protect themselves. On October 4 armed guards invaded the streets of Old Sopris, which is not on mine property, and at the point of their guns broke up a meeting of strikers in a public hall. Everywhere searchlights played all night on strikers' tents, preventing the women and children from sleeping, and driving the men out twenty times a night to defend themselves against the always feared attack. On October 7 it came.

Some strikers went up to Hastings to get their mail. They were cursed and refused admittance to the post office. As they walked back along the road one of the Hastings guards fired two shots over their heads, both of which struck tents in the colony. A few minutes later an automobile containing B. S. Larson, chief clerk of the Colorado Fuel and Iron Company, stopped on the road near the foothills. Twenty shots were fired into the tents. Immediately the colony boiled with shouting, furious men. Only seventeen of them had guns, but the rest armed themselves with rocks and lumps of coal and sticks and swarmed out onto the plain, without plan, without leader. Their appearance was a signal for a volley from the hill above Hastings and from a stone house near the mouth of Hastings canyon. The women and children rushed out of the tent colony and stood fully exposed. Before the furious onslaught of the half-crazed strikers, the guards retreated into the hills. Then the fighting stopped and the men straggled back, worn out with rage and swearing that they were going up and shoot up Hastings that night. But their leaders argued them out of it.

The next morning, about breakfast time, some one fired upon the tents from a passing freight train, and that night the searchlight searched the colony all night, until at four a.m. one of the strikers shot it to pieces. That morning the strikers strolled over as usual to get their mail and watch the train come in. Some of them were playing catch in the baseball field east of the station, when a shot fired from Hastings Hill landed right in the middle of them. One hundred men ran yelling across the field to get their guns, and before they could find them shots began to come from a steel railroad bridge. The strikers came swarming down the track toward the bridge. Forty or fifty ran ahead without any weapons except their bare hands, and the rest straggled along, putting the wrong ammunition into their various makes of gun and trying to make out where the firing came from. They huddled on a coal heap beside the station, uncertain what to do, ignorant of where the firing came from. All this time a fusillade poured from the steel bridge. But the front rank of the armed strikers advanced to Water Tank Hill and, throwing themselves on the ground, blazed away wildly. Suddenly some one shouted, "The militia is coming! The militia is coming! It's a trap! Back to the tent colony! Back to the tent colony!" Crowding and pushing, in a panic, firing back over their shoulders as they ran, the strikers poured back along the track, but not until a rancher, MacPowell, who had been perfectly neutral to both sides, was shot from the steel bridge while riding home.

But the shooting from the steel bridge continued. Then a northbound train stopped at Ludlow, and Jack Maquarrie, special agent for the Colorado and Southern Railroad, told the newspaper reporters that "there was a bunch of deputies down there in the cut trying to start something."

It is interesting to know that the militia had been on the train at Trinidad an hour before the fighting started, and that at the first shot the train left for Ludlow.

Three strikers were wounded. Frantically that afternoon the colonists began digging rifle pits, for upon the arrival of the militia at Ludlow station the guards and deputies had swarmed down from the hill and from the steel bridge, and were boasting that they had taken Ludlow and that before night they would take the tent colony. It was another night of terror for the strikers. No one slept. The men lay in the rifle pits until daylight—some two hundred of them. Only seventeen were armed with rifles; the rest had butcher knives, razors and axes. But the next day the guards returned to the hills, shouting that some night soon they would come down and kill all the red-necks.

Two days later three guards in an automobile emptied their automatic pistols into the tent colony at Sopris. Four days after that the Colorado Fuel and Iron Company mounted a searchlight and a machine gun on the hill above Segundo. A drunken guard who insulted a woman was badly beaten up there, and that same night the machine gun fired on the town for ten minutes. The next day forty-eight strikers, peacefully picketing the Starkville mine, which is owned by James McLaughlin, brother-in-law of Governor Ammons, were arrested, forced to march twelve miles on foot between double rows of armed guards into Trinidad, and thrown into jail.

The outrages continued. In Segundo, Baldwin-Felts detectives invaded the Old Town, which is not on mine property, and broke down the door of a private house with an ax, on the pretext of searching for arms. In Aguilar, mine guards searched the strikers' headquarters at the point of their rifles, and in Walsenburg Lou Miller, a notorious gunman with five murders to his credit, went around the streets with six armed companions, beating up union men. A. C. Felts, manager of the Baldwin-Felts Detective Agency, arrived on the scene and immediately ordered the construction of an armored automobile, mounted with a machine gun, in the Colorado Fuel and Iron Company's steel plant at Pueblo.

Too late the union officials tried to get guns for the strikers. All the ammunition stores had been already cleaned out by the operators, so that by October 15 the twenty-five men at Forbes tent colony, for example, had only seven guns and six revolvers—all of different makes—and very little ammunition. Forbes tent colony lay along the road at the mouth of the canyon leading up to Forbes mine. This place had been fired on several times by snipers from the hills, especially after strikers had refused to allow workmen to pass up to the mine. The men of the colony became so alarmed for the safety of their women and children that they constructed a separate camp for them about three hundred yards away.

On the morning of October 17, a body of armed horsemen galloped down the Ludlow road and dismounted in a railroad cut near the colony. At the same time Felts' armored automobile appeared from the direction of Trinidad, swung around and trained its machine gun immediately on the tents. Astonished and terrified, the strikers swarmed out, dragging their guns with them, but a guard named Kennedy, afterward an officer in the militia, approached with a white flag, shouting:

"It's all right, boys; we're union men." And as the strikers lowered their guns, he said: "I want to tell you something."

They clustered around him to hear what he had to tell them. He cried suddenly: "What I wanted to say was that we are going to teach you red-necks a lesson!" and, lowering the white flag, he dropped it on the ground. At the same time the dismounted horsemen fired a volley into the group, killing one man instantly. In a panic, the strikers poured back to the tents, across the field to a gulch where they had agreed to go in case of attack, and as they ran the machine gun opened up on them. It riddled the legs of a little boy who was running between the tents, and he fell there. The strikers immediately began to fire back, and the battle kept up from two o'clock in the afternoon until dark. Every time the wounded boy tried to drag himself in the direction of the tents, the machine gun was turned on him. He was shot not less than nine times. The tents were riddled, the furniture in them shot to pieces. A little girl, the daughter of a neighboring farmer, was coming home from school. She was shot in the face. At nightfall the shooting stopped and the attacking party withdrew, but all that night the strikers did not dare venture back to their tents. . . .

The terror caused by the brutal attack of the "death special" had about subsided when, five mornings later, the strikers woke up to see it planted in the same position as before, the murderous machine gun trained again on the colony, and three other machine guns within a radius of two hundred yards, completely surrounding the colony. As the sun came up, armed men swarmed down from the hills in every direction. There were more than a hundred of them. Under cover of the guns Under-Sheriff Zeke Martin, of Las Animas County, marched up to the tents and ordered all the men to form in single file and go down to the railroad track. Cursed at and beaten, they were lined up there with the machine gun of the "death special" covering them. Then began a search of the tent colony in which all the strikers' arms were taken, their trunks smashed open, their beds torn to pieces, and money and jewelry stolen. The house of a rancher nearby, a Civil War veteran, who was not connected in any way with the strikers, was entered and ransacked, and his wife was threatened that "if she harbored any more union men her house wouldn't be standing long."

That same night a mob of infuriated miners surrounded a Baldwin-Felts detective in Trinidad and threatened to lynch him. . . .

By this time the strikers in every colony from Starkville to

Walsenburg had determined to rely no more upon the faith or promises of the peace officers, but to get guns and protect their wives and children from the murderous assaults of the mine guards the only way they could. It was a decision born of desperation; few of them had ever seen a gun, much less shot one—and most of them were from countries where the authority of the law is little less than divine. . . .

There were daily threats now by letter, telephone and armed men shouting from the hills that some night soon all the guards from all the mines would come down the canyons and destroy the tent colonies. In Ludlow colony people lived in a continual panic. The men went to Trinidad, begging from house to house for old rifles, rusty pistols—anything, in fact, that would shoot. And it was a strange collection of odd and obsolete weapons that was gathered together in the tent colony. On the advice of their leaders, the colonists dug cellars under their tents, where the women and children could be removed in case of an attack. The enforced watching at night, the insults and occasional shots from mine guards, the beating up of union men whenever they dared go alone outside the colony at night, and the unceasing stories of outrages by the gunmen all along the line, wrought the strikers up to such a pitch that only the pleadings of their leaders prevented them from attacking and annihilating the guards. They returned the latter's threats, and there was terror, too, in the mine camps.

On October 26 the dam of wrath broke. For several days the Ludlow colonists had been expecting an attack, and the settlement was picketed night and day by armed sentries. On Saturday morning, the twenty-fifth, some strikers who had been over to the railroad station reported the arrival of a new searchlight to replace the one shot to pieces on the ninth. Several men exclaimed that it ought not to be permitted to be set up again to spy on them, but the strike leaders insisted that the searchlight must not be interfered with. So it was not molested. Toward afternoon the telephone rang and a voice said: "I'm talking from Hastings.

Look out down there. A big gang has left here on horseback to start something, and a lot more are going to hide at the mouth of the canyon and come out on you when the first shot is fired." Almost the same minute, one of the sentries came running in. "They're coming! The deputies are riding down the canyon—a big bunch!" The men in the camp began to run for their arms. "Don't fight!" cried the leaders, "it's a plant! They're trying to start something!"

"Well, they'll get something then!" answered the men.

"They're not after us," pleaded another. "Leave 'em alone, boys. They're coming in to take that new searchlight back to Hastings."

"No, they don't," shouted a man. "I ain't a-going to have that searchlight on my tent all night. Come on, boys!" And as they hesitated there, uncertain whether to attack or not, the question was decided for them. Twenty armed and mounted men emerged from the canyon road, riding toward the depot. Suddenly one deliberately lifted his rifle and shot— once. It was enough. The strikers poured out of the colony toward the railroad cut and the arroyo, so as to draw the guards' fire away from the tent colony, and began to shoot as they went. Immediately the reserve forces that had been hidden in the canyons poured out, and a battle began which lasted until dark. Outnumbered and outshot, the strikers retreated slowly eastward and north, stopping at the C. and S. Steel bridge. And there the guards tried to dislodge them, when darkness fell; the guards retreated in the night toward the hills and the strikers, some of them, followed. That night almost the entire body of the strikers took to the hills. By Sunday morning, the twenty-sixth, Tabasco mine was besieged by shooting strikers, entrenched on the hilltops. That night word went out up and down the tents of seven thousand strikers that at last the boys had got the guards where they wanted them at Ludlow; and all night long men sifted into camp, walking sometimes twenty-five miles with their guns on their shoulders.

The guards telephoned to Trinidad for help. Twice that

day trains were made up in Trinidad to carry deputies and militia to the reinforcement of Tabasco, but in both cases the train crew refused to carry them. Thirty-six Walsenburg deputies were hurried to Trinidad on a special train, shooting on the Ludlow tents as they passed, and were immediately created deputy sheriffs of Las Animas County in the Coronado Hotel.

But the strikers, without organization or leadership, soon got tired of battle and straggled back across the plain to the tent colony, singing and shouting with the elation of victory. There was a grand banquet and a dance that night, at which all the visitors were entertained, and the warriors told their stories over with much boasting and adulation. But in the midst of the festivities word came that the guards were loading a machine gun into a wagon and were coming down the canyon. The dance broke up in a panic, and all night no one slept. However, there wasn't even a shot fired by either side on the plain until dawn, although desultory rifle fire in the hills indicated that some of the wandering bands were still "sniping" at the guards.

But in the morning it all began again with volleys from the hills. At the same time, authoritative information was phoned from Trinidad of the approach of an armored train of three steel cars equipped with machine guns, such as was driven through Cabin Creek to rain steel into the West Virginia strikers' tents last year. Five hundred men streamed across the plain to wait for that train; they paid no attention to the shooting from the hills. And when the train came within half a mile of Ludlow, such a hail of shots met it that it was forced to back into Forbes mine.

A northeast snow blizzard blotted out the world that night. And in the darkness the strikers left their tents and took to the hills—about seven hundred of them. Before dawn on the twenty-eighth they opened a vicious fire on Berwind and Hastings, killing over ten mine guards and deputies. Closer and closer they drew—fiercer and fiercer waxed their shooting. Telegraph and telephone wires were cut, and a gang was ordered to blow up the railroad leading up from Ludlow. At Tabasco, also, the strikers drove the guards and their families into the mouth of the mine. If they had been permitted to finish what they had begun so thoroughly, there is no doubt that the guards in those three mines would have all been shot. But through the storm couriers came running from the Ludlow colony.

"Stop fighting," they ordered, "and come back to the tents quick. The governor has called out the National Guard!"

And so they straggled back down from the hills and across the plain, discussing this new complication. What did it mean? Would the soldiers be neutral? Would the strikers be disarmed? Would they be given protection against the gunmen? Those that had been in other big strikes were mortally afraid. But the leaders reassured them for the moment, and that evening the men from other tent colonies went home, and the Ludlow men gave in their guns to their leaders so that they could be handed over to the soldiers in the morning. But morning came and no soldiers, nor any news of them. At the same time a man called up from Trinidad to say that seven automobile-loads of armed deputies had left for Ludlow, vowing vengeance for the attack on Hastings and Berwind. And as the day wore on, other and worse rumors multiplied.

"We are lost!" they cried. "The soldiers are coming to take away our rifles. They will shoot us down. That is what they always do in strikes. And first the guards will come to-night. We must send away the women and children." And so the wives and mothers and children were put on the Trinidad train and the men settled down in their empty camp.

"Let's show them we are men. Let us revenge ourselves upon the mine guards, before the soldiers come and kill us. We'll do some real fighting."

There was only a little band now armed, not more than a hundred. Without plans or leaders they sallied out into the storm before dawn; but the guards were now on the alert, and greatly outnumbered the strikers. About seven in the morning they came wearily back and threw themselves on the floor to sleep.

"This militia story was just a trick to leave us unprotected," they said. "There aren't any soldiers coming. Give us all the arms and ammunition and we will wait for the guards here!" And they waited for the end, in cold despair.

But on the morning of the thirty-first the militia troop-train reached a point three miles north of Ludlow, where it stopped while General Chase came to the Ludlow colony under a flag of truce. He informed the leaders of the colony that Governor Ammons' orders were to disarm both sides, to preserve the peace, and that the militia was not to be used to help the operators bring in strikebreakers nor to intimidate the strikers.

The leaders communicated these promises to the men, who, overjoyed at the end of their reign of terror, eagerly turned over their guns to be delivered to the militia, and happily sent for their women and children. So relieved and grateful were they to the soldiers that they planned a magnificent reception.

At the request of the strikers the militia marched into Ludlow in dress uniform. The whole Ludlow colony in its Sunday best went a mile out across the snowy, sunlit plain to the east to meet them. Ahead danced a thousand children, gathered from all the colonies, dressed in white and singing the strike song. A double brass band followed, and then twelve hundred men and women with American flags. They formed two dense, cheering, friendly lines, through which the highly pleased National Guard marched to its camping place. . . .

Chase established his headquarters at Ludlow, the militia camp being across the railroad tracks from the Ludlow tent colony and between it and the mines. He announced that disarmament of both sides would begin at once, and to prove his good faith to the strikers he disarmed the mine guards first. Then he asked the strikers for their guns. They handed over thirty-two—two-thirds of all the firearms in the colony. The reason why the rest were not surrendered was because of a rumor from Trinidad that the guns taken from the strikers there had been turned over to the mine guards at Sopris and Segundo. "Yes," said the militia captain in command at Trinidad, in answer to a question from the strike leaders, "I did turn them over. You see, we have not enough soldiers in the field to protect these mines, and your fellows up there are pretty excited, they tell me." Word also came from Aguilar that the guns taken from the mine guards and Baldwin-Felts detectives had been returned to them for the same reason. Shortly afterward the Ludlow guns were handed over to the guards at Delagua, Hastings, Berwind, and Tabasco. But the strikers didn't make any fuss about it.

The relations between the Ludlow colonists and the militia were very friendly. Teams of soldiers and miners played baseball in the snow and went hunting rabbits together. The strikers gave a dance for the militia in the Big Tent, and the guardsmen visited the different tents and shared in the life of the colony. They were always welcome to dinner. The strikers, too, circulated freely around the militia camp. Among the miners were a number of Greeks and Montenegrins who had fought in the Balkan War. Sometimes the militia officers let them take guns and drill and were astonished at their cleverness.

But this state of things lasted only about two weeks. The main argument of the operators in demanding the militia was that many of the strikers in the tent colonies would be willing to return to work if they could be assured of protection, the operators stating that as soon as the militia entered the field there would be a steady rush of strikers back to the mines. But upon the arrival of the National Guard nothing of the sort happened. Hardly a man deserted. So the operators had to use other tactics.

The attitude of the militia suddenly changed. General Chase, without any warning, announced that the Ludlow strikers were concealing arms and would have to give them all up within twenty-four hours. The militia were ordered to keep away from the tent colony. On November 12, militia and mine guards together, suddenly made a search for concealed arms in the houses of the strikers at Old Segundo. Trunks were smashed and money and jewelry stolen. Word came from Trinidad that three of the most notorious Baldwin-Felts guards had been enrolled as state soldiers. General Chase began to make his rounds in a Colorado Fuel and Iron Company automobile. Strikers were told to keep away from the railroad station and the public roads, so that there would be no dispute between them and strikebreakers going to work in the mines.

There was no state appropriation for paying the National Guard. The coal operators offered to finance it, but Governor Ammons decided it was "not proper." He did, however, allow the Denver Clearing House, through its president, Mr. Mitchell, to advance 250,000 dollars, and that was an indirect way of allowing the coal companies to buy the militia, for Mr. Mitchell is the same president of the Denver National Bank who threatened to call the loans of Mr. Hayden, president of the Juniper Coal Company, if he made terms with the union.

It soon began to be apparent what course the militia intended to pursue. Although martial law had not been declared, and, as a matter of fact, never was, General Chase issued a proclamation in Trinidad creating "the Military District of Colorado," with himself in command, and announced that "military prisoners" would be arrested and disposed of by the militia under his command. The first of these "military prisoners" was a miner who came up to a soldier in the streets of Trinidad and asked where he could join the union. . . .

Chase openly began a campaign of tyranny and intimidation. Just as in former strikes, wholesale arrests followed, and batches of thirty-five to one hundred men and women at a time were thrown into jail without charges and held indefinitely as "military prisoners." Strikers going to the post office at Ludlow to get their mail were arrested. Union men caught talking to strikebreakers were clubbed and jailed. Adolph Germer, Socialist organizer of the United Mine Workers, was placed under arrest when he stepped from the train at Walsenburg, and Mrs. Germer was insulted in her own house by drunken officers. The mine guards, emboldened by the open favor of the militia, began again their interrupted course of making trouble. On the night of November 15, they fired several volleys into the strikers' houses at Picton. A soldier forbade Mrs. Radlich to go for her mail to the Ludlow post office, and when she answered him defiantly he knocked her down with the butt end of his rifle. Lieutenant Linderfelt met a seventeen-year-old boy at the Ludlow station, accused him of frightening militiamen's horses, and beat him with his fists until he couldn't walk.

Even these measures were not violent enough for the operators. Newspapermen at the state capitol heard a group of operators reviling Governor Ammons: "You God damned coward," they said, "we are not going to stand for this much longer. You have got to do something, and do it quick, or we'll get you!" And the embodiment of the will of the people of the sovereign state of Colorado answered: "Don't be too hard on me, gentlemen! I'm doing it as fast as I can." And then the door closed. Shortly after that General Chase issued another proclamation guaranteeing protection for all men wishing to go to work in the mines, and that he intended to establish a secret military court to try and sentence all offenders against the laws laid down by him as Commander of the Military District of Colorado. I think it was that same night that some striker, outraged by the intolerable insolence of Baldwin-Felts Detective Belcher, shot and killed him on the streets of Trinidad. Thirty-five military prisoners were crammed into the stinking cells of the county jail and held there indefinitely without adequate food, water, or heat. Five of them were brought before the military court and charged with murder, and when they would not confess they were tortured. For five days and five nights icy water was thrown on them, and they were prodded with bayonets and clubbed so that they could not sleep. At the end of that time an Italian named Zancanelli broke down and signed his name to a "confession," written by the military officers, which he afterward repudiated and which, of course, was proven false.

The Union made one last desperate attempt to get the operators and strikers together for a conference, but the former refused absolutely to pay any attention to the appeal. General Chase announced that the patience of the militia was exhausted. The strikers discovered to their surprise that a train containing several hundred strikebreakers had been brought into the state and escorted by the militia to the mines. They called up Chase about it. He admitted that Governor Ammons over the telephone had privately modified his order against importing strikebreakers. That was the first the strikers knew of it.

Then began the bringing in of thousands of workmen from the East. Workingmen were assured that there was no strike in Colorado. They were promised free transportation and high wages. Some were hired to work in coal mines, and others were lured west on a land scheme.

Some of these people were union men. Few wanted to be "scabs." But they were told they would not be allowed to leave until they had worked off their transportation and board. An Italian at Primero who tried to escape down the railroad track was shot in the back and killed. Another at Tabasco was murdered because he refused to go to work. Those who really wanted to keep their jobs were forced to work for weeks for nothing. One man, who had some money, paid his transportation in cash, and though he worked twenty days and was credited on the company's books with coal enough to earn him 3.50 dollars a day, he was told at the end of that time that he had made only fifty cents. The militia acted under the orders of the mine superintendents, refusing to allow anybody to leave who had not a "clearance" from the company. You had to have a pass to get in and out of the mine camps. Hundreds of strikebreakers escaped at night over the hills in the snow and sought protection and shelter in the strikers' tent colonies, where they were given union benefits and a tent to live in. . . .

The lawlessness and brutality of the soldiers increased. Two drunken militiamen, one an officer, invaded the house of a rancher while he and his wife were away, made vile suggestions to two small children, broke open trunks and stole everything of value. Although a complaint was made they were not punished. At Pryor tent colony, a Croatian striker named Andrew Colnar wrote a letter to one of his fellow countrymen who was a strikebreaker, asking him to join the union. The militia arrested Colnar, took him to camp, and set him to work digging a hole in the ground under armed guards. They told him that he was digging his own grave and was to be shot at sunrise. Astounded and terrified, the poor man asked to be allowed to see his family for the last time. They told him that he couldn't, and that if he didn't dig his own grave he would be shot immediately. Colnar fainted in the pit that he had dug, and when he came to was cursed and beaten.

This seems to have been a favorite pastime with the militia. Tom Ivanitch, a Pole, was pulled off the train at Ludlow while going to Trinidad and told he must make his grave. There was no charge against him—the militia said they did it for fun!—but he was allowed to write his last letter, and here it is:

Dear Wife:

Best regards from your husband to you and my son and sister Mary and little Kate and my brother Joe. I am under arrest and not guilty and I am digging my own grave today. This will be my last letter, dear wife. Look after my children, you and my brother Joe. There won't be anything more of me unless God helps me. With this world that men have to go innocent and lie in the ground and God bless the ground where I lie. We are digging the grave between the tents and the street. Dear wife and brother Joe, I am telling you to look after my children. Best regards to you and the children and brother Joe and mother-in-law and sister-in-law Mary Smiljimie and to all that's living. If I don't go tonight to Trinidad and see the head men and see if something can be done for us. I think it will be too late. I don't know what to write any more to say good bye for ever. I see now that I will have to go in the grave. God do justice. I got $5 to put in the letter if somebody don't steal it. I got $23.30 from Domenic Smircich. That there is written in a book. Let Joe get that. Best regards to all I know if they are living.

Your husband,
Tom Ivanitch

I am sorrow and broken hearted waiting for the last minute. When you get the money from the society for the children divide it equally.

And here is another from an Italian who was set to the same task:

Dear Louisa:

Best regards from my broken hearted Carlo. This is the last letter I am writing. That's all I have to say. Sorrow. Good-bye, good-bye.

On January 23, the women and children of the strikers held a parade in Trinidad to protest against the imprisonment of Mother Jones, who was then in San Rafael Hospital. They went along gaily enough, singing and laughing, until they turned into Main Street. There, suddenly, a body of militia cavalry blocked their way. "Go to your homes!" they shouted. "Disband! Go back! You can't pass here!" The women stopped uncertainly, and then surged forward, and the body of cavalry slowly advanced upon them with drawn sabers. All the hate of the strikers for the militia surged up in these women. They began to jeer and shout: "Scab-herders! Baldwin-Felts!" The soldiers rode right in among them, herding them. General Chase himself led them, shouting the vilest epithets. A little sixteen-year-old girl stood in the general's way. He rode up beside her and kicked her violently in the chest. Furiously angry, she told him to look out what he was doing. Another soldier galloped at her and struck at her with his saber. A groan and a yell went up from the women. General Chase's horse shied suddenly and the general fell to the ground. The women roared with laughter. "Ride them down! Ride down the women!" screamed the general; and they did. General Chase himself laid open a woman's head with his sword. The steel-shod hoofs of the horses struck women and children, knocking them down. In a panic, the crowd fled along the street, the soldiers among them, striking and yelling like madmen. Throwing themselves off their horses they launched out like madmen with their fists, knocking down women and dragging them along the street. That day the jail was jammed with more than a hundred military prisoners.

Toward the end of February a subcommittee of the Committee on Mines and Mining of the United States House of Representatives came to Trinidad to investigate the strike. Among other things, the most appalling charges against the militia were made by witnesses. Captain Danks, attorney for the militia, promised that he had a wealth of testimony to confute these charges; but at the end of the hearing *he had not even challenged one of them.*

On the last day of the investigation, March 9, a strike-breaker was discovered dead near the Forbes tent colony. The next day the militia, under Colonel Davis, went to Forbes and completely destroyed the strikers' colony, tearing down the tents, smashing the furniture, and ordering the strikers to go out of the state within forty-eight hours. He said he had orders from General Chase to "clean out that tent colony," for the Forbes strikers had been the chief witnesses to militia brutality before the Congressional Committee. More than fifty strikers and their families were turned adrift in the bitterest cold weather of the winter, with no homes to go to and nothing to eat. Two babies died of exposure.

Several days later the militia rounded up ten men from the Ludlow tent colony who had testified against them and marched them up to Berwind. There they beat them, and stood them up against a stone wall with a cannon trained on them, forbidding them to make the least movement and stabbing them with bayonets when they did. They kept them standing there, threatening to shoot them, for four hours, and then got a rawhide whip and lashed them down the canyon, following them on horseback at a gallop. An old miner named Fyler finally became so exhausted that he couldn't run. He stopped, and four soldiers fell upon him and beat him so that he had to crawl back to Ludlow on his hands and knees.

Everything, evidently, was being done to exasperate the strikers. Four times the militia made a pretense of searching Ludlow colony for arms. They would stand two machine guns across the railroad track trained on the colony, and, rushing through the tents, would drag out the men and line them up on the open plain, a mile away, under another machine gun, while the soldiers rode through the camp stealing everything of value they could lay their hands on, tearing up the floors, bursting in the doors and insulting the women.

I don't mean to say that the strikers didn't resent this reign of terror; but I do mean to say that they committed no violence against the militia except to jeer at them and call them names. Nevertheless, they were aroused to a pitch of exasperation that even their leaders couldn't promise to control long. Their homes destroyed and invaded, their women assaulted, robbed and beaten and insulted every minute, they determined that they would not submit any further. General Chase refused to allow the Forbes tent colony to be rebuilt, and the strikers threatened to do it anyway; and this time, they said, they would be prepared to resist in such a manner that the militia would not destroy their homes until they were killed. Frantically, then, all along the fifty miles of tent colonies the strikers began to buy arms. And suddenly, on March 23, the militia was recalled from the field.

The 250,000 dollars advanced by the Denver Clearing House to pay the soldiers had long since been exhausted. Moreover, State Auditor Kenehan had made an investigation, and had found such appalling graft and dishonesty among both officers and privates that he refused to honor the certificates of indebtedness. Many of the soldiers were mutinying because they had received no pay. The mine guards, in uniform, went around the country contracting debts, and signing notes that the state would pay them. There was no discipline whatever. The officers could not control their men.

But before they left two companies of militia were enrolled—Company B in Walsenburg and Troop A in Trinidad. These companies were composed almost entirely of mine guards and Baldwin-Felts detectives. They were paid by the coal companies. The most hardened strikebreakers of the other companies were drafted into a new company—facetiously called Company Q—which had its headquarters at Ludlow. These three companies remained in the field. Many of the men were professional strikebreakers who went to work in the mines in their militia uniforms, leaving their guns at the pit mouth. . . .

Sunday, April 19, was the Greek Easter, and the Greeks at Ludlow tent colony celebrated it. Everybody celebrated it with them, because the Greeks were loved by all the strikers. There were about fifty of them, all young men and all without families. Some of them were veterans of the Balkan War. Because Louis Tikas, a graduate of the University of Athens, was the gentlest and bravest and most lovable of the Greeks he became the leader of the strikers, too. . . .

It was a fine day, the ground was dry, and the sun shone. At dawn the Ludlow people were up, larking around among the tents. The Greeks started to dance at sunrise. They refused to go into the Big Tent, but on a sun-swept square of beaten earth they set flags in the ground; and, dragging their national costumes from the bottom of their trunks, they danced all morning the Greek dances. Over on the baseball diamond two games were in progress, one for the women and one for the men. Two women's teams had decided to play; and the Greeks presented the women players with bloomers as an Easter gift. So, with laughter and shouting, the whole camp took a holiday. Children were everywhere, playing in the new grass on the plain.

Right in the middle of the baseball games, four militiamen came across the railroad track with rifles in their hands. Now, it had been customary for the soldiers to come over and watch the strikers play; but they had never before brought their arms. They slouched up to the men's diamond and took up a position between first base and the home plate, leveling their rifles insolently on the crowd. The strikers paid no attention for a while, until they saw that the soldiers were standing right on the line where the runners had to pass, and interfering with the game. One of the men protested, and asked them to move to one side so that the runners could get by. He also said that there was no necessity for pointing their rifles at the crowd. The militiamen insolently told him it was "none of his damned business," and that if he said another word they would start something. So the men quietly moved their diamond and went on playing. But the militiamen were looking for a row, so they went over to the women's game. The women, however, were not so self-contained as the men. They jeered at the guardsmen, calling them scab-herders, and said that they were not afraid of the guns, and that two women with a popgun could scare them to death. "That's all right, girlie," answered one militiaman. "You have your fun today; we'll have ours tomorrow." Shortly after that they went away.

When the baseball game was over the Greeks served lunch for all the colony. The old meeting tent was not good enough for them on their great holiday. They had magnificently sent to Trinidad and bought new tents for the occasion; tents that had never been used. There was beer for the men and coffee for the women; and whenever a Greek drank he rose and sang a Greek song instead of a toast. Everybody was very happy, because this was the first real day of spring they had had. At night there was a ball; and then about ten o'clock a man came in and whispered to the other men that the militia were riding silently through the colony and listening at the walls of the tents.

The dance broke up. For several days rumors, and even threats, had reached the colonists that the militia intended to wipe them out. In the dark those who had arms gathered in the office tent. There were forty-seven men. They determined not to tell the women and children; because, in the first place, if there was to be a fight, of course the militia would not attack the tent colony, but would allow the strikers to get out into the open plain, as they had in the fall, and fight them there; in the second place, there had been many such threats and nothing had come of them. But just the same they mounted guard around the camp that night; and when morning came everything was quiet, so they went back to the tents to sleep.

About 8:45 the same militiamen who had interrupted the ball game the day before swaggered into camp. They had come, they said, to get a man who was being held against his will by the strikers. Tikas met them. He assured them that there was no man of that name in the colony; but they insisted that Tikas was a liar, and that if he didn't produce the man at once they would come back with a squad and search the colony.

Immediately afterward Major Hamrock called up Tikas on the telephone and ordered him to come to the militia camp. Tikas answered that he would meet the major at the railroad station, which was halfway between the two camps, and Hamrock said all right. But when Tikas got there he noticed that the militia were buckling on their cartridge belts and taking up their rifles; that everywhere was warlike activity, and that two machine guns covering the tent colony had been planted on Water Tank Hill. All of a sudden a signal bomb exploded in the militia camp. The strikers had also seen the machine guns and heard the sound of the bomb; and as Tikas reached the railroad station he saw the forty-seven armed men leaving the tent colony and filing off toward the C. and S. E. Railroad cut and the arroyo. "My God, major! What does this mean?" cried Louis. Hamrock seemed very much excited. "You call off your men," he said nervously, "and I'll call off mine." "But my men aren't doing anything," answered Louis. "They are afraid of those machine guns up on the hill." "Well, then, call them back to the tent colony," screamed Hamrock. And Louis started off on a run to the tents, waving a white handkerchief and shouting to go back. A second bomb went off. He had got halfway, and the strikers had halted in their march, when the third bomb burst; and suddenly without warning, both machine guns pounded stab-stab-stab full on the tents.

It was premeditated and merciless. Militiamen have told me that their orders were to destroy the tent colony and everything living in it. The three bombs were a signal to the mine guards and Baldwin-Felts detectives and strikebreakers in the neighboring mines; and they came swarming down out of the hills fully armed—four hundred of them.

Suddenly the terrible storm of lead from the machine guns ripped their coverings to pieces, and the most awful panic followed. Some of the women and children streamed out over the plain, to get away from the tent colony. They were shot at as they ran. Others with the unarmed men took refuge in the arroyo to the north. Mrs. Fyler led a group of women and children, under fire, to the deep well at the railroad pump house, down which they climbed on ladders. Others still crept into the bulletproof cellars they had dug for themselves under their tents.

The fighting men, appalled at what was happening, started for the tent colony; but they were driven back by a hail of bullets. And now the mine guards began to get into action, shooting explosive bullets, which burst with the report of a six-shooter all through the tents. The machine guns never let up. Tikas had started off with the Greeks; but he ran back in a desperate attempt to save some of those who remained; and stayed in the tent colony all day. He and Mrs. Jolly, the wife of an American striker, and Bernado, leader of the Italians, and Domeniski, leader of the Slavs, carried water and food and bandages to those imprisoned in the cellars. There was no one shooting from the tent colony. Not a man there had a gun. Tikas thought that the explosive bullets were the sound of shots being fired from the tents, and ran round like a crazy man to tell the fool to stop. It was an hour before he discovered what really made the noise.

Mrs. Jolly put on a white dress; and Tikas and Domeniski made big red crosses and pinned them on her breast and arms. The militia used them as targets. Her dress was riddled in a dozen places, and the heel of her shoe shot off. So fierce was the fire wherever she went that the people had to beg her to keep away from them. Undaunted, she and the three men made sandwiches and drew water to carry to the women and children.

Early that morning an armored train was made up in Trinidad, and 126 militiamen of Troop A got on board. But the trainmen refused to take them; and it was not until three o'clock in the afternoon that they finally found a crew to man the train. They got to Ludlow about four o'clock, and added their two machine guns to the terrible fire poured unceasingly into the tent colony. One detachment slowly drove the strikers out of their position at the arroyo, and another attempted in vain to dislodge those in the railroad. Lieutenant Linderfelt, in command of eight militiamen firing from the windows of the railroad station, ordered them to "shoot every God damned thing that moves!" Captain Carson came up to Major Hamrock and reminded him respectfully that they had only a few hours of daylight left to burn the tent colony. "Burn them out! Smoke them out!" yelled the officers. And their men poured death into the tents in a fury of blood lust.

It was growing dark. The militia closed in around the tent colony. At about 7:30, a militiaman with a bucket of kerosene and a broom ran up to the first tent, wet it thoroughly, and touched a match to it. The flame roared up, illuminating the whole countryside. Other soldiers fell upon the other tents; and in a minute the whole northwest corner of the colony was aflame. A freight train came along just then with orders to stop on a siding near the pump house; and the women and children in the well took advantage of the protection of the train to creep out along the right-of-way fence to the protection of the arroyo, screaming and crying. A dozen militiamen jumped to the engineer's cab and thrust guns in his face yelling to him to move on or they would shoot him. He obeyed; and in the flickering light of the burning tents the militia shot at the refugees again and again. At the first leap of the flames the astounded strikers ceased firing; but the militia did not. They poured among the tents, shouting with the fury of destruction, smashing open trunks and looting.

When the fire started Mrs. Jolly went from tent to tent, pulling the women and children out of the cellars and herding them before her out on the plain. She remembered all of a sudden that Mrs. Petrucci and her three children were in the cellar under her tent, and started back to get them out. "No," said Tikas, "you go ahead with that bunch. I'll go back after the Petruccis." And he started toward the flames.

There the militia captured him. He tried to explain his errand; but they were drunk with blood lust and would not listen to him. Lieutenant Linderfelt broke the stock of his rifle over the Greek's head, laying it open to the bone. Fifty men got a rope and threw it over a telegraph wire to hang him. But Linderfelt cynically handed him over to two militiamen, and told them they were responsible for his life. Five minutes later Louis Tikas fell dead with three bullets in his back; and out of Mrs. Petrucci's cellar were afterward taken the charred bodies of thirteen women and children.

Fyler, too, they captured and murdered, shooting him fifty-four times. Above the noise of the flames and the shouting came the screaming of women and children, burning to death under the floors of their tents. Some were pulled out by the soldiers, beaten and kicked and arrested. Others were allowed to die without any effort being made to save them. An American striker named Snyder crouched dully in his tent beside the body of his eleven-year-old boy, the back of whose head had been blown off by an explosive bullet. One militiaman came into the tent, soaked it with kerosene and set it on fire, hitting Snyder over the head with his rifle and telling him to beat it. Snyder pointed to the body of his boy; and the soldier dragged it outside by the collar, threw it on the ground, and said: "Here! Carry the damned thing yourself!"

The news spread north and south like wildfire. In three hours every striker for fifty miles in either direction knew that the militia and mine guards had burned women and children to death. Monday night they started, with all the guns they could lay their hands on, for the scene of action at Ludlow. All night long the roads were filled with ragged mobs of armed men pouring towards the Black Hills. And not only strikers went. In Aguilar, Walsenburg, and Trinidad, clerks, cab drivers, chauffeurs, school teachers, and even bankers, seized their guns and started for the front. It was as if the fire started at Ludlow had set the whole country aflame. All over the state labor unions and citizens' leagues met in a passion of horror and openly voted money to buy guns for the strikers. Colorado Springs, Pueblo, and other cities were the scenes of great citizens' meetings which called upon the Governor to ask the President for Federal troops. Seventeen hundred Wyoming miners armed themselves, and wired the strike leaders that they were ready to march to their help. Letters were received by the Union from cowboys, railroad men, and I. W. W. locals representing a thousand laborers offering to march across the country and help. Five hundred Cripple Creek miners left the mines and started eastward for the Black Hills. . . .

Meanwhile at Ludlow the militia went quite mad. All day they kept the machine guns steadily playing on the scorched and blackened tent colony. Everything living attracted a storm of shots: chickens, horses, cattle, cats. An automobile came down the country road. In it were a man and his wife and daughter touring from Denver to Texas. They did not even know there was a battle going on. Soldiers turned a machine gun on the automobile for two miles, shot the top off and riddled the radiator. To a newspaper reporter Linderfelt screamed: "We will kill every damned red-neck striker and we'll get every damned union sympathizer in this district before we finish." Dead wagons sent out by the union from Trinidad to get the bodies of the women and children were attacked so furiously that they had to turn back. On the still burning ruins of the tents militiamen were seen to throw bodies.

And the strikers, too, were in a frenzy. The United Mine Workers issued a call to arms. By day they lay firing on the summit of the hills in constantly increasing numbers; by night they dug trenches, always getting nearer and nearer to the militia's positions. On Wednesday Major Hamrock telephoned to the mine guards at Aguilar: "For God's sake start something!" he said. "They are pouring in on us from all the tent colonies. All the Aguilar strikers are down here, and you have got to make a play to get them back." So the guards fired a volley into the Aguilar tents from the windows of the Empire Mine boarding house. The effect was astonishing. Three hundred furious strikers and townspeople poured out of the town and swept up toward the mines. Shouting and yelling, they rushed up to the very rifles of the mine guards. They were absolutely resistless. At Royal and No. 9 the guards and strikebreakers fled to the hills. The strikers stormed in and took possession, burning the tipples, destroying the houses, and smashing the machinery with the butts of their rifles. At Empire the general superintendent of the company and some of the guards took refuge in the mine. The strikers sealed them up there, blew up the tipple, and destroyed fifty houses so thoroughly that you could not tell where a house had stood.

All along the line the same thing happened. Strikers' houses in Canyon City were raked with a machine gun. The strikers captured Sunnyside and Jackson mines and melted the machine gun up to make watch-charms, although they did no other damage. At Rouse and Rugby, four hundred strikers attacked the mines.

Two days after the burning of Ludlow, a reporter, some Red Cross nurses, and the Rev. Randolph Cook of Trinidad, were permitted by the militia to search among the ruins of Ludlow tent colony. The battle was still raging, and the soldiers amused themselves by firing into the ruins as close as they could come to the investigators. Out of the cellar under Mrs. Petrucci's tent, which Louis Tikas had tried so hard to reach, they took the bodies of eleven children and two women, one of whom gave birth to a posthumous child. There was no evidence of fire in the cellar, but many of the bodies were badly burned. The truth is that they were burned in their tents—several militiamen have confessed to me that the fearful screaming of the women and children continued all the time they were looting the colony—and the soldiers had thrown them into the hole with others who had been smothered by smoke.

But when the rescuers returned to Trinidad they were told that many other bodies were missing, and one striker informed them that near the northeast corner was a cellar in which eighteen people had perished. So on Saturday they returned. By that time the militia had returned to the field, and General Chase was in command. He welcomed them cordially and asked if they had the authority of the Red Cross Society to carry its banner. They said they had. General Chase courteously asked them to wait a minute while he communicated with Denver and found out. Soon he came back. "It's all right," he said. "I've telephoned to Denver and you can go ahead." So they started down toward the tent colony. Chase followed them through field glasses from his tent, and as they approached the place where they thought the bodies lay he despatched two soldiers after them to bring them back. The General was furiously angry. Without giving any reason he held them under arrest for two hours, guarded by soldiers. At the end of that time they were marched in in single file before him as he sat at his desk. "You're a bunch of damned fakers!" he yelled, waving a telegram. "I have just found out from Denver that you have no authority to carry that Red Cross flag. What the hell do you mean by coming out here and trying to bluff me?" The Rev. Cook ventured to protest that that wasn't fit language to use before ladies. "Pimps, preachers, and prostitutes look all the same to me!" answered the General. "You get to hell out of here back to Trinidad and never come near here again." And it is true that the Red Cross Society of Denver, in a panic at offending the coal operators, had telephoned to Trinidad after the party left for Ludlow and revoked their authorization to use the Red Cross flag. That night the C. and S. Railroad dumped a cargo of quicklime at the militia camp, and several disused wells in the neighborhood were opened. As a matter of fact the strikers themselves have no idea how many people were killed at Ludlow. . . .

The Colorado state government has proven itself inadequate to handle the situation. As we go to press the legislature, called in extraordinary session by the governor to deal with the problem, has adjourned without making the least attempt toward a settlement. The coal companies' machine in the House and in the Senate killed any attempt at remedial legislation, but jammed through a bill authorizing the issue of bonds for one million dollars in order to pay for the militia and mine guards for their splendid work in shooting workingmen down and burning women and children to death. . . .

I want to add one significant fact for the benefit of those who think that Mr. Rockefeller and the coal operators are innocent, though misguided. At the triumphant conclusion of the legislative session, it is said that Mrs. Welborn, wife of

the president of the Colorado Fuel and Iron Company, told
her friends of the "lovely telegram" her husband had received from John D. Rockefeller, Jr. It read, according to
Mrs. Welborn: "Hearty congratulations on the winning of the
strike. I sincerely approve of all your actions, and commend
the splendid work of the legislature."

1914

The Cook and the Captain Bold

"Avast there!" roared a voice that seemed to fill the wide vault of heaven. "Port your helm! What do you think you are? A torpedo boat?"

That voice could belong to only one pair of lungs in the world. I glanced up at a dory, over which leaned a great red face and a pair of enormous shoulders.

"Grampus Bill!" I cried.

"Oh! It's you," he rumbled, "over the side with you!" And as I hauled myself like a seal across the gunwale, Bill sent the boat spinning down the edge of the life lines with one easy heave of his great arms.

"Hi, you!" the voice boomed above the screams of the bathers and the crash of waves. "Inside the lines with you! Don't you know this ocean is private property? Git in before I brain you with an oar!"

He turned to me with a sheepish grin:

"This life-saving certainly does get on a man's nerves!"

"What are you doing at Bath Beach? The last time I saw you—"

"Yaass, I know," said Grampus Bill in a gentle roar. "But history has been made since I seen you last." His large mild eye rolled reflectively over his charges disporting in the holiday surf. "No, lady, this is not the Aquarium. Git inside the ropes before you get bit by a shark!"

"But it seems to me," said I, "that this is rather—er—menial employment—"

"I come down here to get away from people. I'm sore on the human race," reverberated he, spitting.

I held my peace. Ashore lay a stretch of beach backed by

swarming bathhouses, and beyond rose the tawdry minarets and cupolas of the amusement park. Hurdy-gurdy music blotted down the wind and the shouts of ballyhoo men.

"Human nature," continued Bill, "is a damn disappointing bill of goods, and the bigger the human the worse the nature. In a fat man it seems more aggravated than in most. If it wasn't for a fat man I'd be cap'n of a good schooner, along with part of a million dollars." A look of vast melancholy settled over his face as he visualized these unattainable delights.

"I lost out," continued Grampus Bill, with a sigh like the first mutterings of a norther, "on account of the meanest man in the world; and I claim it was a good scheme, too. You know? Well, it was like this. A man by the name of Elmira G. Peters, who owned the schooner, *Ladies' Harp*—she was a heirloom in his family," said Bill, "for she was anyway forty-five years old—well, as I was sayin', this man Peters had a great idee of getting ice up in Maine in the early spring, and taking it down to Jamaica, where it's hot and tropical all the year round, and selling it to the abrigines at six hundred per cent profit. Early spring ice is cheaper in Maine than arguments to a woman. No!" he bellowed suddenly, "you ain't drowning! Take hold of the rope, you pirate! Wrap your fingers round it!"

"You say this Peters was the meanest man in the world?" I asked, unable to control myself.

"Lord, no!" boomed Grampus Bill in the exasperated tones of an impatient mother to a squalling child. "I'm a-coming to that. You hit the nail when you said that this was no job for a man like me, that has got the rep of being the best mate on the New York waterfront. Peters, he knew that, so he told me if I would take the *Ladies' Harp* down south, he'd make me cap'n next trip."

At this point a man ventured a short distance beyond the life lines. Bill callously pointed his dory at the swimmer and drove him with a few sharp pulls in vicious silence. We rested on the bosom of the placid sea.

"Well," Bill went on, "we stood up to the mouth of the Kennebec in fair good weather. Right away that made me feel sort of gloomy. 'Too much good luck,' I says to myself, laying in my bunk. 'No good never come of fine weather yet.' Old man Peters himself was cap'n, and often I gave vent to these here presentiments: 'Cap'n,' I says, 'we're shooting straight for hell and disaster. The wind's been good, the crew ain't kicking, and it looks like we're all goin' to make a pile of money. As for me,' I says, 'I don't like it. There's a Jonah on board this craft,' I says.

"But he wouldn't heed me. And as often as the cook came into the cabin carrying our food, this cook, he allowed his feelin's of disbelief and contempt to be freely seen. He laughed at me, this slumgullion did, with scarce a' attempt to conceal his sentiments.

"Now, I'm a patient man, and I can enjoy a joke on myself as well as other men. Fortunately, there ain't many. This here cook, however, he didn't have no joke on me. He just naturally had a nasty disposition. 'Cap'n,' I says, 'I never been on a voyage yet with a good wind which didn't end bad. There's a Jonah on this ship,' I says. 'Tee-hee!' says the cook. The time had come. I says firmly, 'I know who that Jonah is.' So I rose from the table, and I pasted that cook under the bunk."

Grampus Bill doubled up a fist like a ham, and gazed affectionately at his knuckles.

"Things brightened up considerable for me after that. We run into a spell of bad weather and got our jib-topsail blowed away. A whole lot of the men what had only been to sea on ferryboats before got seasick. For a couple of days I stood by at the wheel and emptied my mind on them cab drivers. Then that cook, he showed a commendable manly spirit by putting green paint in my soup; and I towed him up and down the deck six times at the end of a halyard with real respect."

Grampus Bill smiled reminiscently. "After that he seemed properly subdued, but the beggar was stewing a piece of treachery in his mind as mean as ever I heard of."

A shade of cosmic sadness for the human race cast Bill's face into a temporary gloom.

"Well, about the first of February we was sliding down the Kennebec for the open sea, loaded up with ice. A good many of the crew had deserted—but that only showed my discipline was good. Five of them went away without their wages, so the old man was pleased, too. But we was ten miles out to sea, standing southeast by east two points south, with our starboard rail awash, when four bells sounded, and I went below to git my dinner. Then the awful truth burst upon us. That cook had went—slipped ashore somewhere at the mouth of the river. In the middle of the cabin table we found a note, stuck on with green paint. It says: 'I ain't going to be housemaid no more for a couple of bullsharks. I'm going to be a prizefighter, where I can hope for a little peace and relaxation. I have took the cabin lamps, the cap'n's trousers, and the mate's shoes as part of my wages, and would have took two brass ventilators and the ship's compass, only I couldn't get them off.'

"Now this is very important to remember," Grampus Bill wagged a finger like a coupling pin. "Them ventilators and that compass was in a shocking state. We never did get that compass right again. And that explains why we sailed into the Sargasso Sea with us thinking all the time we were heading straight for Jamaica. But the most horrible misfortune of all was that we didn't have no cook. 'Cap'n,' I says, 'I told you all along that damned anarchist was a Jonah. And you didn't believe me. If you had let me run things,' I says, 'I'd have walloped that cook from the fo'c's'le head clear back to the binnacle,' I says, 'every day immediately after dinner. Then we would have had no trouble,' I says.

"Now, living in the city and all," continued Grampus Bill, impressively, "p'r'aps you don't realize that a man's stomach is the most important part of life at sea. I been cast on a desolate island for three months with nothing but sand fleas for company; I been wrecked in the Arctic Ocean, where every wave turned to ice just before it broke and battered ships to pieces; I swum a half mile race with two sharks in the Indian Ocean; I been attacked by cannibals in the South Seas and forced to devour several of them in self-protection. You may call me weak and you may call me womanish—but I tell you, when I heard that cook had deserted the ship, I blenched, sir, and I winched. I begun to think of the horrors of the bo's'n cooking—he was a Eyetalian. I shuddered to think that maybe I might have to cook myself. 'Cap'n,' I says, 'if we don't put back to take on a cook, I'm going to wreck this vessel on the first convenient rock so's to have something to do to take my mind off my food.' The upshot of it was we put back to Portland for a cook.

"I was foolish enough to think we had slipped Old Man Trouble with that cook," continued Bill bitterly. "I must 'a' ben mad. It's simply ridickelous to change one Jonah for another, ain't it now? And that's wot we done. For, would you believe it, there wasn't no cooks to be had in Portland—nothing but a fat man by the name of Flinders, who come aboard and said he had a passion for the sea.

"'How do you mean "passion?"' says I. 'Have you ever sot foot on a ship in the hull course of your wuthless life?'

"'Of course not,' he says, coldly. 'But I ben a-taking lessons to be a Capting in a correspondence school,' says he. 'I can already splice a rope on paper, and if I ever lay my hooks on a sextet,' says he, 'I bet I can ferret out a latitude or a longitude if there's one anywheres around. Besides,' he says, 'there ain't a current or a shoal in the hull Seven Seas I ain't got by heart. Question 33: In wot direction, if any, flows the Semilinear Equatorial North Atlantic Current during the Winter Solstice? Answer: Fetching west by south after picking up Cape Near Light in a direct line with the old sycamore, bearing a point and a half north around the Windward Islands.' I give him a look, and he broke off and cowered. 'And I can box the compass,' he finished, weak and low.

"'Hold yourself in, Bill,' orders the Old Man. 'Look here, you ignorant assemblage of intestines,' he says mildly, 'we don't want no more cap'ns aboard this schooner.'

"'Oh!' says Flinders, disappointed.

"'But can you cook?'

"'In the course of my efforts to secure enough funds to complete my education,' chirps Flinders, 'I have cooked in a lumber camp. In fact, I just come from there. . . .'

"'All right,' says the Old Man. 'Bring your dunnage aboard. We sail in half an hour.'

"'Cook!' says the fat man, contemptuously. 'Cook! And I knowing probably more navigation than anybody here!'

"The Cap'n motioned me to sit down again. This Flinders stared thoughtfully at the floor for a space. 'Why not?' says he, speakin' like to himself. 'It would be a chancet. I can work up to be capting. Is the promotion rapid?'

"'It's more than that,' I says. 'You can git promoted from where you sit, through the skylight, under the binnacle, down the fo'c's'le companion, soused through a lot of odds and ends in the forepeak and end up in the galley, all inside of an hour.' So saying, I made a couple of hostyle moves. But Flinders got up.

"'Capting!' he yells, all pasty. 'This here person, a total stranger to me, is, I gather, threatening me with pussonal violence. I demand an apology!'"

Grampus Bill lowered his voice impressively to correspond with the astounding revelation he made.

"Cap'n Peters apologized," he said quietly. "But that ain't the wust. The Old Man says, 'Bill, remember your stomich.' And—I apologized! But I says to myself, 'Oncet I git you on the high seas, George, all the fathers of the church can't save you from pussonal hell!'

"My attentions being occupied with teaching some of the new men their position as dorgmeat, I didn't run up against this Flinders until eight bells, when I went below for lunch. I'm not a man to nurse a grudge, so I was peaceable-disposed toward him. Well, what do you think? There sat the Cap'n, lookin' sort of purple 'round the gills, a-taring at the cabin table, which same was entirely bare of forks and plates.

"'Wot the hell?' says I.

"'Tar my seams if I know,' he says in a dazed voice. 'I just made fast here myself. When I come down, there was that cook a-setting here with five or six books spread open in front of him, *doin' sums!*

'I sings out, "Where the hell's my grub?" He sort of starts, and says, "Oh, beg pardon, Capting, I got so everlastingly engrossed in my triggernometry—" and off he beats it to the galley.

"'Flinders!' I roars, quite insane with hunger and discouragement. He appears in the door, humming a song like this:

> In my little shallop I
> shall ride
> With white wings on
> the blue sea-tide—

"'You ornery shark's gullet,' says I, 'wot do you mean by not having my dinner ready?'

"'Well,' says he, kind of snippy, 'you needn't make such a fuss. If you want me to cook your meals you'd better post up a little schedule in the kitchen: Breakfast, 7:30 to 9:30; Lunch, 12:30 to 2:00; Dinner, 6:00 to 8:30, and so on. In the lumber camp we had lunch early; and you'd feel a good deal better if you et say an hour earlier. By the bye, I don't know what right *you* got to interfere in a merely personal matter between my employer and myself.'

"Man," said Bill, "you can't imagine how I had to smother myself. But it was before lunch, and if I'd hit him then, we wouldn't 've had no grub. 'Wait till I've grubbed,' I kept telling myself. But all I says was, 'You immaterial piece of hellfire, I'm the mate! Un'erstand? One more crack like that and the schoolgirls of Gloucester will cast another wreath off the pier for a unknown corp'. Another thing. Every time you open your head henceforth you emit a "sir!"'"

"'There,' says Flinders, 'now I *am* hurt. Just for that you'll get no dinner!

"'*Wot!*' I says.

"'You've hurt my feelings,' he says. 'I shall not serve

you. I'm accustomed to cooking for gentlemen, I'll have you know.'

"Well, I just hauled off and swiped him under the ear, and down he went, like a sack of clams. Would you believe it, he bust out crying—bawling like a baby. There he set, a-blocking up the companionway, screeching fit to bust, and shakin' all over like a closet-hauled sail when the wind shifts. I didn't know what to do.

"'Git up out of that,' I yells, 'and git forrad before I slap you another!' But he never moved, just sobbed and sobbed, crying out, 'Never, never, have I been so humiliated! Wot would my poor old mother think? O my! O my!' I called him every name I could lay tongue to, and even tried to hit him. But Lord! You can't hit a jellyfish; it ain't human!

"By that time I didn't have no appetite left. An' to make matters wuss, the crew sent a committee aft to find out why they wasn't getting no food. Then it come on to blow all of a sudden, and up on deck I could hear the booms slatting around and the sails cracking. I grabbed aholt of that fat glubbering man to pull him out of the way so as I could git on deck—and I swear to goodness I couldn't budge him. He must 'a' weighed four hundred pound. I lost my temper then, and kicked and hit him, but he never moved.

"'I'm going to set right here,' says he, 'until that brute has begged my parding!'

"An' the upshot of it was I had to crawl out through the cabin skylight. . . ."

Grampus Bill was plunged in melancholy reminiscence. He sighed, and the waters around showed whitecaps.

"The skipper give Flinders a talking-to while I was gone. He said he'd discharge him right in mid-ocean if he didn't obey orders. Anyway, it was some kind of argument like that which this male chambermaid could understand. Because inside of a half-hour he had dinner on the table, and was moving around that cabin like a pale, outraged mountain. I will say it was A-one food, too.

"It didn't take long for Flinders to chipper up. A day or

so later I was taking a trick at the wheel when we sighted a couple of whales. Just then this great cook waddled out on deck, a-wiping his hands on his apron. He come aft, where no cook never dared put his foot on my ship before, nodding brightly.

"'Ah, whales!' he says. 'I studied all about whaling in my second-year course. I suppose,' he says, 'you never studied about whales much?'

"'I ben mate of three whaling-ships in my time,' I says, sarcastic and bitter. But he never noticed.

"'There is three species of whales,' he begun, 'thrasher whales, right whales, and sperm whales. The first is of absolutely no value commercially. The second, the right whale, yields often forty or fifty barrels of oil. But the sperm whale is the most eagerly sought after. His habitat is now restricted almost entirely to the Arctic regions. Formerly, however, he flourished in the temperate seas. One such animal yields sometimes hundreds of barrels of oil. Besides oil, other products of the whale are whalebone, ambergris, which is–'

"'You git forrad into that galley!' I screamed. 'And if you even stick your head out I'll throw the rudder at you!'

"Then another time the Cap'n was taking observations, and I was working out the position of the ship, when Flinders come softly up behind, leaned over my shoulder and breathed onions on me.

"'Dear, dear!' he says, like he pitied me, 'how quaint and old fashioned! Why don't you use logarithms, old man? You see, you don't git the scientific value out of your false horizon at all. Let me show you–' And he grabbed the thing out of my hand! I ordered the port watch onto the capstan, hitched the cargo derrick onto that cook, and we doused him over the side, kicking and screeching, in the North Atlantic.

"But even that didn't seem to do no good. Right in the middle of dinner he'd come down the companion with a tray and say, 'Capting, do you realize what this wind is? It's the tail end of the Northeast Trade, which sweeps you out of the Carribbean through the Florida Straits during February, and is deflected by the current of warm air carried by the Gulf Stream, and again by the cold blast generated by the Labrador Current,' and so on, until I couldn't stand it no longer and handed him a swipe in the chops. Then he'd set down on the floor right in the companionway and blubber—and you couldn't git past him or move him. Often I've stayed there an hour waiting for Flinders to move, because we didn't dare to open up the skylight. I'm just telling you these here incidents so you can understand how exasperated we all felt. And the crew was the same way. Wot with the uncertainty of getting anything to eat, and his patronizing them because they was only common sailors and he was going to be a capting, all hands was wild with hate at that cook. They took to putting roaches in his bunk. And then they discovered a better way to git even. They never noticed him. Acted just like he wasn't there when he spoke to them. Of course he couldn't fly into a temper at that, but it hurt his feelings something dreadful. Pretty soon nobody was speaking to Flinders at all, but you just couldn't make him clap a stopper on his jaw-tackle. Every meal he'd ladle out a piece of information in a way to make your stomach turn.

"Well, we first begun to notice something was wrong three days out to sea. Observation at noon showed us always at least three points off our course; and we'd correct the reckoning only to find the same thing happen next day. I thought it was the wheelman getting careless, and acting on that theory, I walloped the living sin out of a quartermaster or so. But still she kept a-yawing off; and wot with shifting winds and this Flinders contemptuous of our ignorance of navigation, I was in a fair sweat all the time. So one day I says, 'Wotever else I accomplish in this mis-spent life,' I says, 'I'm going to git my name writ down in history as the man that closed your porthole. Flinders,' I says, 'the next time you open your trap in my presence except in administering to the legitimate lusts of the flesh,' I says, 'I'm going to Desdemona you with a mass of plum duff. I mean it this time.' And thereafter there was peace for a while.

"The way we was running, we was due at Jamaica in eleven days; but with correcting our course and all, I calculated it would take us a day or two longer. But six days out the sky was overcast and we couldn't take no more observation; so we had to go by the needle—and, as I told you, the needle wasn't correct. We didn't know that, however. Well, she stayed cloudy day after day, and we went a-blowing along. Five days we went steady, then five more, and still no sight of land, and cloudy as ever. It begun to git warm. 'Well,' says the Old Man, 'we're a-getting south anyhow. It don't have to be Jamaica—any hot island will do. Wot we want is the tropics—Tropic of Cancer or Tropic of Paprika, it don't make no difference.' We sailed on, it gitting warmer and warmer, and the breeze dropping every day more, for ten days. It was fair hot. Pretty soon we begun to notice that we didn't see no ships. I got worried. By all odds, we must 'a' sailed past Jamaica, going that long. I wondered why we hadn't seen no islands. The water we took over the side for swabbing decks was so hot it almost burned you. We hadn't loaded up for no long voyage, neither, and drinking water begun to git low. To make it wuss, the wind fell away to a flat calm, and one morning I come on deck to see us fouled in a mess of thick seaweed, stretching away east'ard as fur as you could see.

"Then the sun come out, for the fust time in two weeks or more, and we took the reckoning. *We was four hundred miles south and eight hundred east of Jamaica!* Flinders was giving us grub and he heard us talking it over. He got so excited he dropped the soup on the cabin floor. 'Capting!' he cried, 'I know all about it. It come in lesson 654, *The Equatorial Calms and Vicinity*. This here is the Sargasso Sea! It is formed by the conjunction of the circular motions of the Canary Current and the Gulf Stream. Many derelicts—' Here I gave him a horrible grimace and he shut up like a sea anemone. But he was right. There we was, a half a thousand sea-miles off the track of ships, becalmed, with water low and none too much food.

"And just then a man come running yelling 'There's fourteen feet of water in the hold!' This Flinders opened his mouth to speak, but I roars, 'Shut up!' Which he did. But all of a sudden he begun to grin to himself, the treacherous scoundrel!

"Well, we pried off the main hatch—and all we saw was a great black mess of water swilling around below, with ice-cakes floating on top. 'My God!' yells Peters, 'we've sprung a terrible leak. Man the pumps!' And we fell to, like demons. We pumped all that day, and all night, and then sounded her again. The water was eighteen feet deep, and all the ice-cakes was melted. By this time the deck was nearly awash. It was sure we'd have to abandon the ship, if we didn't all want to sink. Ol Peters run around like a horseshoe crab at low tide, not wanting to make up his mind. But meanwhile the tanks was almost empty of fresh water, and food was going fast.

"In that thirty-six hours I done some terrible hard thinking. Here we was, with little water and food, hundreds of miles out of the steamer lanes, and more from land. Most likely we would run out of grub, because anyway you can't pack enough in a boat to last a five-hundred-mile row. Most likely we would have to devour a companion. So I looks around for the most eligible companion and my eyes light on Flinders. Nine-tenths of that man was pure fat, and the only person that would ever mourn his absence would be the correspondence school.

"So I ranged alongside him on deck and says, 'Flinders, when we leave the ship, you are to come in my boat.'

"'Why?' says he, surprised. 'Thank you very much. But I'm a-going with the bo's'n.'

"'You don't want to go with the bo's'n,' I says, kindly. 'He is only a common sailor. You want to go with the *mate*.'

"'Much obliged,' says he. 'But the bo's'n says I won't have to row any in his boat. I just *hate* physical exertion,' he says.

"I seen then that the bo's'n was thinking just like me, the underhanded sculpin. 'Well,' I says, 'you don't have to row in my boat neither. Wot's more, I'll give you full rations as long as they last.'

"'Hum,' says he, looking puzzled, 'I don't see why everybody wants to be so good to me. I tell you, it's a hearty relief to notice such a change in people since we come here. Everybody has ben so kind I can't thank you all for your generosity. I *knew* you'd understand me some day,' he says. ('Uh-huh!' says I, 'so everybody's taking a hand, hey?')

"Along about two bells Flinders come up to me and says, 'I'm real sorry I can't go along with you in your boat. The quartermaster he offered me half of the water besides, and a umbrella over me to keep the sun off.'

"I lost my temper. 'You git in my boat, you understand,' I shouted, 'or I'll stove a hole along your waterline!' Just then Old Man Peters emerged from the cabin companionway. 'Wot's the trouble?' he ast. Flinders he had a grievance. 'All these gentlemen ben inviting me to go in their boats,' says he, 'because I know so much about navigation. I never knew I had so many friends. And then this here mate orders me to go with him, and threatens me with pussonal violence. So I just said I wouldn't go, and I won't!'

"I seen Peters' eye begin to light with understanding, as he surveys the steaks, chops, hams, and cutlets of the fat man. 'You're perfectly right,' says he. 'Mr. Mate, I'm ashamed of you sir! As for you, Mr. Flinders, I shall feel happy if you will come in *my* boat.'

"'I'm certainly most honored,' says Flinders. 'But the quartermaster he offered me—'.

"' I will be happy to offer you just what the quartermaster did, and whatever else you can think of.'

"'Well,' says Flinders, 'now you know I want to be a capting some day. So if—now—I could be capting of any ship you happen to next be owner of—'

"'All right,' says the skipper, who didn't own no other ship and had no intention of doing so. 'Shake on it. You go in my boat.' At the same time I seen him calculating the number of days before that cook would vanish off the list of eligible capn's in any navy. I had a sudden panic, and hastily thought about myself.

"'Cap'n,' says I, 'you don't want no crowd in your boat. Let's take the dingy,' I says, 'and you and me and good old Flinders'll all go together in her alone.' Peters and I looks at each other with good fellowship and the hungry eye of perfect understanding. 'All right,' he says. 'And now, let's cast off. In about an hour we'll all be drowned, the water's gaining that fast.'"

Here Grampus Bill squinted horribly, in an effort to find words in which to convey to me the picture which rose in his mind.

"I shall not dwell," he boomed, "upon the casting-off of them boats, and the uproars which erupted out of the bo's'n and quartermaster when they found their prey had slipped his cable. Their mutterings died away in the distance as boat after boat pulled off from the *Ladies' Harp* and disappeared all over the horizon. The skipper and me we fixed a lot of cushions comfortable-like in the stern of that dinghy, rigged up Peters' green umbrella over it, and stowed this wuthless hulk of a sea-cook there. Then we cast off, and leaving the schooner wallowing in the wash, fell to the oars, Peters weeping openly. Flinders, he wep' also—out of pure sympathy, he said. So we give way over a sea smooth as glass, the sun beating down something fierce, a stink of seaweed such as I never smelled in all my travels, and the only sounds being a albatross cawing impatient-like overhead hopeful for a corp' or so, and them two idiots blubbering soft.

"Pretty soon Flinders he dried his eyes and says, 'Well, earth to earth, and dust to dust. No use crying over spilt ice. In order to take your minds off this sad event,' he says, 'I'm a-going to enliven the dull hours by imparting useful information garnered from my studies,' he says. 'Now this here Sargasso Sea is peculiar in many respecks. The various weeds and water-growths, carried by the two main ocean currents of the South Atlantic, is whirled by centrifiggal force to their inner circumferences,' says he, 'where they gathers in the calm center known as the Sargasso Sea. This sea, like the hub of any wheel, continual revolves from right to left, north to west to south to east and so on, and it is the dreadful fate of derelicts to follow around this here course for ever and ever–' Like that he kep' on for a couple of hours, until I nearly screamed out loud. But I kep' hold on my humors by the consoling idee that soon the internal machinery wot produced that idle chatter would be digesting in my intestines. And soon this Flinders luxurious fell drowsy to sleep, while the Cap'n and me sweated and got dizzy rowing in the sun.

"Now we figgered as how we was near the south side of the Sargasso Sea, and so instead of picking out a precarious passage through the seaweed acrost the center of it, we laid a course south by east, with the intention of passing clean around it going with the current, and a-trying to fetch the Canaries off the coast of Africa. Along about sundown we et a biskit and drunk a swaller of water, resting for a space. The *Ladies' Harp* was hull down in the north. Then we fell to again. Pretty soon Flinders he woke up and devoured five biskits and a pint of water–which was horrible! But we didn't dare to say nothing, because we had promised him full rations. After eating he lit his pipe and says, looking up at the sky, 'Sailors in the old days found their way about the sea at night by means of the North Star,' he says, 'and the Southern Cross. The North Star is, of course, invisible from these latitudes, but if you will look sharp,' he says, 'you will observe the Dipper in the northwest quarter of the heavens. The two small stars at the end of the handle is called the Pointers,' he says, 'because they point direct to the North Star, whose other name,' he says, 'is Arcturus; and up there is a constellation called Cassiopeia's Chair. Almost immediately above our heads is the so-called Southern Cross, whose value to sailors has been acknowledged since the remotest antiquity. It–' Well, mercifully for that fat man, he dozes off again. I kep' my temper, because I wanted to eat him fresh when the time come.

"He woke up again about dawn and wrapped himself

around a half-dozen biskit, two cans of potted ham, and a pint and a half of water. I ventured to remonstrate. He looks at me grieved, and gazes down at hisself. 'Wot's two cans of potted ham amongst me?' he ast. Peters, he whispers hoarsely, 'Leave him be. We got to keep him in condition.' Then the sun leaps up like a red hot stove in the east, and we fell to a-drooping. As we pulled, this Flinders shifted his carcass around to git comfortable, and begins, 'I was most interested,' he says, 'in a series of preliminary lectures concerning the general subjeck of the composition of the sea,' he says. 'It was called *Oceans: Their Whys and Wherefores,* and is of immense value to seamen in general. Did you men ever take that course?' he says. We didn't dare open our heads. 'Well,' he goes on, 'the ocean contains in solution various chemicals, of which the most important is sodium–salt. This here sodium is washed down by the rivers along with various other constituents of the earth in small quantities. How do you suppose,' he says, 'that the ocean comes to be so salty?' We said nothing. 'You do not know,' he says, with scorn. 'It is because of the continual evaporation of the sea water by the sun, which evaporation does not draw off the chemicals, which are left in constantly increasing solution in a constantly diminishing quantity of H_2O,' he says, 'which is continually replenished by the evaporated moisture falling upon the earth in the form of rain, and rejoining the oceans in the form of rivers, which in turn carry down more chemicals–'

"I want to say right here," remarked Grampus Bill, "that the sufferings of the early Christian martyrs was nothing but fiddle-de-dee alongside of us. We was treated to this kind of bilge until I slavered like a mad dorg most of the time. But most of the time Flinders he slep' under the umbrella on the cushions, and Peters and me, we pulled them oars. We pulled all that day, reeling in the sun, and all the next night, and the next day, and the next night– But why go further? It got so after a while that life wasn't nothing but a long dragging at them oars with muscles so sore you give a screech every time you pulled, and your head swimming round and round in the sun, and the voice of Flinders a-coming from way off, saying, 'Seven-eighths of the earth's surface is water.' Sometimes he would sing in a horrid, cracked voice, to cheer us up, he said—songs like this:

> Jolly boating weather,
> Row, row together,
> With your bodies between your knees. . . .

All in time to me and Peters pulling, until we almost bust into tears. About the second morning Flinders woke up and et a huge meal, and drank out of the barrel until I thought he never would get done. 'Why,' he says, putting it down, 'why, I declare! It's empty!'

"'*Wot!*' we screamed, not able to believe our ears. It was. That cook had drunk up all the water we thought would last a couple of days more. Peters and me sat there, dazed, horrified at wot we'd heard. Presently Flinders he fell asleep, and the Old Man turned around to me, with a wild gleam in his eye. 'Now is the time,' he says. 'It's too damn bad we can't keep him to eat. But we'd better lay him out now and drink his blood.'

"I was just getting an oar loose when Flinders woke up sudden. 'I don't know,' he says drowsily, feeling his neck, 'but I think I'm getting a boil. Wot with this here inactivity,' he says, 'and the irregularity of meals, I don't think my blood is in very good condition. You don't happen to have a little sulphur and iron in the boat, do you?' he says.

"I went quite insane. Jumping up and down in the boat I shouted, 'Sulphur and iron be damned!' I bawled. 'You insignificant hunk of God-help-us,' I says, 'you know wot you've done? You went and drunk up all the fresh water in this boat, you guzzling water-logged hulk of a coal barge,' I says. 'That's wot you done!'

"'Well,' says he, 'I call it very careless of you not to bring along more. If I called myself a sailor,' says he, 'I wouldn't own up to no such negligence—'

"'More!' cried Peters, faint from rage and disappointment. 'Hold on to me, somebody. More! Don't you know there wasn't no more in the tanks?'

"'Then why didn't you dip it out of the hold?' says Flinders. 'All you had to do was to lower down a bucket.'

"'Don't hit him,' says Peters. 'He's mad. Presently he'll give a screech and jump overboard, and we'll have the pleasure of seeing him slowly drown.'

"'Mad my stepfather,' says Flinders warmly. 'You mean to tell me you parlor-sailors didn't know that water in there was the ice-cakes melting because of the warm ocean we was in?' he says.

"It seemed we set there, Peters and me, gazing at each other for a couple of hours.

"'Why—why didn't you tell us?' whispers the skipper.

"'I tried to,' says Flinders, 'but this uncultured mate here uncouthly tells me to stow my jabber.'

"The only word wot will describe the ensuing is pande-momianum."

Grampus Bill passed a trembling hand athwart his features, and it come away wet with perspiration. He continued finally:

"We each got an oar and was going to beat this Flinders to death," he said, "when the latter suddenly cries out:

"'Don't you dare to hit me!' he says, 'or I'll leave you to your fate on the high seas. Nobody but me knows these here currents of the Sargasso Sea, and nobody can't find that ship again unless I tell 'em how!'

"'My God!' says Peters, groaning. 'It's true, Bill. Set down!' I done it, despairing.

"'Remember your promise,' says Flinders, setting up sudden. 'I'm capting of this here craft, and of the *Ladies' Harp*, too, if we find her! Give way now, hearty. We'll lay her northeast by a point north. You remember wot I told you about that revolving centrifiggal current? Well, that there current is a-carrying the ship toward us every minute, and by tomorrow morning we'll sight her!'

"He had us dead to rights. So we done wot he told us. My God, but it was a shameful thing to see—two strong, able-bodied sailors of more than common capacity obeying the orders of a fat cook wot had never ben to sea! But I was thinking that all was not yet lost. Once we got on that schooner, we could brain that cook with a belaying pin impuniously, there being no crew handy to see the crime. However, I hadn't counted on the treachery of Elmira G. Peters. He was sore all over, a-blushing with shame and rage. And being reluctant to blame hisself, he looked around for somebody to fasten it onto. And that somebody was me. Along about sunset, when Flinders was asleep, I leaned over and proposed my plan for disposing of that cook.

"'Hush up!' he says, furious. 'Don't you never dare to talk such things to me again, you black-hearted scoundrel!' he says to me. 'If it hadn't ben for you stopping Flinders from talking, we'd never had had this here trouble and worry!' And that," mourned Grampus Bill, "was wot soured me forever on human nature.

"The rest of the story is just one long tale of meanness and ingratitude. About morning, sure enough, we sighted the *Ladies' Harp,* no more sunk than we'd left her; and about noon we was sucking water through a hose out of the hold. Nice fresh water, too, just like he said, the deceitful slumgullion! And then, all of a sudden, a little breeze come up. 'Fall to the pumps,' says Flinders, taking the wheel—and we fell to, all wore out with hardships as we was. Next day we picked up the bo's'n's boat, and the day after the quartermaster's. And would you believe it? Not one of them would listen to any plan to kill the cook, but like dorgs they turned on me, when I was down, and said they was glad to git revenge for all the discipline I had taught 'em. But the thing that almost busted my heart," said Grampus Bill, choking, "was when Peters and Flinders made me turn to and cook. . . .

"Of course I couldn't stand that long. One night as we was standing north by west I seen the lights of a steamer headed so she'd cross our bows. So I dropped the dinghy overboard without anybody seeing, and managed to git picked up."

Bill bent his roving glance upon a bather who was frolicking just outside the life lines, and his face took on the fierce joy of a tiger about to leap upon its prey, as he silently rowed in that direction.

"And that ain't all," he said, briefly. "That diabolical Flinders he stopped them pumping, and druv north until they found an iceberg wot had drifted down from Greenland. He ranged the schooner alongside and grappled her to the iceberg until the water in the hold all friz up again to ice-cakes. Then he bore away south by west and fetched up at Jamaica, where I heard tell that the profits was a million dollars...."

Having crept up behind the unsuspecting swimmer, Bill suddenly gave vent to a series of frightful hoots and struck at him viciously with an oar. "Inside the lines with you," he roared in a voice that dominated the shouts of the bathers and the crash of the surf. "Take yourself and your shameful naked limbs out of this ocean oncet! And don't come around bothering me and my ocean no more, you miserable apology for a sandab!"

1914

The War in Eastern Europe*

THE EASTERN GATE OF WAR

By here passed the American Red Cross units, the foreign Medical Missions, on their way to typhus-stricken Serbia—veteran doctors and big, robust nurses laughing at the danger and boasting what they would do; and by here the gaunt, shaking survivors drifted back to tell how their comrades died.

Still they came. While we were in Salonika three new British expeditions passed through, one hundred and nineteen strong. Fresh young girls, untrained and unequipped, without the slightest idea what they must face, explored the colorful streets and the bazaars.

* A month after Reed returned from the western front as a correspondent for the *Metropolitan Magazine,* he left to cover the war in Eastern Europe. He was accompanied by Boardman Robinson, a Canadian artist assigned by the *Metropolitan* to illustrate Reed's stories. They had planned to be away for three months but were gone seven—from April to October 1915—and did not witness any of the grand dramatic climaxes they had anticipated. From Italy they went to Salonika, from there to Serbia, and then to Bucharest where once again there was little action. They crossed into Russia and finally landed in Petrograd after some exasperating experiences with the tsarist authorities. Once more in Bucharest, Reed determined to see Constantinople. There he was unofficially asked to leave Turkey because he had been seen talking with too many Armenians. When Bulgaria proved uneventful, and their return to Serbia and Salonika even more so, they took ship for Italy and home. Ironically, just as they left hostilities flared up, with the German and Austrian armies entering Serbia, and Bulgaria coming under attack.—*Ed.*

"No, I never had any experience in nursing," said one, "but one just nurses, doesn't one?"

A British Royal Army Medical Corps lieutenant who heard her shook his head in despair.

"The damned fools in England to let them come!" he cried. "It is almost certain death. And they are worse than useless, you know. They are the first to fall sick, and then we have to look after them."

Of course, there was a new rumor every five minutes. Day and night ephemeral newspapers flooded the streets and cafés with huge scareheads reading:

CONSTANTINOPLE FALLS
FORTY THOUSAND ENGLISH SLAUGHTERED
ON THE PENINSULA!
TURKISH REVOLUTIONISTS MASSACRE THE
GERMANS!

One evening an excited mob of soldiers with flags swept cheering along the sea wall shouting: "Greece declares war!"

Spies infested the city. Germans with shaved heads and sword-cuts all over their faces pretending to be Italians; Austrians in green Tyrolean hats passing as Turks; stupid-mannered Englishmen who sat drinking and talking in the cafés, eavesdropping the conversation in six languages that went on about them; exiled Mohammedans of the Old Turk party plotting in corners, and Greek secret service men who changed their clothes fourteen times a day and altered the shape of their mustaches.

Occasionally out of the East a French or British warship grew slowly from the flat world of the sea, moored at the docks, and made repairs. Then the city was full of drunken sailors day and night.

For Salonika was anything but neutral. Besides the army officers on the streets, every day saw the arrival of British ships full of ammunition for the Serbian front. Every day cars loaded with English, French, and Russian cannon disappeared into the somber mountains northward. We saw the

English gunboat on its special car begin the long journey to the Danube. And through this port went the French airplanes, with their hundred pilots and *mécaniciens;* and the British and Russian marines.

And all day long the refugees poured in; political exiles from Constantinople and Smyrna, Europeans from Turkey, Turks who feared the grand smash-up when the empire should fall, Greeks of the Levant. From Lemnos and Tenedos the refugee boats carried the plague brought there by the Indian troops—even now it was spreading in the crowded lower quarters of the town. Always you could see pitiful processions crawling through the streets—men, women, and children with bloody feet limping beside broken-down wagons filled with the dilapidated furniture of some wretched peasant's hut. Hundreds of Greek popes from the monasteries of Asia Minor shuffled by, their threadbare black robes and high hats yellow with dust, their feet bound with rags, and all their possessions in a gunny sack over their shoulders. In trampled courtyards of old mosques, under pillared porticos painted red and blue, half-veiled women with black shawls on their heads crowded, staring vacantly into space or weeping quietly for their men, who had been taken for the army; the children played among the weed-grown tombs of the *hadjis;* their scanty bundles of belongings lay heaped in the corners.

Late one night we walked through the deserted quarter of docks and warehouses, so filled with shouting movement by day. From a faintly lighted window came the sound of pounding and singing, and we peered through the grimy pane. It was a waterfront saloon, a low-vaulted room with a floor of hard packed earth, rough table and stools, piles of black bottles, barrel-ends, and one smoking lamp hung crazily from the ceiling. At the table sat eight men, whining a wavering Oriental song, and beating time with their glasses. Suddenly one caught sight of our faces at the window; they halted, leaped to their feet. The door flew open—hands reached out and pulled us in.

168

"Entrez! Pasen Ustedes! Herein! Herein!" shouted the company, crowding eagerly about us as we entered the room. A short, bald-headed man with a wart on his nose pumped our hands up and down, babbling in a mixture of languages: "To drink! To drink! What will you have, friends?"

"But *we* invite *you*–" I began.

"This is my shop! Never shall a stranger pay in my shop! Wine? Beer? *Mastica?*"

"Who are you?" asked the others. "French? English? Ah– Americans! I have a cousin–his name Georgopoulos–he live in California. You know him?"

One spoke English, another harsh maritime French, a third Neapolitan, a fourth Levantine Spanish, and still another pidgin German; all knew Greek, and the strange patois of the Mediterranean sailor. The fortunes of war had swept them from the four corners of the Middle World into this obscure backwater on the Salonika docks.

"It is strange," said the man who spoke English. "We met here by chance–not one of us has ever known the other before. And we are all seven carpenters. I am a Greek from Kili on the Black Sea, and he is a Greek, and he, and he– from Ephesus, and Erzurum, and Scutari. This man is an Italian–he lives in Aleppo, in Syria–and this one a French-man of Smyrna. Last night we were sitting here just like now, and he looked in at the window like you did."

The seventh carpenter, who had not spoken, said something that sounded like a German dialect. The proprietor translated:

"This man is Armenian. He says all his family is killed by the Turks. He tries to tell you in the German he learned working on the Baghdad Railway!"

"Back there," cried the Frenchman, "I leave my wife and two kids! I go away hiding on a fisherboat–"

"God knows where is my brother." The Italian shook his head. "The soldiers took him. We could not both escape."

Now the master of the house brought liquor, and we raised our glasses to his beaming countenance.

"He is like that," the Italian explained with gestures. "We have no money. He gives us food and drink, and we sleep here on the floor, poor refugees. God will certainly reward his charity!"

"Yes. Yes. God will reward him," assented the others, drinking. The proprietor crossed himself elaborately, after the complicated fashion of the Orthodox Church.

"God knows I am fond of company," he said. "And one cannot turn away destitute men in times like these, especially men of pleasing talents. Besides, a carpenter gains good wages when he works, and then I shall be repaid."

"Do you want Greece to go to war?" we asked.

"No!" cried some; others moodily shook their heads.

"It is like this," the English-speaking Greek said slowly: "This war has driven us from our homes and our work. Now there is no work for a carpenter. War is a tearing down and not a building up. A carpenter is for building up—" He translated to the silent audience, and they growled applause.

"But how about Constantinople?"

"Constantinople for Greece! Greek Constantinople!" shouted two of the carpenters. But the others broke into violent argument.

The Italian rose and lifted his glass. "*Eviva* Constantinople Internazionale!" he cried. With a cheer everybody rose. "Constantinople Internazionale!"

"Come," said the proprietor, "a song for the strangers!"

"What was that you were singing when we came?" demanded Robinson.

"That was an Arab song. Now let us sing a real Turkish song!" And throwing back their heads, the company opened their noses in a whining wail, tapping with stiff fingers on the table while the glasses leaped and jingled.

"More to drink!" cried the excited innkeeper. "What is song without drink?"

"God will reward him!" murmured the seven carpenters in voices husky with emotion.

The Italian had a powerful tenor voice; he sang *La donna*

e mobile, in which the others joined with Oriental improvisations. An American song was called for, and Robinson and I obliged with "John Brown's Body"—which was encored four times.

Later dancing displaced music. In the flickering light of the fast-expiring lamp the proprietor led a stamping trio in the *kolo,* dance of all the Balkan peoples. Great boots clumped stiffly down, arms waved, fingers snapped, ragged clothes fluttered in brown shadow and yellow radiance ... Followed an Arab measure, all swaying bodies and syncopated gliding steps, and slow twirlings with closed eyes. At an early hour of the morning we were giving the company lessons in the "Boston," and the turkey trot ... And so ended the adventure of the Seven Carpenters of Salonika. . . .

SERBIA

We rubbed ourselves from head to foot with camphorated oil, put kerosene on our hair, filled our pockets with moth balls, and sprinkled naphthalene through our baggage; and boarded a train so saturated with formalin that our eyes and lungs burned as with quicklime. The Americans from the Standard Oil office in Salonika strolled down to bid us a last farewell. . . .

These were the ordinary precautions of travelers bound for Serbia, the country of the typhus—abdominal typhus, recurrent fever, and the mysterious and violent spotted fever. . . .

Already the warm weather and the cessation of the spring rains had begun to check the epidemic—and the virus was weaker. Now there were only a hundred thousand sick in all Serbia, and only a thousand deaths a day—besides cases of the dreadful post-typhus gangrene. In February it must have been ghastly—hundreds of dying and delirious in the mud of the streets for want of hospitals.

The foreign medical missions had suffered heavily. Half a hundred priests succumbed after giving absolution to the dying. Out of the four hundred odd doctors with which the Serbian army began the war, less than two hundred were left. And the typhus was not all. Smallpox, scarlet fever, scarlatina, diphtheria raged along the great roads and in far villages, and already there were cases of cholera, which was sure to spread with the coming of the summer in that devastated land; where battlefields, villages, and roads stank with the lightly buried dead, and the streams were polluted with the bodies of men and horses. . . .

The gorge of the Vardar, as if it were a sterile frontier between Greek Macedonia and the high valleys of New Serbia, broadened out into a wide valley rimmed with stony hills, beyond which lay mountains still higher, with an occasional glimpse of an abrupt snow peak. From every canyon burst rapid mountain streams. In this valley the air was hot and moist; irrigation ditches, lined with great willows, struck off from the river, across fields of young tobacco plants, acres upon acres of mulberry trees, and plowed land of heavy, rich clay that looked like cotton country. Here every field, every shelf of earth, was cultivated. Higher up, on bare slopes among the rocks, sheep and goats pastured, tended by bearded peasants with huge crooks, clad in sheepskin coats, spinning wool and silk on wooden distaffs. Irregular, white, red-roofed villages meandered along rutted spaces where squat little oxen and black water buffaloes dragged creaking carts. Here and there was the galleried *konak* of some wealthy Turk of the old regime, set in yellow-green towering willows, or flowering almond trees heavy with scent; and over the tumbled little town a slender gray minaret, or the dome of a Greek church.

All sorts of people hung about the stations—men turbaned and fezzed and capped with conical hats of brown fur, men in Turkish trousers, or in long shirts and tights of creamy homespun linen, their leather vests richly worked in colored wheels and flowers, or in suits of heavy brown wool ornamented with patterns of black braid, high red sashes wound round and round their waists, leather sandals sewed to a circular spout on the toe and bound to the calf with leather ribbons wound to the knees; women with their Turkish *yashmak* and bloomers, or in leather and woolen jackets embroidered in bright colors, waists of the raw silk they weave in the villages, embroidered linen underskirts, black aprons worked in flowers, heavy overskirts woven in vivid bars of color and caught up behind, and yellow or white silk kerchiefs on their heads. Many wore a black kerchief—the only sign of mourning. And always and everywhere gypsies—the men in a kind of bright turban, the women with gold pieces for earrings and patches and scraps of gay rags for dresses, bare-footed—shuffling along the roads beside their caravans, or lounging about the rakish black tents of their camps.

A tall, bearded man in black introduced himself in French as a Serbian secret service officer whose job was to keep us under observation. Once a dapper young officer came aboard and questioned him, nodding to us. The other responded.

"*Dobra!* Good!" he said, clicking his heels and saluting.

"That station," remarked the secret service man as the train moved on again, "is the frontier. We are now in Serbia."

We caught a glimpse of several big, gaunt men lounging on the platform, rifles with fixed bayonets slung at their shoulders, without any uniform except the soldier's kepi.

"What would you?" shrugged our friend, smiling. "We Serbians have no longer any uniforms. We have fought four wars in three years—the First and Second Balkan Wars, the Albanian revolt, and now this one . . . For three years our soldiers have not changed their clothes."

Now we were passing along a narrow field planted with small wooden crosses, that might have been vine poles, spaced about three feet apart; they marched beside the train for five minutes.

"The typhus cemetery of Gievgieli," he said laconically. There must have been thousands of those little crosses, and each marked a grave!

There came in sight a great, tramped-down space on a hillside beyond, honeycombed with burrows leading into the brown earth, and humped into round hutches of heaped-up mud. Men crawled in and out of the holes, ragged, dirty fellows in every variety of half-uniform, with rifle belts crisscrossed over their breasts like Mexican revolutionists. Between were stacked rifles, and there were cannon with ox-yoke limbers and half a hundred springless oxcarts ranged along the side, while farther on the hobbled oxen grazed. Below the mud huts, at the bottom of the hill, men were drinking from the yellow river that poured down from a score of infected villages up the valley. Around a fire squatted twenty or more, watching the carcass of a sheep turn in the flames.

"This regiment has come to guard the frontier," explained our friend. "It was here that the Bulgarian *comitadjis* tried to break through and cut the railroad last week. At any moment they might come again . . . Is the Bulgarian government responsible, or did the Austrians pay them? One can never tell, in the Balkans."

And now, every quarter-mile we passed a rude hut made of mud and twigs, before which stood a ragged, hollow-cheeked soldier, filthy and starved-looking, but with his rifle at present arms. All over Serbia one saw these men—the last desperate gleaning of the country's manhood—who live in the mud, with scanty food and miserable clothing, guarding the long-deserted railroad tracks.

At first there seemed no difference between this country and Greek Macedonia. The same villages, a little more unkempt—tiles gone from the roofs, white paint chipped from the walls; the same people, but fewer of them, and those mostly women, old men, and children. But soon things began to strike one. The mulberry trees were neglected, the tobacco plants were last year's, rotting yellow; cornstalks stood spikily in weedy fields unturned for twelve months or more. In Greek Macedonia, every foot of arable land was worked; here only one field out of ten showed signs of cultivation. Occasionally we saw two oxen, led by a woman in bright yellow headdress and brilliantly colored skirt, dragging a wooden plow carved from a twisted oak limb, which a soldier guided, his rifle slung from his shoulder.

The secret service man pointed to them. "All the men of Serbia are in the army—or dead—and all the oxen were taken by the government to draw the cannon and the trains. But since December, when we drove the Austrians out, there has been no fighting. So the government sends the soldiers and the oxen over Serbia, wherever they are wanted, to help with the plowing."

Sometimes, in details like these, there flashed before our imaginations a picture of this country of the dead; with two bloody wars that swept away the flower of its youth, a two months' hard guerrilla campaign, then this fearful struggle with the greatest military power on earth, and a devastating plague on top of that. . . .

Gievgieli shared with Valieva the distinction of being the worst plague spot in Serbia. Trees, station, and buildings were splashed and spattered with chloride of lime, and armed sentries stood guard at the fence, where a hundred ragged people pressed murmuring—for Gievgieli was quarantined. We stared through the fence at a wide, rough street of cobbles and mud, flanked by one-story buildings white with disinfectant; at almost every door flapped a black flag, the sign of death in the house. . . .

On the station a bell was ringing. The stationmaster blew a horn, the engine whistled, the train began to move. . . .

Late in the afternoon we halted on a siding to let a military train pass—twelve open flatcars packed with soldiers, in odds and ends of uniforms, wrapped in clashing and vividly colored blankets. It had begun to rain a little. A gypsy fiddler played wildly, holding his one-stringed violin before him by the throat, which was carved rudely to represent a horse's head; and about him lay the soldiers, singing the newest ballad of the Austrian defeat. . . .

Every regiment has two or three Gypsies, who march with the troops, playing the Serbian fiddle or the bagpipes, and accompany the songs that are composed incessantly by the soldiers—love songs, celebrations of victory, epic chants. And all through Serbia they are the musicians of the people, traveling from one country festa to another, playing for dancing and singing. Strange substitution! The Gypsies have practically replaced old-time traveling bards, the *goosslari*, who transmitted from generation to generation through the far mountain valleys the ancient national epics and ballads. And yet they alone in Serbia have no vote. They have no homes, no villages, no land—only their tents and their dilapidated caravans.

We tossed some packages of cigarettes among the soldiers in the cars. For a moment they didn't seem to understand. They turned them over and over, opened them, stared at us with heavy, slow, flat faces. Then light broke—they smiled, nodding to us. *"Fala,"* they said gently. *"Fala lepo!* Thanks beautifully!" . . .

THE VALLEY OF CORPSES

It was the summit of Goutchevo that the Austrians seized and entrenched at the time of the second invasion. In the face of their withering fire the Serbians climbed its eastern side, foot by foot, until their trenches were also upon the narrow crest, and along a front of ten miles on top of a savage mountain was fought that strange Battle Above the Clouds which lasted fifty-four days, and ended with the retirement of the Serbs, only because the third invasion had broken their lines down by Krupaign. After the rout at Valievo the Austrians abandoned Goutchevo without a stand.

The genial young captain who escorted us had once been a *comitadji* officer, sent by the government to organize revolt—first in Macedonia, and then in Austrian Bosnia and Herzegovina.

"Before we volunteered for *comitadji* service," he said, "we were sent to the universities in Berlin and Vienna to study the organization of revolutions, particularly of the Italian *Risorgimento*. . . ."

176

Our road turned to rough country way, deep in mud, then to a mere track where only mules and pedestrians could pass—winding upward through immense oaks and ashes, lost in swift mountain brooks and choked with brush. An hour's hard climb brought us to the summit of the first mountain, from which we could see the precipitous peak of Eminove Vode—"Waters of Emin," as the old Turks named it—rising tremendous from the little valley that lay between, and splendid with the vivid green of young leaves, and great shining knobs of black rock.

In the high valley of the hills the white houses of a village lay half hidden in a sea of riotous plum blossoms. Their windows gaped wide—their doors swung idly to and fro. Behind some wall which we could not see a feminine voice was wailing shrilly, flatly, with hysterical catches, the monotonous song of mourning for the dead. The captain pulled up his horse and hallooed loudly—finally a thin, gaunt woman came slowly through the orchard.

"Have you *rackia*, sister?"

"*Ima.* I have." She went back and returned with a stone jug and a long-necked vase for us to drink from.

"What is this place?"

"It is the Rich Village of the Rackia-Makers."

"Where are all the people?"

"They are dead, of the spotted heat (typhus)."

We spurred forward through the golden silence, heavy with the scent of the plum trees and with humming bees. The wailing died behind. Here the traveled road ended, and beyond was a mountain path untraveled save by hunters and the goatherds of high Goutchevo, but now scarred and rutted by the feet of thousands, and the passage of heavy bodies dragged through the rocks and brush.

"By here the army climbed Goutchevo," said the captain, "and those marks are the marks of cannon that we took up there." He pointed to the towering height of Eminove Vode. "Horses were no good—and the oxen fell dead of fatigue. So we pulled them up by men—a hundred and twenty to each gun."

The path wound upward along the flank of the mountain and through a leaping stream which we waded. Here it ceased; but on the other side the deeply scored hillside rose almost straight for five hundred feet. We dismounted and led the stumbling, winded mountain horses, zigzagging from shelf to shelf of earth and crumbling rock.

"It took them three days to haul the cannon up here," panted the captain.

Resting and walking, and for level spaces riding a short distance, we climbed up through the forest of the mounting crest perhaps a thousand feet higher, over ground strewn with brass cartridge shells, trace leathers, bits of Serbian uniforms, and the wheels of shattered cannon limbers. Everywhere in the woods were deserted huts thatched with leaves and the branches of trees, and caves in the ground, where the Serbian army had lived for two months in the snow. Higher up we noticed that the lower parts of the trees were covered with leaves, but that their tops were as if dead; slowly as we climbed the dead part descended, until half the forest lifted gaunt, broken spikes where the vicious hail of bullets had torn off their tops—and then came trees naked of branches. We crossed two lines of deep trenches, and emerged on the bare summit of Goutchevo, which had also once been wooded, but where now nothing but jagged stumps studded with glistening lead remained.

On one side of this open space were the Serbian trenches, on the other side the Austrian. Barely twenty yards separated the two. Here and there both trenches merged into immense pits, forty feet around and fifty feet deep, where the enemy had undermined and dynamited them. The ground between was humped into irregular piles of earth. Looking closer, we saw a ghastly thing: From these little mounds protruded pieces of uniform, skulls with draggled hair, upon which shreds of flesh still hung; white bones with rotting hands at the end, bloody bones sticking from boots such as the soldiers wear. An awful smell hung over the place. Bands of half-wild dogs slunk at the edge of the forest, and far away we could see two tearing at something that lay half-covered on the ground. Without a word the captain pulled out his revolver and shot. One dog staggered and fell thrashing, then lay still—the other fled howling into the trees; and instantly from the depths of the wood all around came a wolfish, eerie howling in answer, dying away along the edge of the battlefield for miles.

We walked on the dead, so thick were they—sometimes our feet sank through into pits of rotting flesh, crunching bones. Little holes opened suddenly, leading deep down and swarming with gray maggots. Most of the bodies were covered only with a film of earth, partly washed away by the rain—many were not buried at all. Piles of Austrians lay as they had fallen in desperate charge, heaped along the ground in attitudes of terrible action. Serbians were among them. In one place the half-eaten skeletons of an Austrian and a Serbian were entangled, their arms and legs wrapped about each other in a death grip that could not even now be loosened. Behind the front line of Austrian trenches was a barbed wire barricade, significant of the spirit of the men pinned in that deathtrap—for they were mostly Serbians from the Austrian Slav provinces, driven at the point of a revolver to fight their brothers.

For six miles along the top of Goutchevo the dead were heaped like that—ten thousand of them, said the captain. From here we could see for forty miles around—the green mountains of Bosnia across the silver Drina, little white villages and flat roads, planes of fields green and yellow with new crops and brown with plowing, and the towers and bright houses of Austrian Svornik, gleaming among lovely trees at the bend of the river; southward in long lines that seemed to move, so living were they, lifted and broke the farther peaks of Goutchevo, along which wriggled to the end of vision the double line of trenches and the sinister field between. . . .

We rode through fruit orchards heavy with blossoms, between great forests of oaks and beeches and blooming chestnuts; under high wooded hills, whose slopes broke into a hundred rippling mountain meadows that caught the sun like silk. Everywhere springs poured from the hollows, and clear streams leaped down canyons choked with verdure, from Goutchevo, which the Turks called "Mountain of Waters"— from Goutchevo, saturated with the rotting dead. All this part of Serbia was watered by the springs of Goutchevo; and on the other side they flowed into the Drina, thence into the Save and the Danube, through lands where millions of people drank and washed and fished in them. To the Black Sea flowed the poison of Goutchevo. . . .

RUSSIA

Cholm. Somewhere among those crowded roofs and spires was the headquarters of General Ivanov, commander-in-chief of all southwestern Russian armies, next in power to the Grand Duke Nikolai Nikolaievich himself. At last here was a man with authority to let us visit the front. . . .

The sentry at staff headquarters said that every one had gone for the night.

"*Loutchaya gostinnitza!*" we told the driver. Mechanically we looked for the Hotel Bristol, which is to be found in every city, town, and village of the continent of Europe—but it had suffered the common decline of Hotel Bristols. The best *gostinnitza* turned out to be a three-story, lath-and-plaster structure halfway down a steep street in the crowded Jewish quarter, with a sign in Russian: "English Hotel." Of course, no one spoke English there—no English-speaking guest had ever visited the place. But a black-mustached little Pole, who bounced perspiring to answer the "*Nomernoi!*" of impatient guests, knew two phrases of French: "*Très jolie*" and "*tout de suite*"; and the *Hashein* or housemaster spoke Yiddish.

As we were dressing next morning appeared an officer with a shaven head, and asked us politely to accompany him to the staff. No less than four persons, he said, had heard us speak German and reported the presence of spies at Cholm.

We were ushered into a room where, at a small table, sat a pleasant-faced man who smilingly shook hands and spoke French. We gave him the passes and a card of introduction from Prince Troubetskoi.

"The governor general of Galicia advised us to come here and ask General Ivanov for permission to go to the front."

He nodded genially. "Very good. But we must first telegraph the grand duke—a mere formality, you know. We'll have an answer in two or three hours at the most. In the meanwhile, please return to your hotel and wait there."

Our room was on the third floor, up under the roof, with a sloping ceiling and two dormer windows. Beyond were shabby, patched tin roofs of the huddled Jewish town, and rising over them the heavily wooded hill, crowned with the towers and golden domes of the monastery. A cobbled street on the right led up the hill to the gates of the monastery park, between wretched huts and tall tenements. To the left the view soared over housetops to wide-flung plains that stretched forever north—patches of deep woods, fields, villages, and nearby, the railroad yards alive with shuttling trains.

We waited all day, but no one came. Before we were up next morning the bald-headed officer entered, bowing.

"The grand duke has not yet answered," he said evasively, "but doubtless he will in the course of the day—or maybe tomorrow."

"Maybe tomorrow!" we cried together. "I thought it was a matter of two or three hours!"

He looked everywhere but at us. "His highness is very busy—"

"Can't his highness spare a few minutes from planning retreats to attend to our case?"

"Have patience, gentlemen," said the officer hastily and uncomfortably. "It is only a matter of an hour or so now. I promise you that there will be no delay . . . And now I am ordered to ask you to give me all your papers—of whatever nature."

Were we suspected of being spies? He laughed uneasily and answered no, as he made out a receipt.

"And now," said he, "I shall have to demand your word of honor not to leave the hotel until the answer comes."

"Are we under arrest?"

"Oh dear, no. You are perfectly free. But this is an important military post, you understand—" Muttering vaguely, he made off as fast as he could, to avoid answering any more questions.

Fifteen minutes later the *Hashein* walked unceremoniously into our room with three Cossacks, big fellows in tall fur hats, pointed boots, long caftans open at the chest; in each belt a silver-worked long dagger hung slantwise in front, and a long, silver-hilted Cossack sword at the side. They stared at us with expressionless faces.

"What do they want?" I asked in German.

The *Hashein* smiled conciliatingly. "Only to look at the gentlemen. . . ."

A little later when I went downstairs one of the Cossacks was pacing up and down before our door. He drew aside to let me pass, but leaned over the stair rail, and shouted something in Russian; another, standing in the hall below, came forward; and from the street door I saw a third peering up.

We wrote an indignant note to General Ivanov. The colonel came at midnight and said that the Cossacks would immediately be withdrawn, with the general's apologies. (Next morning they *had* been withdrawn—to the bottom of the stairs, where they glowered at us suspiciously.) As for our detention, the colonel explained that that was all a very grave matter. We had entered the zone of military operations without the proper passes.

"How were we to know which passes were proper? They were signed by generals, and honored by Prince Bobrinski at Lemberg. What have we done that's wrong?"

"For one thing," said he, "you have come to Cholm, which is forbidden to correspondents. Secondly, you have discovered that Cholm is General Ivanov's headquarters, and that is a military secret."

Saturday morning our friend the shaven lieutenant appeared, looking gloomier than ever.

"I have, gentlemen, to announce to you some very disagreeable news," he began formally. "The grand duke has answered our telegram. He says: 'Keep the prisoners under strict guard.'"

"But what about our going to the front?"

"That is all he replied." He hurried on. "So unfortunately you will be compelled to keep to this room until further orders. The guards at the door will attend to your wants."

"Look here," said Robinson. "What's the matter with your silly grand duke—"

"Oh—" interjected the officer, with a shocked face.

"What are you shutting us up for? Does the grand duke think we're spies?"

"Well," he returned doubtfully, "you see, there are curious things, inexplicable things among your papers. In the first place, there is a list of names—"

We explained impatiently for the hundredth time that those were the names of American citizens reported to be caught by the war in the parts of Bucovina and Galicia held by the Russians, and that the American minister in Bucharest had given us the list to investigate.

The officer looked sympathetic but uncomprehending. "But many of them are Jewish names."

"But they are American citizens."

"Ah!" said he. "Do you mean to say that Jews are American citizens?" We affirmed this extraordinary fact, and he didn't contradict us—but you could see he didn't believe it.

Then he gave his orders. We were not to leave the room under any circumstances.

"Can we walk up and down the hall?"

"I am sorry"—he shrugged his shoulders.

"This is absurd," I said. "What is the charge against us? I demand that we be allowed to telegraph our ambassadors."

He scratched his head vaguely and went out, muttering that he would ask his chief. Two Cossacks immediately mounted the stairs and began to pace up and down in the little hall outside our door; another one stood on the landing below; a fourth at the front door; and the fifth man mounted a shed in the yard of the Jewish house, three stories sheer drop below, and fixed his stolid gaze upon our window.

After consultation, Robinson and I sat down and composed a diplomatic note to the Russian government–in English, so as to give them the trouble of translating it–formally notifying all concerned that from this date we refused to pay our hotel bill. Summoning a Cossack, we told him to take it to the staff.

It was now about noon. Over the wide Polish plain the June sun swam slowly up, beating down on the sloping tin roof immediately over our heads. We stripped, garment by garment, and hung out of the window gasping for air. Word had spread abroad of the illustrious captives in the top floor of the "English Hotel," and the Jewish family that inhabited the house below us swarmed out of the door, and stood gazing up at us. Beyond the yard fence was a silent crowd of townspeople, almost all Jews too, staring at our window in silence. They thought we were captured German spies. . . .

That night the shaven officer returned with permission for us to telegraph our ambassadors, and with General Ivanov's reply to our note: He did not know why the grand duke ordered us imprisoned. As for the hotel bill, that would be arranged.

Meanwhile the telegrams disappeared into the vast unknown, and for eight days no answer came. For eight days we inhabited that malodorous chamber under the hot tin roof. It measured four strides wide by five across. We had no books except a Russian-French dictionary and the *Jardin de Supplice*, which exhausted their charm after the sixth perusal. Along about the fifth day the *Hashein* discovered somewhere in the town a pack of cards, and we played double-dummy bridge until even now I shriek at the sight of a card. Robinson designed me a town house and a country house to while away the time; he designed luxurious city residences for the Cossacks; he drew their portraits. I wrote verses; elaborated impossible plans of escape; planned a novel. We flirted from the window with the cook of the Jewish house below; we made speeches to the townspeople gathered in the street; we screamed curses to the surrounding air, and sang ribald songs; we walked up and down; we slept, or tried to sleep. And every day we spent a happy hour composing insulting communications to the tsar, the Duma, the Council of Empire, the grand duke, General Ivanov and his staff—which we forced a Cossack to take to headquarters.*

Early in the morning appeared the *Hashein*—a young Jew with a dark, handsome, expressionless face covered by a silky brown beard—followed by a suspicious Cossack.

"*Morgen!*" he would shout at us in broken German, as we stuck our noses out of the bedclothes. "*Was wollen sie essen heute?*"

"What can we have?" we would invariably reply.

"*Spiegeleier–biftek–kartoffeln–schnitzel–brot–butter–chai.*"

Day after day we took the Russian-French dictionary, and labored with him to change the diet; but he could not read Russian, and refused to understand it when we pronounced the words. So we alternated between eggs, tough steak, and veal, with always the eternal tea at least six times a day. A samovar operated on the balcony below our window, and from time to time one of us rushed to the door, pushed the Cossack out of the way, leaned over the stairs and bellowed, "*Hashein!*" There was a running and calling of anxious Cossacks, doors opened and guests popped their heads out, and cries came echoing up from below.

"*Chto!*"

* After waiting sixteen days, Reed and Robinson were released and permitted to go to Petrograd.–*Ed.*

"Chai!" we bellowed. *"Dva chaya–skorrey!"*

We tried to have eggs for breakfast, but the *Hashein* refused. "Eggs for lunch, eggs for dinner, but no eggs for breakfast," he announced calmly. "Eggs for breakfast are very unhealthy. . . ."

Sometimes in the breathless evening, when the Cossack in the yard below had got tired of watching and slipped off for a drink, we would climb out of our window onto the steep peaked roof and look down on the tin roofs and teeming overcrowded streets of the town. Southward on the hill were the two ancient spires of the grand old Catholic church, remnant of the days of glory when John Poniatowski was king of Poland. Down on a dark side street was the squat, unmarked building that held the Jewish synagogue and the *heder*–the Jewish sacred school–and from this building ascended day and night the whining drone of boys chanting the sacred books, and the deeper voices of *ravs* and *rebbes* hotly discussing the intricate questions of the law. The tide of Russia was rising and overflowing this city of old Poland. We could see from our roofs colossal military barracks and institutions–immense buildings with façades a quarter of a mile long, as they are in Petrograd; and eight churches building or completed lifted grotesque onion-shaped towers into the air, colored red and blue, or patterned in gay lozenges. Directly before our window was the Holy Hill. Above a rich mass of green trees six golden bulbs rose from the fantastic towers of the monastery, and at evening and on Sunday deep-toned and tinkly bells galloped and boomed. Morning and night we watched the priests going up and down the street–fanatic-faced men with beards and long curly hair falling upon their shoulders, dressed in gray or black silk coats falling to their feet. And the Jews on the sidewalk stepped out of their way. Now the monastery was a military hospital. Groups of girls in the lovely white headdress of the Russian Red Cross hurried in and out of the great gates where two soldiers always stood guard; and there was always a silent knot of people peering curiously through the iron fence. Occasionally a wide-open yelling siren could be heard rising and deepening out of the distance, and presently an automobile would rush furiously up the steep street, full of wounded officers. Once it was a big open machine, in which the body of a huge man writhed in the grip of four nurses who were trying to hold him down. Where his stomach had been was a raw mass of blood and rags, and he screamed awfully all the way up the hill, until the trees swallowed the automobile and his screams simultaneously.

During the day the uproar of the teeming town obscured all other sound. But at night we could hear, or rather feel, the shocking thunder of the enemy's guns less than twenty miles away.

Immediately under our eyes was enacted every day the drama of Jewish life in Russia. Our Cossack guard paraded superciliously about the yard of the house below, the children making wide detours as they passed him, the young girls bringing him glasses of tea and trying to smile at his coarse familiarities, the old people stopping politely to talk with him and casting looks of hate at him behind his back. He strutted about like a lord, he the humblest slave of the Russian military machine. We noticed that every two or three days all the Jews, young and old, wore upon their breasts a little paper medallion. One morning the *Hashein* came to our room with one: It was a cheap electrogravure of the tsar's daughter, the Grand Duchess Tatiana.

"What is that?" I asked him, pointing to it.

He shrugged his shoulders in a bitter kind of way. "It is the grand duchess's birthday," he said.

"But I have seen the people wearing it already twice this week."

"Every two or three days," he answered, "is the grand duchess's birthday. At least that is what the Cossacks say. The Cossacks make every Jew buy a picture of the grand duchess on her birthday and wear it. It costs five rubles. We are only poor Jews, too ignorant to know what day is the grand duchess's birthday. But the Cossacks are Russians, and they know."

"What if you refuse to buy it?" I asked.

He drew his finger significantly across his throat and made a gurgling noise.

It was a filthy place, that yard, full of the refuse of two Jewish houses and whatever the hotel guests threw out of their windows. A high board fence separated it from the street, with great wooden gates closed by a strong bar. The door and the lower windows of the house were also protected by heavy wooden shutters fastened from the inside. These were for defense against pogroms. Against the fence a slanting platform of planks had been erected, where all day long innumerable dirty little children climbed up and slid down, shrieking with laughter, or lay on their stomachs with their noses over the fence to watch the Cossacks ride by. Babies wailed and sprawled in the mud of the yard. From the open doors and windows ascended the odors of perpetual cooking.

But every Friday at noon the house was all of a bustle, as was every Jewish house in the town, preparing for the Sabbath. All the women put on their oldest working clothes; slops were emptied into the yard, and a tin tub of steaming water stood on the doorstep, out of which bucketfuls were carried inside, whence came sounds of scrubbing, sweeping, the slap of wet mops, and the rhythmic songs of Jewish women at work. The buckets, now full of dirty water, were poured back in the tin tub, and after its contents had become brown and thick like soup, all the family receptacles were brought—pans, crockery, knives and forks, cups and glasses—and washed there. The fountain was too far away to waste water. And after that the children each filled a bucket from the tub and went in to bathe, while the rest scoured the door jambs and the window sills and the two stone steps below the door, swaying in unison to a minor chant.

The linen hanging on the clothesline was taken in. A feeling of joy and release was abroad; the terrorized gloom of weekdays seemed to lift. All the little Jewish shops closed early, and the men came home walking in little friendly knots like people whose work is done. Each put on his best long coat and peaked cap, his most shiny boots, and went out to join the ever-thickening steady stream of sober, black-robed people that flowed toward the synagogue.

In the house the dirty carpets were rolled up to reveal the white floor, which is always covered except on the Sabbath, and on the days of great religious feasts. And one by one the women, girls, and little children came laughing and chattering out of the purified house in their best clothes, and went out on the street, where all the other women and children were gathered, to gossip together and show off their finery.

From our window we could see a corner of the kitchen, with the wrinkled old dowager of the house superintending the sealing of the oven; could hear the jangling of the keys being put out of sight for the Holy Day, and look full upon the dining room table with its row of candles lit for Candle Prayer, and the Sabbath loaf covered with doily, the wine flask, and *kiddush* cup. . . .

After supper the children played quietly, stiffly in their Sabbath clothes, and the women gathered in front of the houses; as the darkness grew, from every window of a Jewish house a light beamed, to show the wayfarer that the spirit of God brooded over that roof. And we could look into the windows of a long, bare room on the second story, empty during the week, where the men-folks gathered with great books spread out before them on the table, and sang together deep-toned, Oriental-sounding psalms until late into the night.

On the Sabbath the men went in the morning to the synagogue. It was a day of much visiting between houses in Sabbath clothes; of an interminable dinner that lasted the greater part of the afternoon, with gay songs sung by the whole family to clapping of hands; of dressed-up families, down to the last baby, straggling along the road that led around the base of the Holy Hill toward the open country . . .

189

And then night and the unsealing of the oven, the putting down of the carpets, little Yakub repeating his lessons to his teacher in a singsong wail, the opening of the shops, old clothes again, dirt, and terror.

Every day or so a tragic little procession would pass up the street that led to the prison beyond the monastery: two or three Jews in their characteristic long coats and peaked caps, shuffling along with expressionless faces and dejected drooping shoulders, preceded and followed by a great shambling soldier with a bayoneted rifle in the hollow of his arm. Many times we asked *Hashein* about these people; but he always professed ignorance. Where were they going? "To Siberia," he would mumble, "or perhaps—" and he would gesture the pulling of a trigger. The *Hashein* was an extremely prudent person. But sometimes he stood for a long time in our room, looking from Robinson to me and back again, as if there was much to say if only he dared. Finally he shook his head, sighed, and went out past the watchful Cossack, devoutly touching the paper prayer nailed up at the door jamb.

1916

Sold Out*

The Editor of the New York *Evening Mail* was advising the German-Americans to vote for (Theodore) Roosevelt. Someone asked him why. He replied, "I know he is anti-German, but the Germans should support Roosevelt because he is the only exponent of German *Kultur* in the United States."

When Theodore Roosevelt was president, a delegation from the state of Michigan went to Washington to plead with him the cause of the Boer Republic, then fighting for its life against the British government. One of the delegates told me that Roosevelt answered them cold as ice: "No, the weaker nations must yield to the stronger, even if they perish off the face of the earth."

When Germany invaded Belgium, Colonel Roosevelt in *The Outlook,* told us that was none of our business and that our policy of isolation must be maintained even at the expense of the Belgian people.

These instances showed the peculiar Prussian trend of the

* In 1916, as correspondent of the *Metropolitan Magazine* and the *Masses,* Reed attended the presidential nominating conventions of the Democratic, Republican, and Progressive parties. It was at the latter convention that Reed saw Theodore Roosevelt's betrayal of the Progressives. Under the impact of a widespread antimonopoly movement, they had fought for Roosevelt's nomination at the Republican convention in 1912. When the Republican hierarchy pushed through the renomination of William Howard Taft, the Republican dissidents, taken in by Roosevelt's sham liberalism, formed the Progressive Party and nominated Roosevelt for the presidency. Four years later he openly returned to his rampant imperialism and helped to crush the Progressives.—*Ed.*

colonel's mind, and we were at a loss when he subsequently took up cudgels for that same Belgium which he had so profoundly damned, and came forward as the champion of the "weak nations." Could it be chivalry? Could it be a sympathy with the cause of democracy? We held off and waited, skeptical as we were, and soon the snake was discovered gliding through the colonel's grass. All this talk about Belgium insensibly changed into an impassioned pleading for enormous armies and navies in order that we might live up to our international obligations, and into a violent attack upon the Wilson administration for not doing what the colonel had told it to in the first place. And the particular point he kept emphasizing was the administration's cowardly refusal to crush the Mexican people!

After General Leonard Wood and the ambitious military caste in this country had whispered in the colonel's ear, and after the munitions makers and the imperialist financiers had given the colonel a dinner, and after the predatory plutocrats he fought so nobly in the past had told him they would support him for president of the United States, "Our Teddy" came out for the protection of weak nations abroad and the suppression of weak nations at home; for the crushing of Prussian militarism and the encouragement of American militarism; for all the liberalism, including Russia's financed by the Anglo-American loan, and all the conservatism of the gentlemen who financed it.

We were not fooled by the colonel's brand of patriotism. Neither were the munitions makers and the money trust; the colonel was working for their benefit so they backed him. But large numbers of sincere people in this country who remembered Armageddon and "Social Justice" imagined that Roosevelt was still on the side of the people. Most of these persons had flocked to his standard in 1912 flushed with a vision of regenerated humanity, and had given up a good deal of their time, money, and position to follow democracy's new Messiah. Four years of dictatorship by George W. Perkins and the steel trust, four years in which the colonel had patently allowed his crusaders to perish politically in droves, four years of contradiction and change until he was screaming at the top of his lungs for blood-thirstiness, obedience, and efficiency, had not dimmed their faith. These people were not militarists; they were for peace, not war; they were not for universal service of any kind, nor obedience to corporations. They were for Roosevelt; they thought that, after all, he stood for Social Justice. So they blindly swallowed what he advocated and shouted, "We want Teddy!"

In 1912, Theodore Roosevelt issued his Covenant with the American People, assuring them that he would never desert them, and affirming the unalterable principle of Social Justice for which he stood. This Covenant was the Progressive Party's reason for being. Indeed, if they had not believed the Covenant with the American people would be resuscitated, I doubt if the Progressives, after those four long years of silence and neglect, would have risen to blindly follow Colonel Roosevelt again. They had had their knocks. They had made their sacrifices. They knew that as Progressives they could not come to power in 1916. But when that call came, all over the country in a million hearts the spark of almost extinct enthusiasm burst into flame, and the feeling of a holy crusade of democracy which had stirred men and women four years ago again swept the country.

Not the intelligent radicals—no matter how much they wanted Teddy, they knew he would betray them when it suited him—but the politically backward and inexperienced people, the backwoods idealists, as it were—they trusted Teddy. Hadn't he said he would never desert them? It was to be another Armageddon, and they would sacrifice to the cause as they had sacrificed before.

Little did they know that Theodore Roosevelt, in New York, was referring to them as "rabble," and planning how he could shake himself free from enthusiasts, from idealists, from the dirty and stupid lower classes. Little did they know that he was saying impatiently about them, "You can't build a political party out of cranks. I have got to get rid of the 'lunatic fringe.'" And by "lunatic fringe" he meant those people who believed in Social Justice and wanted to put it into effect.

The call to the Progressive convention spoke of trying to reach a basis of understanding with the Republican Party. To this the Progressives assented; some because they wanted to get back into the Republican fold, and others because they wanted to force Roosevelt and Social Justice upon the Republicans and upon the country. And if the Republicans would not take Teddy and progressivism why then hadn't Teddy made a covenant with them? They would go it alone again as they had in 1912—the Party of Protest, the noble forlorn hope. And so they came to Chicago, inarticulate, full of faith, stirred by a vague aspiration which they would put into words later. Teddy was not Teddy to them; he was democracy—he was justice and fairness and the cause of the poor. Also he was Preparedness; but if Teddy said Preparedness meant Justice and Liberty, then Teddy must be right. The platform of the party shows how completely these crusaders of 1912 had replaced principles with Roosevelt—there is no social justice in it.

I looked down from the platform of the Auditorium in Chicago upon the turbulent sea of almost holy emotion; upon men and women from great cities and little towns, from villages and farms, from the deserts and the mountains and the cattle ranches, wherever the wind had carried to the ears of the poor and the oppressed that a healer and mighty warrior had risen up to champion the Square Deal. The love of Teddy filled those people. Blind and exalted they sang "Onward Christian Soldiers" and "We Will Follow, Follow Teddy!" There was virility, enthusiasm, youth in that assembly; there were great fighters there, men who all their lives had given battle alone against frightful odds to right the wrongs of the sixty per cent of the people of this country who own five per cent of its wealth. These were not revolutionists; for the most part they were people of little vision and no plan—merely ordinary men who were raw from the horrible injustice and oppression they saw on every side. Without a leader to express them, they were no good. We, Socialists and revolutionists, laughed and sneered at the Progressives; we ridiculed their worship of personality; we derided their hysterical singing of revival hymns; but when I saw the Progressive convention, I realized that among those delegates lay the hope of this country's peaceful evolution, and the material for heroes of the people.

On the platform was another crowd—the Progressive leaders. Now at the Republican convention I had seen Barnes and Reed, Smoot and Penrose, and W. Murray Crane and those other sinister figures who fight to the death against the people. Well, the crowd on the platform of the Progressive convention looked much the same to me; George Perkins of Wall Street, James Garfield, Charles Bonaparte, etc. Among this furtive, cold group of men there was no spark of enthusiasm, no sympathy for democracy. Indeed, I passed close to them once and I heard them talking about the delegates on the floor. They called them "the cheap skates!" And yet this inner circle, whose task it was to use the Progressives as a threat to the Republicans, but not to permit them to embarrass the colonel, were, as I knew, Theodore Roosevelt's confidants, his lieutenants in the convention.

The Republican convention was sitting only a few blocks away, thoroughly controlled by Penrose, Smoot, Crane, Barnes, et al. This the Progressive delegates learned; and they learned that Theodore Roosevelt could not under any circumstances be nominated there. They clamored for Teddy. Roaring waves of sound swept the house. "We want Teddy! Let's nominate Teddy now!" Only with the greatest difficulty did the Gang persuade them to wait. "The call for a convention," they said, "had emphasized the necessity of getting together with the Republicans in order to save the country. We ought to appoint a committee to confer with the Republican convention as to a possible candidate that both parties might support."

"We want Teddy! We want Teddy!"

"Wait," counseled Perkins, Penrose, Garfield, and the rest of the Gang, "it will do no harm to talk with them."

Governor Hiram Johnson of California thundered to the delegates: "Remember Barnes, Penrose, and Crane in 1912! We left the Republican convention because the bosses were in control. They are still in control. The only word we should send to the Republican convention is the nomination of Theodore Roosevelt!"

"It won't do any harm to talk it over with them," counseled the Gang. "We have here a telegram from Theodore Roosevelt recommending that we discuss matters with the Republicans." And they read it aloud.

Flaming Victor Murdock leaped to the stage. "You want Teddy," he cried. "Well, the only way you will get him is to nominate him now."

"I will tell you the message we ought to send to the Republican convention," shouted William J. McDonald. "Tell them to go to hell!"

Well did they know—Murdock, McDonald, and Johnson—that the colonel was liable to sell them out. Well did they know that the only way to put it up squarely to Roosevelt was to nominate him immediately, before the Republicans had taken action.

"Wait!" counseled the Gang, cold, logical, polished, and afraid. "It will do no harm to appoint a committee to consult with the Republicans. If we go it alone, Theodore Roosevelt and Social Justice cannot be elected."

And so the committee of conference was appointed, because the delegates trusted Perkins, Garfield, Bonaparte—and Roosevelt. What the Republicans thought was indicated in the composition of their committee: Reed, Smoot, W. Murray Crane, Nicholas Murray Butler, Borah, and Johnson.

"God help us!" cried Governor Hiram Johnson. "Tonight we sit at the feet of Reed, Smoot and Murray Crane!"

And literally he did: for he was appointed as one of the Progressive committee upon which sat George W. Perkins and Charles J. Bonaparte.

Upon the platform of the Progressive convention the next morning word was spread quietly around that the colonel, over the telephone, had requested that his name not be put in nomination until the Republicans had nominated their man. The committee made its report, inconclusive from every point of view, and little by little the feeling that Roosevelt must be nominated grew as the time went on. Only the Gang held the convention in check by insisting that the committee must have another session with the Republicans. And then, like a thunderbolt, came Roosevelt's second message from Oyster Bay, recommending as a compromise candidate the name of Senator Henry Cabot Lodge of Massachusetts! Henry Cabot Lodge, the heartless reactionary, who is as far from the people as any man could be! It threw a chill over the assembly. They could not understand. And now the nominations had begun in the Republican convention, and the Gang in control of the Progressives could control no longer. Bainbridge Colby of New York was recognized and nominated Theodore Roosevelt; Hiram Johnson seconded the nomination; and in three minutes the rules had been suspended and Roosevelt was adopted by acclamation. "Now," said Chairman Raymond Robins, "the responsibility rests with Colonel Roosevelt, and I have never known him to shirk any responsibility, no matter how insignificant or tremendous it might be. I believe that Colonel Roosevelt will accept." And the convention adjourned until three o'clock.

How the Republicans nominated [Charles E.] Hughes by an overwhelming majority is now ancient history; and how the Progressives, full of hope and enthusiasm and girding themselves for the great fight, returned to receive Roosevelt's acceptance, I saw. The bands played and exultingly, like children, the standards moved up and down the aisles. Professor Albert Bushnell Hart of Harvard raced about the hall waving a huge American flag.

"No one man or two men or three men can own the Progressive Party," shouted Chairman Robins, referring directly to George W. Perkins. "This is to be a people's party financed by the people. I call for subscriptions to the campaign fund from the floor." In twenty minutes, with a burst of tremendous enthusiasm, 100,000 dollars had been pledged by the delegates in the gallery. It was a magnificent tribute to the spirit of the "cheap skates."

And then it began to be whispered about the platform that Theodore Roosevelt's answer had arrived; it said that if the convention insisted upon an answer at once, he must decline—that before accepting the Progressive nomination, Colonel Roosevelt must hear Justice Hughes' statement; that he would give the Progressive National Committee his answer on June 26; that if the committee thought Justice Hughes' position on Preparedness and Americanism was adequate he would decline the Progressive nomination; however, if the committee thought Justice Hughes' position inadequate, he would consult with them on what was best to be done. This we, the newspapermen, and George Perkins and the Gang knew for an hour before the convention adjourned, yet not one word was allowed to reach the delegates on the floor. Skilfully, Chairman Robins announced that in accordance with the will of the delegates, he was going to see that the convention adjourned at five o'clock sharp—though no one had asked for this. The collection of money went merrily on, and those who gave did so because they thought Theodore Roosevelt was going to lead them in another fight. Only Governor Hiram Johnson and Victor Murdock sounded the note of bitterness and the certainty of betrayal.

"God forgive us," cried Governor Johnson, "for not acting the first day as we ought to have acted!"

Victor Murdock was even more disillusioned. "The steam roller has run over us," he cried. "We must never again delay making our decisions."

And then, at four minutes to five o'clock, Chairman Robins announced perfunctorily another communication from Theodore Roosevelt, and read it; and before the convention had time to grasp its meaning, it had been adjourned and was pouring, stunned and puzzled, out through the many doors into the street. It took several hours for the truth to get into those people's heads that their Messiah had sold them out for thirty pieces of political silver. But they did understand finally, I think.

That night I was in the Progressive headquarters. Big bronzed men were openly weeping. Others wandered around as if they were dazed. It was an atmosphere full of shock and disaster. Yes, the intelligent radicals had known it would come this way, so contemptuously, so utterly. They thought that the colonel would have left them some loophole as he left himself one. They did not realize that the colonel was not that kind of man, that his object was to break irrevocably with the "cranks" and the "rabble"—to slap them in the face by the suggestion of Henry Cabot Lodge as a Progressive candidate. But now they were left, as one of them expressed it, "out on a limb and the limb sawed off."

As for Colonel Roosevelt, he is back with the people among whom alone he is comfortable, "the predatory plutocrats." At least he is no longer tied to democracy. For that he undoubtedly breathes a sigh of relief. And as for democracy, we can only hope that some day it will cease to put its trust in men.

1916

This Unpopular War

It was one of those moist, stifling summer nights they have in Washington. After a perfect dinner we adjourned to the library and peeled off our coats, for comfort's sake. The butler brought ice, siphons, and tall glasses, and things to smoke.

There were four or five of us; myself the stranger, and the others, clever youngsters a year or so out of college, now doing volunteer work on the Munitions Board, Hoover's Food Administration, or one of the innumerable subcommittees of the Council of National Defense.

They were well enough off to be able to do war work in Washington. None of them had had any real experience of competition for existence. Their minds inclined more to psychology and literary criticism than to political expediency. They had accepted the war and conscription as steps in the working out of a political theory whereby brains would ultimately rule mankind. Let me add that each was prepared to "do his bit," even to the extent of dying for his country. One was going to enlist in the aviation corps; the others thought they would be more serviceable in advisory or organizing positions than in the trenches.

"No one of any intelligence," one boy was saying, "thinks the war is popular.

"The other night a bunch of us dined together—Joe and George and Newton, some of the War Department men, and a few of the big business men in the subcommittees of the Council of National Defense.

"We wanted to think up a 'talking point,' as drummers call it, to 'sell the war.' For three solid hours we sat there cudgeling our brains, but we couldn't think of a single reason not patently a lie which was important enough to excite the patriotism of the man on the street. Of course, our own reasons were sufficient, but for an advertising campaign they are much too—well, 'highbrow.'"

The aviation enthusiast spoke up, lying on his back and blowing expensive cigar smoke at the ceiling.

"Do you know what is needed? Only one thing—the same that did the trick for England. Casualties. At first it was impossible to interest the English masses in the war; they could not be made to see that it was their affair. But when the lists of dead, wounded, mutilated, began to come back—and, by the way, England ought to be grateful for the German atrocities—then hatred of the Germans began to soak into the whole people from the families of the wounded and the dead. This social anger is patriotism—for war purposes.

"If I had the job of popularizing this war, I would begin by sending three or four thousand American soldiers to certain death. That would wake the country up."

Now if this young man could wake up America by the simple process of immolating himself, I think he would not hesitate to play Curtius—although he has no romantic illusions, and would only be playing upon public sentimentalism to accomplish a highly rational end. However, he knows well that nothing he could do—even if action were not foreign to his temperament—would stir the American people in the slightest degree. The only thing which *would* stir them is pain, grief, a sense of unutterable loss. So, for our own good, let's slaughter several thousand boys.

Life is cheap now, and if by destroying some thousands of young men—less than a day's toll on the world's battle lines— one clear step could be taken toward the freedom of mankind, I know where to find men for the job—and not conscripts, either. But to be compelled or to be lured by cheap extravagances into furthering political theories too complicated or too subtle to fire the mass of the people, seems to me the same old undemocratic string-pulling which set Europe aflame.

I spent a year and a half in the various countries and on the various battle fronts, visiting all the belligerent capitals and seeing action on five fronts. One of my best friends has accused me of not grasping the significance of the war, of not being impressed with the tremendous human contrasts of this universal cataclysm. He says I went over there with the fixed socialist idea that the capitalistic ruling classes had cynically and with malice tricked their people into war; and that I refused to see anything else.

I admit I went abroad with an idea, and that my idea *was* substantially that. Everybody had at least one theory at the beginning of the war. But I was soon disillusioned; I found that the various peoples were not reasonable enough to make trickery necessary—even the socialists and antimilitarists shedding their beliefs like old skins when the colors and the drums swept down the street.

I'm afraid I never did properly understand the drama and the glory of this war. It seemed to me, those first few weeks coming up through France, as if I would never get out of my mind again those beflowered troop trains full of laughing, singing boys—the class of 1914—bound so gaily, unthinkingly to the front. And then Paris—not stern, stoical, heroic, as the reporters all described it; but sick with fear, full of civilian panic, its citizens trampling down women and children in their wild rush to get on the trains for the South.

I saw so many ugly things—rich people putting their handsome houses under the protection of the Red Cross, and later when the Germans had retreated to the Aisne, withdrawing them. Small tradesmen making money out of things needed by the soldiers. Little political fights between the military medical corps and the Red Cross, whereby thousands of beds in the city were vacant, and the wounded died lying out on the cobbles in the rain at Vitry.

Against that, what? A nation rising *en masse* to repel invasion, but without much stomach for a slaughter most people, I think, felt to be utterly stupid and useless. The flags, the emptiness, the spy crazes, the wild-eyed women, the German airplanes dully dropping bombs from overhead into the streets. The shock, and then the slow inevitable dislocation of ordinary life, the growing tension. Later on, the one-armed, one-legged, the men gone mad from shellfire; in side streets the lengthening lines of wretched poor at the public kitchens.

The battle of the Marne was something to go wild with delight about—but by that time there was no one left in Paris to celebrate. Decked with thousands of flags, the city lay smiling vapidly in the bright sunlight, her streets empty, her nights black. There were no glorious tidings, no heroism, no tolling bells and public rejoicings. Those things cease to be when the whole of a nation's manhood is drained into the trenches. There is no such thing as heroism when millions of men face the most ghastly death in such a spirit as the armies of Europe have faced it these three years. Millions of heroes! It makes military courage the cheapest thing in the world.

Why is it I saw this kind of thing? I tried to see the picturesque, the dramatic, the human; but to me all was drab, and all those millions of men were become cogs in a senseless and uninteresting machine. It was the same on the field. I saw a good deal of the battle of the Marne, I was with the French north of Amiens during the beginning of trench warfare. Almost always it was the same mechanical business. At first we were curious to know what new ways of fighting had been evolved; but the novelty soon wore off, as it did to the soldiers in the trenches.

At the battle of the Marne I spent the evening with some British transport soldiers at the little village of Crécy, in sound of the great guns stabbing the dark away off to the north. These "Tommies"—why had they gone to war? Well, they didn't rightly know, except that Bill was going, and they wanted to get away from home for a spell, and the pay was good.

Along about October 1, 1914, I had to stay the night in Calais, and out of sheer loneliness found my way finally to the town's one and only "joint," where there was liquor, song, and girls. The place was packed with soldiers and sailors, some of them on leave from the front. I fell into conversation with one *poilu*, who told me with great pride that he was a socialist–and an internationalist, too. He had been guarding German prisoners, and waxed enthusiastic as he told me what splendid fellows they were–all socialists, too.

"Look here," I said. "If you belonged to the International why did you go to war?"

"Because," he said, turning his clear eyes upon me, "because France was invaded."

"But the Germans claim that you invaded Germany."

"Yes," he answered gravely, "I know they do say that. The prisoners tell me. Well, perhaps it is true. We were probably both invaded. . . ."

London, plastered with enormous signs, "Your King and Country Need You! Enlist for the War Only!" In all open spaces, knots of young men drilling–bank clerks, stockbrokers, university and public school men, the middle and upper middle classes; for at this time the workers and the East End were not interested in the war. The first Expeditionary Force had been wiped off the face of the earth coming down from Mons; England was getting mad, at the top, and "Kitchener's Mob" was forming.

The great masses of the people of England knew little about the war and cared less. Yet it was up to them to fight, volunteer or conscript. Business and manufacturing concerns began to discharge their employees of military age, and a patriotic blacklist saw to it that they got no other work; it was "Enlist or Starve." I remember seeing a line of huge trucks sweep through Trafalgar Square, full of youths and placarded "Harrods' Gift to the Empire." The men inside were clerks in Harrods' Stores, and they were being driven to the recruiting station.

There were other things in London which nauseated one. The great limousines going down to the City of a morning with recruiting appeals on their windshields, and overfed, overdressed men and women sitting comfortably inside. The articles for sale in the shops, with the "Made in Germany" signs torn off and new cards affixed, "Made in England"; the Rhine and Moselle wines they served in restaurants, their labels painted out, the immensely snobbish Red Cross benefit concerts and dances that made the fall of 1914 "London's gayest autumn."

All the talk of "German militarism," and "the rights of small nations," and "Kaiserism must go"—how sickening to know that the rulers of England really did not believe these pious epithets and platitudes! It was only the great masses of simple folk who were asked to give their lives because "Belgium was invaded," and the "scrap of paper" torn up. Just as in this our own country, where persons of intelligence cannot help smiling—or weeping—when President Wilson talks of American "democracy," and the "democracy" America champions in this war.

Berlin was less patently charged with hypocrisy, as one might expect; for Berlin had been getting ready for this for years. There was less need for advertising than there was in either London or Paris—the Germans had less differences of opinion about the war. And yet to see those hundreds of thousands of gray automatons caught inevitably and irreparably in that merciless machine, hurled down across Belgium in mile-wide, endless rivers, and poured against the scraps of death-rimmed fortresses in close-marching battalions, was more horrible than what I saw in other countries.

Will anyone now dare to claim that the German people were told the truth about the war, or even told anything to speak of? No. The whole nation was sent to the trenches, without opportunity to know, to object, a little more ruthlessly than other nations—except Russia.

I was at the German front, where men stood up to their hips in water, covered with lice, and fired at anything which moved behind a mud bank eighty yards away. They were the color of mud, their teeth chattered incessantly, and every night some of them went mad. In the space between the trenches, forty yards away, was a heap of bodies left over from the last French charge; the wounded had died out there, without any effort being made to rescue them; and now they were slowly but surely sinking into the soft mud, burying themselves. At this place the soldiers spent three days in the trenches and six days resting back of the lines at Comines, where the government furnished beer, women, and a circulating library.

I asked those mud-colored men, leaning against the wet mud bank in the rain, behind their little steel shields, and firing at whatever moved–who were their enemies? They stared at me uncomprehendingly. I explained that I wanted to know who lay opposite them, in those pits eighty yards away. They didn't know–whether English, French, or Belgians, they had not the slightest idea. And they didn't care. It was Something that Moved–that was enough.

Along the thousand-mile Russian front I saw thousands of young giants, unarmed, unequipped, and often unfed, ordered to the front to stop the German advance with clubs, with their defenseless bodies. If anyone thinks the Russian masses wanted this war, he has only to put his ear to the ground these days when the Russian masses are breaking their age-long silence, and hear the approaching rumble of peace.

No one will ever describe the unimaginable brutality of the old-time Russian military system, through whose machinery went Russia's young men. I have seen an officer on the streets of Petrograd knock in the teeth of a soldier who didn't salute with just the proper amount of servility. Soldiers were treated like animals, as a matter of course. To the Russian peasant, what harm was in the Japanese, the Persian, the Turk, the Austrian, or the Prussian–before whose cannon his body crumpled down in alien lands far from his pleasant home? What care he if Serbia were invaded by Austria–or Belgium by the Germans? Hear him now, in those simple tones so exasperating to the "democracies" of the west:

No annexations, no indemnities.

Every people has a right to dictate its own form of government.

In Serbia, I was struck first by the unbelievable damage wrought by war and pestilence among a people of "still unbroken men;" and secondly, by the evidences of the network of intrigue in which the great powers had enmeshed the rulers of Serbia, driving straight to war. One young Serbian told me how the plot to kill the Austrian archduke had been formed, and how the Serbian government tolerated the conspiracy, and all about the money paid by the Russian minister. . . .

Happily, I was in Bulgaria when she was forced into the war by her king and German diplomacy; and I had an opportunity to study a modern nation in the act of tricking its people. For seven out of the thirteen political parties in Bulgaria, representing a majority of the people, were against going to war, and through their regularly appointed delegates conveyed their position to the king, demanding the calling of parliament. But the king, ministers, and the military authorities responded by suddenly decreeing mobilization—with a stroke of the pen converting a nation into an army—and from that moment all communication between citizens, all protest, ceased—or was choked in blood.

I could go on telling of Italy, of Rumania, of Belgium under the Germans, how everywhere I saw the one main fact, repeated over and over again, that this was not a war of the peoples, that the masses in the different countries had, and have, no motive in continuing the struggle except defense, and revenge; and that even now the millions of men on all the fronts would stop fighting, lay down their arms and go home, at a word of command. . . .

Perhaps the most significant thing I noticed in Europe was the stubborn persistence of internationalism, in spite of the war. Especially in those neutral countries between belligerents was it so. There citizens of enemy countries met in natural friendly communion, bound a little closer, it seemed to me, by the blind grapple of their fatherlands. It was wonderful to perceive by a thousand signs the truth that internationalism is an instinct in mankind. In Holland I have seen even British and German interned soldiers, who could not speak each other's language, fraternizing; while in Switzerland, and in far Rumania, Germans and Frenchmen met to talk the business out, and pledge each other a deeper friendship.

Soon it will be hard for us in America to realize that we ever had German friends, or ever will have them. The casualty lists of the great conscript army will begin to come in, and what my scientific young friend in Washington described will begin to happen to us; we will begin to hate—"the social anger that is patriotism." Already we've had a taste of what will come a thousand times intensified, in the beating of "pacifists" by soldiers and sailors—and in arbitrary arrests and suppressions by the police everywhere. It is getting to be as much as a man's liberty is worth to say that this is not a popular war, and that we are not going democratically about "making the world safe for democracy."

Yet both those things are true. In all the nations of the world—even including Germany—this war was not a popular war; nor is there one place left on the face of the globe where the government has dared to put it up to the fighting men whether they would begin the war, and having begun it, whether they will fight on. In all these embattled nations, whose proud crests just now flaunt in chief the word *Democracy,* a small class of immensely wealthy people own the country, while an enormous mass of workers are poor. Belgium, the ravished innocent among nations, was in times of peace the cruelest industrial oligarchy in Europe, with the poorest, most exploited people. And it was this laboring proletariat which was thrown against the might of imperial Germany, to defend its masters.

Now comes our turn. Now millions of young American men are to go to Europe and kill Germans or be killed, in the name of "democracy." Most of these young men are workers, who may or may not know that their employers' patriotism never prevented them from squeezing the ultimate energy from "factory fodder." They may or may not realize that political power without economic power makes "democracy" a hollow sham. It may perhaps have occurred to them that the democratic way to make war is to ask the consent of those who are to do the fighting.

It will be said that it is easy to complain of the "undemocratic" methods of our government—but what was to be done? I think President Wilson could have stopped and asked almost any man he met on the street—he would have told him that.

Here is the way I diagnose the common man's attitude. At the outbreak of the war he felt pretty neutral as between the two belligerents. Later on his sympathies swung to the Entente cause—but never strongly enough to persuade him to bleed and die for it. Certainly, whether you like it or not, Wilson was elected because "he kept us out of war."

The common man's program was this. His conscience hurt him a little at the shipping of arms and ammunition to Europe —or anyway, he felt that it was unfair. He would have cheerfully embargoed our munitions export trade. He thought Americans had no business traveling in the war zone, any more than playing tag in a pesthouse and he was all for warning them to keep out of there, or anyway, to keep off the vessels of belligerent nations. Compulsory military service he regarded as distinctly un-American, to say the least.

I don't say this frame of mind lasted three years, with the entire press, the churches, the universities, the banks and business agencies all screaming one endless chorus of fear and hatred, overwhelmingly unanimous. No, he couldn't stick it out; pretty soon he simply threw up his horny hands and began to believe that the Allies were right and all the autocracy was in Berlin. But nevertheless, the simple ideas I have outlined above were the common man's reactions to the war; and I think that if he'd been consulted about what to do, the course of American history would have been changed. Anyway, the common man's cerebrations seem to me a perfectly valid, sensible and wise comment on the war. . . .

In the exclusive club to which I belong, a group of Plattsburghers were sitting at cocktail time, one day just before the president read his war message in Congress. The papers said that the Germans had torpedoed another American ship, and that American citizens had been drowned.

"It's true," one youth was drawling, "that they have been destroying our ships and killing our citizens—but I must confess that my ardor was somewhat dampened when I read that one of the victims was a Negro. . . ."

1917

The I.W.W. in Court

In the opening words of his statement why sentence of death should not be pronounced upon him, August Spies,* one of the Chicago martyrs of 1887, quoted the speech of a Venetian doge, uttered six centuries ago—

I stand here as the representative of one class, and speak to you, the representatives of another class. My defense is your accusation; the cause of my alleged crime, your history.

The Federal courtroom in Chicago, [1918] where Judge Landis sits in judgment on the Industrial Workers of the World,** is an imposing great place, all marble and bronze and mellow dark woodwork. Its windows open upon the heights of towering office buildings, which dominate that courtroom as money power dominates our civilization.

Over one window is a mural painting of King John and the Barons at Runnymede, and a quotation from the Great Charter:

No freeman shall be taken or imprisoned or be disseized of his freehold or liberties or free customs, or be outlawed or

---

* August Spies, though clearly innocent, was sentenced to death along with other militant Chicago labor leaders in the frame-up case growing out of the Haymarket affair of 1886—a major phase in the national labor struggle for the eight-hour day.—*Ed.*

** The I.W.W. was formally charged with conspiring to violate the criminal syndicalist laws. Ninety-three of the defendants, victims of wartime terror, were subsequently given sentences ranging from four to thirty-eight years and fined from twenty to thirty thousand dollars.—*Ed.*

exiled or any otherwise damaged but by lawful judgment of his peers or by the law of the land—

To no one will we sell, to no one will we deny or delay right or justice. . . .

Opposite, above the door, is printed in letters of gold:

These words the Lord spake unto all your assembly in the mount out of the midst of the fire, of the cloud, and of the thick darkness, with a great voice; and he added no more. And he wrote them in two tables of stones, and delivered them unto me. . . .—Deut. V. 22.

Heroic priests of Israel veil their faces, while Moses elevates the Tables of the Law against a background of clouds and flame.

Small on the huge bench sits a wasted man with untidy white hair, an emaciated face in which two burning eyes are set like jewels, parchment skin split by a crack for a mouth; the face of Andrew Jackson three years dead. This is Judge Kenesaw Mountain Landis, named for a battle—a fighter and a sport, according to his lights, and as just as he knows how to be. It was he who fined the Standard Oil Company thirty-nine million dollars. (No, none of it was paid.)

Upon this man has devolved the historic role of trying the Social Revolution. He is doing it like a gentleman. Not that he admits the existence of a Social Revolution. The other day he ruled out of evidence the Report of the Committee on Industrial Relations, which the defense was trying to introduce in order to show the background of the I.W.W.

"As irrelevant as the Holy Bible," he said. At least that shows a sense of irony.

In many ways a most unusual trial. When the judge enters the courtroom after recess no one rises—he himself has abolished the pompous formality. He sits without robes, in an ordinary business suit, and often leaves the bench to come down and perch on the step of the jury box. By his personal order, spittoons are placed beside the prisoners' seats, so they can while away the long day with a chaw; and as for the prisoners themselves, they are permitted to take off their coats, move around, read newspapers.

It takes some human understanding for a judge to fly in the face of judicial ritual as much as that. . . .

As for the prisoners, I doubt if ever in history there has been a sight just like them. One hundred and one *men*—lumberjacks, harvest-hands, miners, editors; one hundred and one who believe that the wealth of the world belongs to him who creates it, and that the workers of the world shall take their own. I have before me the chart of their common-wealth—their industrial democracy—One Big Union.

One Big Union—that is their crime. That is why the I.W.W. is on trial. If there were a way to kill these men, capitalist society would cheerfully do it; as it killed Frank Little, for example—and before him, Joe Hill. . . . So the outcry of the jackal press, "German agents! Treason!"—that the I.W.W. may be lynched on a grand scale.

One hundred and one strong men. . . .

These hundred and one are outdoor men, hard-rock blasters, tree fellers, wheat binders, longshoremen, the boys who do the strong work of the world. They are scarred all over with the wounds of the industry—and the wounds of society's hatred. They aren't afraid of anything. . . .

In the early morning they come over from Cook County Jail, where most of them have been rotting three-quarters of a year, and march into the courtroom two by two, between police and detectives, bailiffs snarling at the spectators who stand too close. It used to be that they were marched four times a day through the streets of Chicago, handcuffed; but the daily circus parade has been done away with.

Now they file in, the ninety-odd who are still in jail, greeting their friends as they pass; and there they are joined by the others, those who are out on bail. The bail is so high—from 25,000 dollars apiece down—that only a few can be let free. The rest have been in that horrible jail—Cook County—

since early last fall; almost a year in prison for a hundred men who love freedom more than most.

On the front page of the *Daily Defense Bulletin,* issued by [I.W.W.] headquarters, is a drawing of a worker behind the bars, and underneath, "Remember! *We are in* here *for* you; *you are out* there *for* us!" . . .

Inside the rail of the courtroom, crowded together, many in their shirt sleeves, some reading papers, one or two stretched out asleep, some sitting, some standing up; the faces of workers and fighters, for the most part, also the faces of orators, of poets, the sensitive and passionate faces of foreigners—but all strong faces, all faces of men inspired, somehow; many scarred, few bitter. There could not be gathered together in America one hundred and one men more fit to stand for the Social Revolution. People going into that courtroom say, "It's more like a convention than a trial!" True, and that is one of the things that gives the trial its dignity; that, and the fact that Judge Landis conducts it in a cosmic way. . . .

And then I noticed the clumps of heavy, brutish-faced men, built like minotaurs, whose hips bulged and whose little eyes looked mingled ferocity and servility, like a bulldog's; the look of private detectives, and scabs, and other bodyguards of private property. . . .

And I saw the government prosecutor rise to speak—Attorney Nebeker, legal defender for the great copper-mining corporation; a slim, nattily dressed man with a face all subtle from twisting and turning in the law, and eyes as cold and undependable as flawed steel. . . .

And I looked through the great windows and saw, in the windows of the office buildings that ringed us round, the lawyers, the agents, the brokers at their desks, weaving the fabric of this civilization of ours, which drives men to revolt and dream, and then crushes them. From the street came roaring up the ceaseless thunder of Chicago, and a military band went blaring down invisible ways to war. . . .

*

Talk to us of war! These hundred and one are veterans of a war that has gone on all their lives, in blood, in savage and shocking battle and surprise; a war against a force which has limitless power, gives no quarter, and obeys none of the rules of civilized warfare. The Class Struggle, the age-old guerrilla fight of the workers against the masters, worldwide, endless ... but destined to end!

These hundred and one have been at it since in their youth they watched their kind being coldly butchered, not knowing how to resist. They have mastered the secret of war—the offensive! And for that knowledge they are hunted over the earth like rats.

In Lawrence a policeman killed a woman with a gun, a militia man bayoneted a boy; in Paterson the private detective thugs shot and killed a worker standing on his own porch, with his baby in his arms; on the Mesaba Range armed guards of the steel trust murdered strikers openly, and other strikers were jailed for it; in San Diego men who tried to speak on the streets were taken from the city by prominent citizens, branded with hot irons, their ribs caved in with baseball bats; in the harvest fields of the great Northwest workers were searched, and if red [I.W.W.] cards were found on them, cruelly punished by vigilantes. At Everett, the hirelings of the lumber trust massacred them. . . .

The creed of the I.W.W. took hold mostly among migratory workers, otherwise unorganized; among the wretchedly exploited, the agricultural workers, timber workers, miners, who are viciously underpaid and overworked, who have no vote, and are protected by no union and no law, whose wage and changing abode never allow them to marry, nor to have a home. The migratory workers never have enough money for railway fares; they must ride the rods, or the "side-door Pullman"; fought not only by Chambers of Commerce, manufacturers' associations, and all the institutions of the law, but also by the "aristocratic" labor unionists. The natural prey of the world of vested interest; of this stuff the I.W.W. is building its kingdom. Good stuff, because tried and refined;

without encumbrances; willing to fight and able to take care of itself; chivalrous, adventurous. Let there be a "free speech fight" on in some town, and the "wobblies" converge upon it, across a thousand miles, and fill the jails with champions.

And *singing*. Remember, this is the only American working class movement which *sings*. Tremble then at the I.W.W., for a singing movement is not to be beaten. . . .

When you hear out of a freight train rattling across a black-earth village street somewhere in Iowa, a burst of raucous, ironical young voices singing:

> O I like my boss,
> He's a good friend of mine,
> And that's why I'm starving
> Out on the picketline!
> Hallelujah! I'm a bum!
> Hallelujah! Bum again!
> Hallelujah! Give us a hand-out
> To revive us again!

When at hot noontime along the Philadelphia waterfront you hear a bunch of giants resting after their lunch, in the most mournful barbershop rendering that classic: *Whadda Ye Want Ta Break Yer Back Fer the Boss For?*

Or, *Casey Jones—The Union Scab.*

I can hear them now:

> Casey Jones kept his junk pile running,
> Casey Jones was working double time;
> Casey Jones, he got a wooden medal
> For being good and faithful on the S. P. line!

They love and revere their singers, too, in the I.W.W. All over the country workers are singing Joe Hill's songs, "The Rebel Girl," "Don't Take My Papa Away From Me," "Workers of the World, Awaken." Thousands can repeat his "Last Will," the three simple verses written in his cell the night before execution. I have met men carrying next their hearts, in the pocket of their working clothes, little bottles with some of Joe Hill's ashes in them. Over Bill Haywood's desk in national headquarters is a painted portrait of Joe Hill, very moving, done with love . . . I know no other group of Americans which honors its singers. . . .

Wherever, in the West, there is an I.W.W. local, you will find an intellectual center—a place where men read philosophy, economics, the latest plays, novels; where art and poetry are discussed, and international politics. In my native place, Portland, Oregon, the I.W.W. hall was the livest intellectual center in town . . . There are playwrights in the I.W.W. who write about life in the "jungles," and the "wobblies" produce the plays for audiences of "wobblies."

What has all this to do with the trial in Chicago? I plead guilty to wandering from the point. I wanted to give some of the flavor that sweetens the I.W.W. for me. It was my first love among labor organizations. . . .

It was in September, 1917, that the I.W.W. manhunt began. From that time until April, 1918—seven months—the boys lay in jail, waiting for trial. They were charged with being members of an organization, and conspiring to promote the objects of this organization, which were, briefly, to destroy the wage system—and not by political action.

All this leading inevitably to the "destruction of government in the United States." . . . This main count in the indictment would have been highly ludicrous if it hadn't been mixed up with the sinister "obstructing the War Program of the Government"; and there were dragged in the twin sins of sedition and opposing the draft. . . .

And while the hundred and twelve were rotting in jail, a ferocious hunt was launched throughout the country; I.W.W. halls were raided, conventions jailed; papers were seized; workers were herded into bull pens by the thousand; and every organization of police, volunteer or regular, joined the campaign of violence and terrorization against the I.W.W., so widely labeled as German agents. . . .

Of course the "treason" phase of the case broke down

completely. It was only inserted to disguise the real nature of the prosecution, anyway. The blood-curdling revelations of German intrigue promised the world by the prosecution at the opening of the trial did not materialize. The government experts who examined the books and accounts of the organization admitted that all was in order. Finally, it was not proven that there was an I.W.W. policy concerning the war, or even concerted opposition of opinion to conscription. . . .

Among other farcical incidents was the loudly heralded arrival in Chicago of ex-Governor Tom Campbell of Arizona, with a "suitcase full of proofs that the I.W.W. was paid by Germany." For weeks he stood off and on, waiting to be called to the witness stand. Then of a sudden he announced in the newspapers that the famous "suitcase" had been stolen by an I.W.W. disguised as a Pullman porter! . . .

In order that there should be no opportunity for sentimentality, the prosecution dismissed all indictments against women defendants; in order that the I.W.W. should not be able to testify about the worst outrages perpetrated against the workers, not one of the Bisbee deportees was put on trial, and not one of the Butte strikers who might testify to the Speculator mine fire. . . . But because of the latitude allowed by Judge Landis, and the skill of [the defense attorneys] Vandeveer and Cleary, the defense has been one long bloody pageant of industrial wrong; Cœur d'Alene, San Diego, Everett, Yakima Valley, Paterson, Mesaba Range, Bisbee, Tulsa. . . .

From the very beginning, behind shallow legal pretexts loomed the Class Struggle, stark and implacable. The first battle was in the choice of a jury, which dramatically revealed the position of both sides. In examining talesmen, the attorney for the prosecution asked such questions as these:

"Can you conceive of a system of society in which the workers own and manage industry themselves?"

"Do you believe in the right of individuals to acquire property?"

"You believe, do you not, that all children should be taught respect for other people's property?"

"You believe, do you not, that the founders of the American Constitution were divinely inspired?"

"Don't you think that the owner of an industry ought to have more say-so in the management of it than all his employees put together?"

Any prospective juror who admitted a familiarity with labor history, with economics, or with the evolution of social movements, was peremptorily challenged by the prosecution. The questions of the defense were invariably objected to, and the prosecution made a series of extraordinary speeches to the court, in which were remarks such as the following:

"Karl Marx, father of that vicious doctrine—the cesspool into which the roots of the I.W.W. have gone for much nourishment."

"This case is an ordinary criminal case, in which a number of men conspired to break the law ... Their crime consists in the fact that they conspired to take from the employer what is constitutionally his, and in the ownership of which the law supports him."

"The wage system," said Mr. Clyne, of the prosecution, "is established by law, and all opposition to it is opposition to law."

Another time [prosecutor] Nebeker delivered himself of the following: "A man has no right to revolution under the law." To which Judge Landis himself made remark, *"Well, that depends on how many men he can get to go in with him— in other words, whether he can put it over."*

The defense sternly held to the class war issue. Among questions asked the jurymen by Vandeveer and Cleary were:

"You told Mr. Nebeker that you had never read any revolutionary literature. Have you never read, in school, about the American Revolution of 1776? Or the French Revolution which deposed the king and made France a republic? Or the

219

Russian Revolution that overthrew the autocracy and the tsar?"

"Do you recognize the right of people to revolt?"

"Do you recognize the idea of revolution as one of the principles of the Declaration of Independence?"

"You have told Mr. Nebeker that you don't think it is right to take away property from those who own it. In our own Civil War, do you think it was right for Congress to pass a law which took away from the people of the South several million dollars' worth of property in the form of chattel slaves—without compensation?"

"You don't believe then that property interests are greater than human interests?"

"Suppose these defendants believed that a majority of the people would be right in abolishing modern property rights in the great industries in order to free a great number of workingmen from industrial slavery—would that prejudice you against them?"

"Do you believe workers have the right to strike?"

"Do you believe they have the right to strike even in war times?"

"Which side usually starts violence in a labor dispute?"

"Would you be opposed to the application to industry of the underlying principles of American democracy?"

"Do you consider that one individual has an inalienable right to exploit two hundred or three hundred men and make protected profits off their labor?" . . .

And so on, for a whole month. What an education that jury had; except that the jackal press has "hushed up" or perverted utterly the story of the I.W.W. trial. Publicity could not help but win the case for the "wobblies"; and so the great prostituted newspapers ignore the most dramatic legal battle since Dred Scott—one whose implications are as serious, and whose sky is banked with thunderheads. . . .

Day after day, all summer, witness after witness from the firing line of the Class Struggle has taken the stand, and helped to shape the great labor epic; strike leaders, gunmen, rank and file workers, agitators, deputies, police, stool pigeons, secret service operatives.

I heard Frank Rogers, a youth grown black and bitter, with eyes full of vengeance, tell briefly and drily of the Speculator mine fire, and how hundreds of men burned to death because the company would not put doors in the bulkheads. He spoke of the assassination of Frank Little, who was hung by "vigilantes" in Montana, and how the miners of Butte swore to remember. (In the general headquarters of the I.W.W. there is a death mask of Frank Little, blind, disdainful, set in a savage sneer.)

Oklahoma, the tar-and-feathering of the workers at Tulsa; Everett, and the five graves of Sheriff McRae's victims on the hill behind Seattle . . . all this has come out, day by day, shocking story on story. I sat for the better part of two days listening to A. S. Embree telling over again the astounding narrative of the Arizona deportations; and as I listened, looked at photographs of the miners being marched across the arid country, between rows of men who carried rifles in the hollow of their arms, and wore white handkerchiefs about their wrists.

Everyone knows how the deportees were loaded on cattle cars, how the engineer, protesting, was forced to pull the train out, and how finally, arriving at Columbus, New Mexico, the train was ordered back and finally halted in the desert, where United States troops saved the wretched people from exposure and starvation. Many of the deportees had wives, families, and property in Bisbee, some were not I.W.W.'s at all, and others had no connection with the labor movement in any way; a large number of the men owned Liberty bonds, and many were registered in the draft. . . .

I sat listening to a very simple fellow, an agricultural worker named Eggel, who was telling how the "vigilance committees" and the gunmen from the towns of the Northwest hunted the I.W.W. farm hands. Without emotion Eggel described how he and others were taken off a train at Aberdeen, South Dakota, and beaten up.

"One man would sit on your neck, and two men on your arms, and two on your legs, while a detective, Price I think was his name, beat us up with a two-by-four, and it was criss-crossed, notches made on it, this way and that way, so it would raise welts on a man ... beat you over the back and your hips. . . .

"So they took me away in one automobile, and they took Smith in another, and then they gave me another beating. So after that third beating I came back to Aberdeen, and slunk in at night, and I slept beneath a livery barn, and the next day I crept down to the depot and took a train for North Dakota. . . ."

Listen to the scriptural simplicity of this:

"Well, they grabbed us. And the deputy says, 'Are you a member of the I.W.W.?' I says, 'Yes'; so he asked for my card, and I gave it to him, and he tore it up. He tore the other cards up that the fellow members along with me had, so this fellow member says, 'There is no use tearing that card up, we can get duplicates.' 'Well,' the deputy says, 'we can tear the duplicates up too.'

"And this fellow worker says, he says, *'Yes, but you can't tear it out of my heart.'*"

The humility of the workers is beautiful, the patience of the workers is almost infinite, and their gentleness miraculous. They still believe in constitutions, and the phrases of govern-ments—yes, in spite of their preamble, the I.W.W. still have faith in the goodness of mankind, and the possibility of jus-tice for the righteous. . . .

1918

With Gene Debs on the Fourth

"What'll it be, Mr. Sparks?" asked the drug clerk, with the familiarity of common citizenship in Terre Haute, Indiana, and the respect due to a successful politician.

"Gimme a nut sundae, George," said the lawyer, who lived around the corner on Sycamore Street. Sparks is not his real name. He was dressed up in a new gray suit, adorned with a small American flag, buttons of the First and Third Liberty loans, and a Red Cross emblem. "Reg'lar Fourth o' July weather, hey George?"

Through the windows of the drug store Eighth Street looked extremely animated; with families trooping toward the center of the town, flags aslant in children's hands, mother and pa in holiday attire and sweating freely; with patriarchal automobiles of neighboring farmers, full of starched youngsters and draped with bunting. Faintly came the sound of an occasional firecracker, and the thin strains of martial music from the parade. A hot, sticky wind blew occasional puffs of yellow dust up the street.

"Yes, we got a spell of heat all right," responded George. "We're going to close pretty soon and go up town to see the p'rade." He scooped ice cream and went on gossiping. "They say Gene Debs has got arrested up to Cleveland."

Everyone in the place stopped talking and looked up.

"Yes," said the lawyer in a satisfied tone. "Ye-e-es, I guess from what the papers say Gene stepped over the line this time. I guess they'll shut him up now."

An old man in a stiff white shirt, with gray whiskers sticking out of a shrewd, smooth-shaven face, looked up from a table in the corner.

"Do ye think they're agoin' to put Gene in jail?" he queried, a little anxiously.

"He'll have to pay the penalty of breakin' the law just the same as other folks," answered Sparks, virtuously. "If he's agoin' to make trouble for the gov'ment, trouble is what he'll get. This ain't any time to talk socialism. . . ."

George paused in his concoction of a milk shake. "You know Hank, the policeman; well he was in here last night, and he says Gene Debs ought to ben locked up twenty-five years ago."

There were mutters of approval at this.

"It's bad for the town," announced Mr. Sparks. "Why with all the money Gene Debs has made out on the Chautauqua, he ain't bought a single Liberty bond. . . ."

A raw-boned, brick-colored youth who sat with two giggling girls in muslin finery, spoke out fiercely:

"I bet the Kaiser would give him the Iron Cross if he ever heard about Gene Debs!"

The old man with the chin-whiskers mildly intervened.

"We-e-ell, that's goin' a leetle strong," he remarked. "Everybody knows Gene Debs. He ain't no traitor, Gene ain't. Only jest a trifle flighty, that's all's a matter with Gene Debs. . . ."

Everybody knows Gene Debs in Terre Haute. Sixty-two years ago he was born in Terre Haute, of parents who came to America from Alsace. Gene's father was of upper middle-class family, and owned mills in Colmar. He fell in love with a girl who worked in one of his mills, and renounced his heritage to marry her. They came to Indiana as immigrants, and lived through hells of poverty. . . .

This was all before 1870. But old man Debs never admitted that Alsace could be German. On his tombstone he had engraved, "Born at Colmar, Alsace, France."

Gene, his father, and his mother went through their political and economic evolution together. Together Gene and his father voted for the Greenback Party, then for the Populists ... and that way, the characteristically American way, Gene Debs and his father and mother came to socialism. ...

Terre Haute is a rich little country town in the Hoosier land, where Eugene Field came from, and James Whitcomb Riley, and a whole raft of novelists and poets. Going through that country on the train I can never resist the feeling that after all, *this* is real America. Trim villages, white farmhouses set in trees, fields of tasseled corn; shallow rivers flowing between earthen banks, little rolling hills spotted with lazy cows, bare-legged children; the church spires and graveyards of New England, transported hither by Protestant folk, mellowed and grown more spacious by contact with the South and West; rural schoolhouses, and everywhere hideous and beloved monuments commemorating the Civil War; locusts jarring in the sycamores, an almost overwhelming fertility rioting in the black earth, steaming in the procreative heat of flat-country summer, and distilling a local sweetness that is distinctively American—sentimental and humorous.

The Middle West, with its tradition of settled, country-living folk, and behind that, the romance of the Civil War, and still further back, the epos of the race moving West and conquering. ...

Here lives Gene Debs, authentic kin of Field and Riley, American, Middle Western, shrewd, tender-hearted, eloquent and indomitable. When I was a small boy my conception of Uncle Sam was just what I found Gene Debs to be—and I'm not at all sure my instinct was wrong.

It was on the Fourth of July that Art Young* and I went to Terre Haute to see Gene. Barely a month before, the terrible rumor had gone round, chilling all our hearts—"Gene Debs is going back on the party!" That lie he nailed in the ringing statement published in the New York *Call*.** ... Then came his tour through the middle states, menaced

* The great American artist and social cartoonist.—*Ed.*
** Socialist Party newspaper founded in 1909.—*Ed.*

everywhere with arrests, violence, even lynching . . . and Debs calmly speaking according to schedule, fearless, fiery and full of love of people. . . . Then his Canton speech,* a clear internationalist manifesto, and the Cleveland arrest.

"Gene Debs arrested! They've arrested Gene!" people said everywhere, with a shock, a feeling of pity, of affection, of rage. Nothing that has happened in the United States this year has stirred so many people just this way. The long sentences given to conscientious objectors, the suppression of the Socialist press, the indictment of editors, lecturers, Socialist officials under the Espionage and Sedition Acts—people didn't seem to be deeply moved by these things; but the arrest and indictment of Gene Debs—of Gene Debs as a traitor to his country! That was like a slap in the face to thousands of simple people—many of them not Socialists at all—who had heard him speak and therefore loved him. Not to mention the hundreds he has personally befriended, helped or even saved from every sort of evil. . . .

"Gene Debs arrested! Our Gene! That's going too far!"

It appears that Allan Benson** had come out with a piece in the paper criticizing the authorities for arresting Debs at the moment when he was "just on the point of going over to the National Party!" Sitting there in his darkened sitting room, with the busts of Voltaire, Rousseau, and Bob Ingersoll just behind him, he chuckled over Mr. Benson's perspicacity. I couldn't help seeing a ludicrous mental picture of Gene Debs in the company of pious Prohibition preachers and Socialist renegades. "Cheap skates," was Gene's dismissal of the whole tribe.

He was in bed when we arrived, but insisted on getting up. Not very well, his wife said; had not been well a whole year. How gaunt and tall he was, how tired his long burned-up

* Debs' famous anti-war speech made at the state convention of the Socialist Party at Canton, Ohio, June 16, 1918. As a result of this speech, he was arrested and sentenced to ten years in prison.—*Ed.*

** A former leader of the Socalist Party and its candidate for president in 1916.—*Ed.*

body looked; and yet with what a consuming inward radiance he came forward and greeted us, holding both his hands on ours, looking at us so eagerly, as if his affection for us was so deep . . . We felt wrapped in Gene Debs' affection. I had never met him, but I had heard him speak. How from that body and soul then he had poured out vitality, flaming across all his time, warmth and courage and belief!

Now he was older, more ravaged by the strain of giving and fighting; but his smile was still as delighted, and his sympathy as wonderful, and the tides of his indomitability at the service of anyone. . . .

Gene talked. You who have never heard him talk don't know just what that means. It isn't erudition, fine choice of words, or well-modulated voice that makes his charm; but the intensity of his face, glowing, and the swift tumbling out of his sincere words. He told about his trip, describing with boyish pleasure how he outwitted the detectives watching for him in Cleveland; and how mayors and patriotic committees in little towns had warned him not to speak—and he had spoken; just the same.

"Aren't you afraid of lynching?" I asked him.

Gene smiled. "Now that's a funny thing," he said. "I just don't happen to think about it, some way. I guess I'm sort of psychically protected, anyway. I know that so long as I keep my eye on them, they won't dare to do anything. As a rule they're cowardly curs anyway. Keep your eye on them, that's all. . . ."

Outside as he talked to us the automobiles went by, covered with flags, and the sound of the parade came drifting down . . . Looking through the darkened windows we watched the people. As they passed the house they motioned or pointed toward it, with expression compounded half of eager malice, and half of a sort of fear. "That's where Gene Debs lives," you could see them saying, as one would say, "The House of the Traitor. . . ."

"Come on," said Gene, suddenly. "Let's go out and sit on the porch and give 'em a good show, if they want to see me."

So we went out on the porch, and took off our coats. And those who passed only looked furtively our way, and whispered, and when they caught Gene's eye, bowed over-cordially.

The old man told us how the people of Indiana, and indeed, of all the Middle States, were will-broken and terrorized by "Loyalty" leagues, citizens' committees, vigilantes—and whipped into hysteria besides ... The old frankness which still characterized Hoosier farmers before the war, was now all gone. No one dared speak his mind to anyone. Many, many loved him, Gene Debs, who dared not testify in any other way except by anonymous letters ... He spoke of leaders of the people who, after being beaten by mobs, or tarred-and-feathered, abandoned their rebellion and conformed to the view of the majority.

"If they did that to me," said Gene, "even if I changed my mind I don't think I could say so!"

There was something tragic, and funny, in the way Terre Haute regarded Gene. Before the war Gene added luster to the name of the town, as well as having an immense personal popularity. In the beginning, practically the whole population, all through that section, was against going to war ... But since the war the usual phenomenon has happened in Terre Haute. The whole place has been mobilized physically and spiritually. Except Gene Debs. The simpler people couldn't understand it. The bankers, lawyers and merchants felt for him a terrible rancor. Even the ministers of the gospel, who had often implored him to address their conventions, now held meetings denouncing "the enemy in our midst."

No names were mentioned. No one dared to call Gene Debs "enemy" to his face. When he went down the street, everyone was studiously polite. Department of Justice operatives, volunteer detectives of all sorts, Liberty loan agents, prowled all around his house—but did not dare to enter and front the old lion. Once a businessmen's "patriotic" committee descended upon a German-born workman, and threatened him. Gene heard about it, and sent word to the committee: "Come down to *my* house, why don't you, instead of to the place of a poor man. I have a shotgun waiting for you fellows." The committee did not come. . . .

I have a picture of Gene Debs, his long bony head and shining face against a background of bright petunias in a box on the rail, his lean hand lifted with the long, artist's fingers giving emphasis to what he said:

"Say, isn't it great the way most of the boys have stood up? Fine! If this can't break them down, why then I know nothing can. Socialism's on the way. They can't stop it, no matter what they do. The more breaks the other side makes, the better for us. . . ."

And as we went down the steps, wringing our hands, clapping us on the shoulder, winning and warm, he said—and all the neighbors could hear him, too . . .

"Now you tell all the boys everywhere who are making the fight, Gene Debs says he's with you, all the way, straight through, *without a flicker!*"

1918

The Peace that Passeth Understanding . . .
a Fantasy

Scene: *The Salon de l'Horloge in the Palais d'Orsay, Paris—meeting place of the Peace Conference. At back a heavily ornate mantel of white marble, surmounted by a clock, above which rises the marble statue of a woman holding a torch; by some called "Victory," by others "Liberty," "Enlightenment," "Prohibition," etc. The clock is fifty years slow.*

The dialogue is carried on by each Delegate in his native tongue—but this presents no difficulties, as all understand one another perfectly.

During the action of the play incidental music may be provided, consisting of patriotic airs played softly.

Discovered: *Seated at the Peace Table, President Wilson, Premiers Clemenceau, Lloyd George and Orlando, and Baron Makino, the Japanese Delegate. As the curtain rises there is general laughter, in which Orlando does not join.*

Wilson: I had no idea the lower classes were so extensive . . . That explains my speech at Turin. I said, "The industrial workers will dictate the peace terms. . . ." (*Renewed mirth. Orlando looks sour.*)

Orlando (*gloomily*): Corpo di Bacco! Yes. You put me in a hell of a fix. I was forced to suppress that speech. We almost had a revolution! You must remember that the Italian workingmen are not educated—*we* have no Samuel Gompers.* . . .

---

* President of the American Federation of Labor—with the exception of one year—from 1882 to 1924.—*Ed.*

Lloyd George (*to Orlando*): Oh, I say, old cock! Don't take yourself so seriously. They're *always* talking revolution—in England, too—but so long as we can keep them *voting*. . . .

Clemenceau (*to Wilson, with Gallic charm*): Saperlotte! What a man! And that League of Nations—*quelle idée!* At first I thought you some sort of Henri Ford . . . Who but you could have explained that Balance of Power and the League of Nations are identical?

Wilson: Yes, yes . . . May I not insist that it is the *phrase* we must strive to attain? The advertising business is very highly developed at home. . . .

Makino: *Banzai.* Open Door in China.

Wilson (*modestly*): A trifling achievement. Why in America, my second campaign was won by the phrase, "He kept us out of war." (*General hilarity.*)

Orlando (*pounding the table*): *Per dio!* That's what we need in Italy! Couldn't you make another trip explaining that Italian treaty the Bolsheviki published?

Lloyd George (*briskly*): Well, gentlemen, I am reluctant to interrupt this pleasant diversion, but I suggest that we get to work on what our American colleague calls "the solemn and responsible task of establishing the peace of Europe and the world." (*Laughter.*) I don't want to be late for the *Folies Bergères;* going to the theater is another method of government which we have learned from Mr. Wilson. (*He bows to the President.*)

Clemenceau (*taking his place at the head of the table*): The Peace Conference will now come to order. Let the room be searched.

(*The Delegates look under the table, behind curtains, tapestries, pictures, and the statue above the clock. Orlando emerges first from beneath the table, holding the Serbian Delegate by the ear.*)

Orlando (*severely*): What are you doing here? Don't you realize that this is the Peace Conference?

Serbian Delegate: But we fought in the war.

231

Orlando: That was *war!* This is *peace!* (*The Serbian Delegate is ejected.*)

(*Clemenceau drags from behind the clock the Belgian Delegate.*)

Clemenceau (*shaking him*): Eavesdropping again, eh? How many times must you be told that this is a private affair?

Belgian Delegate: But the war was *about us*, wasn't it?

Clemenceau: War? War? Don't you know that the war is over? (*The Belgian Delegate is ejected.*)

(*Concealed in the folds of tapestry Makino discovers the Czechoslovak Delegate.*)

Makino (*indignantly*): Once more and you'll be de-recognized!

Czechoslovak Delegate: But the Fourteen Points—

Makino: They have not yet been interpreted. Run along now back to Siberia and shoot Bolsheviki until you're sent for! (*The Czechoslovak Delegate is ejected.*)

(*Lloyd George appears, grasping the Rumanian Delegate by the collar.*)

Rumanian Delegate: But you promised us Transylvania!

Lloyd George (*testily*): In the Wilsonian sense! In the Wilsonian sense! (*The Rumanian Delegate is ejected.*)

(*During this time Wilson is in the fireplace, thrusting up the chimney with a poker. Three persons come rattling down, covered with soot. As they are seized and brought forward, they can be identified as the Armenian Delegate, the Yugoslav Delegate, and the Polish Delegate.*)

Armenian Delegate: We thought the independence of Armenia—

Wilson (*firmly*): May I suggest that the Conference take note of the ingratitude of this person? At this very moment we are raising a Relief Fund in the United States!

Orlando (*to the Yugoslav*): What do you mean, butting in here?

Yugoslav Delegate: But thousands of our people fought in the Italian Army.

Orlando: Well, what more do you want?

Clemenceau (*to the Pole*): You be careful, young man, or we'll take away your pianist and give you a flute player!

(*The Armenian, Yugoslav, and Polish Delegates are ejected.*)

Makino (*to Wilson*): I think somebody's calling you.

(*Wilson crosses over and opens the window. A shrill clamor of Spanish voices from the Delegates of the Central American Republics can be heard.*)

Wilson (*loftily*): We are here to see, in short, that the very foundations of this war are swept away . . . Those foundations were the aggression of great powers upon the small. . . .

Delegates of Colombia, Panama, San Salvador, Nicaragua, Guatemala, Santo Domingo, etc.: How about the taking of the Panama Canal? Why do the United States Marines control elections in Nicaragua? Why does the American government disregard the decisions of the high court which the American government set up? Why did the United States abolish the Santo Domingan Republic and set up an American military dictatorship? Nicaraguan canal route—Brown Brothers—United Fruit Company—etc., etc.

Wilson: Nothing less than the emancipation of the world . . . will accomplish peace. (*With a noble gesture he sweeps the Latin-American Delegates off the sill and closes the window.*)

Clemenceau (*wiping the perspiration from his brow*): The Peace Conference is now safe for Democracy!

Wilson: Select classes of men no longer direct the affairs of the world, but the fortunes of the world are now in the hands of the plain people! (*Laughter.*)

Makino: It is worth coming all the way from Japan just to hear him!

Clemenceau: Now, gentlemen, before we get down to dismembering Germany, fixing the amount of the indemnity and stamping out Bolshevism, I should like to ask Mr. Wilson to interpret some of his Fourteen Points ... Of course, *we* know it's all right, but there is anxiety in certain quarters ... Rothschild telephoned me this morning. ...

For instance, will our distinguished colleague explain how in hell he proposes to get around Point One—*Open covenants of peace, openly arrived at, after which there shall be no private understandings of any kind, but diplomacy shall proceed always frankly and in the public view?*

Wilson: Well, gentlemen, are we not "openly arriving?" Everybody knows that we're holding a Peace Conference ... And then the word "understanding"; that means something people can *understand.* Assuredly it is not our intention to establish *that* kind of a peace! *(Applause from all.)*

Lloyd George: Point Two has been bothering the Admiralty a bit—*Absolute freedom of navigation upon the seas, outside territorial waters, alike in peace and war, except as the seas may be closed in whole or in part by international action for the enforcement of international covenants.* It sounded to us just a leetle pro—well, pro-any-nation-except-England, if you catch my meaning. ...

Wilson: May I not call attention to the fact that Great Britain consists of England, Scotland and Wales? "International"—do you follow me? What could be more international than England, Scotland, and Wales? *(Cheers and hand-shaking among the Delegates, and especially among Lloyd George.)*

Makino: As to Point Three—*The removal, so far as possible, of all economic barriers, and the establishment of an equality of trade conditions among the nations consenting to the peace and associating themselves for its maintenance.* You see—our interests in China—our position in the Pacific—

Wilson: Really elementary, my dear fellow. May I not

direct attention to the innocuous phrase, "so far as possible?" You and I, Baron, are aware of the possibilities... And while we are upon this subject, consider Point Four—*Adequate guarantees given and taken that national armaments will reduce to the lowest point consistent with domestic safety.* Why do you think I slipped in "consistent with domestic safety"? *(The applause is absolutely deafening.)*

Lloyd George: Mr. Wilson *must* make a lecture tour explaining who started the war!

Clemenceau: Just to clarify Point Five—about the colonies, you know—

Lloyd George and Makino: Ah!

Clemenceau: Exactly what does it mean? *Free, open-minded and absolutely impartial adjustment of all colonial claims, based upon a strict observance of the principle that in determining all such questions the interests of the population concerned must have equal weight with the equitable claims of the government whose title is to be determined.* I take it that this does not apply to Chinese or Negroes....

Wilson: For the purposes of the Peace Conference, may we not regard the Albanians as Mongolian Hittites?

Lloyd George *(doubtfully)*: But the Irish—

Wilson *(thoughtfully)*: The Irish vote in New York is not despicable. If I were to run for a third term—

Lloyd George: The Irish are very literal.

Wilson *(brightening)*: May I be permitted to point out the idealistic phrase, "the population concerned"? What is the "population concerned" in the case of Ireland? The English, naturally—are very much concerned, too!

Lloyd George *(admiringly)*: If I had only been brought up as a professor!

Wilson: At this point allow me to call your attention to the fact that the United States is also accumulating a fewer—shall we say "adopted children?" I have accommodated you gentlemen as regards Negroes and Orientals; it is only fair that you permit me to add to the list our Latin Americans. . . .

Clemenceau: By all means.

The others: Certainly, with pleasure.

Makino (*diffidently*): A delicate question, but one full of interest to my government—

Lloyd George: And mine—

Makino: The German colonies—in the Pacific—

Clemenceau: And in Africa—

Lloyd George (*coldly*): German colonies in Africa? Really, you must be mistaken. I don't recall any. . . .

Makino: Our troops captured a place called Kiau-Chao.

Clemenceau: But that is in China, isn't it?

Makino (*blandly*): Oh, no—in Germany.

Wilson: Gentlemen, we cannot return to the old ways. I have made definite statements—that is, definite for me. For instance, I have said, "No nation shall be robbed . . . because the irresponsible rulers of a single country have themselves done deep and abominable wrong."

(*All stare at him in astonishment.*)

Orlando: But how do you propose to do it then?

Wilson (*softly, with a gentle smile*): The League of Nations. . . . The League of Nations will take over the German colonies.

Lloyd George: Preposterous! I refuse to accept—

Makino: The Japanese government will not withdraw—

Wilson: One moment, one moment, gentlemen! The League of Nations turns over the colonies to agents—I have coined a word, "mandatories." *You* are the mandatories—

Lloyd George: Responsible to the League of Nations? Never!

Wilson: Only in a sense. It is a Wilsonism. The League of Nations lays down certain rules for the administration of these colonies. Every five hundred years the mandatories report to the League. *We* are the mandatories—and we are the *League of Nations!*

(*The Delegates embrace one another.*)

Makino (*to Lloyd George*): And the Pacific?

Lloyd George: We English are a sporting race, Baron. Have you a set of dice?

(*Immediately all produce dice.*)

Lloyd George: Thank you, I prefer my own.

Makino: I am used to mine, too.

(*The telephone rings. Clemenceau answers.*)

Clemenceau (*to Wilson*): Gompers on the wire. He brings you greetings from King George, and wants to know what the Peace Conference has done about labor.

(*Wilson goes to the telephone.*)

Wilson: Good afternoon, Samuel. I am as keenly aware, I believe, as anybody can be that the social structure rests upon the great working classes of the world, and that those working classes in several countries of the world, have, by their consciousness of community of interest, by their consciousness of community of spirit, done perhaps more than any other influence to establish a world opinion which is not of a nation, which is not of a continent, but is the opinion, one might say, of mankind. Cordially and sincerely yours, Woodrow Wilson. Please give that to the press. Good-bye. (*He hangs up.*)

Lloyd George (*looking at his watch*): Can't we hurry along, old dears? I've a dinner engagement with half a dozen kings.

Clemenceau: Point Six is, you will admit, the most important of all. The one about Russia—

(*Chorus of groans, snarls, and epithets in four languages.*)

Clemenceau (*reading*): *The evacuation of all Russian territory*—Does that mean by the Germans?

Wilson: That is hardly the meaning of the phrase. It stands to reason that if the Germans withdraw, the Russians might invade Russia. . . .

Lloyd George: It means that Russia must be evacuated by everyone except foreigners and the Russian nobility.

Clemenceau (*continuing*)—*and such a settlement of all questions affecting Russia as will secure the best and freest cooperation of the other nations of the world in obtaining for her an unhampered and unembarrassed opportunity for the independent determination of her own political development and national policy*—Excuse me, surely you don't mean—

Wilson: Certainly not.

Clemenceau (*continuing*)—*and assure her of a sincere welcome into the clutches*—I beg your pardon, my mistake —*into the society of free nations under institutions of her own choosing.* Excuse me, but isn't there a little too much "independent determination" and "institutions of her own choosing" in the document?

Wilson: On the contrary. If you will note the present state of the public mind, I think you will realize that it is especially necessary at this time to repeat this formula as much as possible.

Clemenceau (*continuing*)—*and, more than a welcome, assistance also of every kind that she herself may need and may herself desire.* Do I understand by that—?

Makino: The Omsk government is already manufacturing vodka. So far as we can discover, Russia's only other need seems to be a tsar—and we're arranging that as speedily as we can.

Clemenceau: I see. I thought perhaps—

Wilson: Oh, no. May I not comment on the amateurish quality of European diplomacy? At home we think nothing of putting fifteen hundred people in jail for their opinions, and calling it free speech. . . .

Clemenceau (*reading*): *The treatment accorded Russia by her sister nations in the months to come will be the acid test of their good-will, of their comprehension of her needs as distinguished from their own interests, and of their intelligent and unselfish sympathy.* That sort of thing won't go down in France. We have billions in Russian bonds—

Wilson: May I call attention to the inexpensiveness of adjectives?

Makino: But there are a number of embarrassing nouns. What *shall* we do about Russia?

Lloyd George: There is a flock of Grand Dukes out in the hall. Suppose we ask them in.

Wilson: It is inadvisable. One of them might be infected with Bolshevism—no one seems to be immune. Who knows that even *we*— (*All shudder*). If we learned the facts about Russia they might influence our judgment. . . .

Clemenceau: Let us pretend that Russia is divided among warring factions, and invite all of them to send representatives to a Conference at the headwaters of the Amazon—

Wilson (*nodding*): You are improving. "To confer with the representatives of the associated powers in the freest and frankest way."

Orlando: The Bolsheviki talk well. . . .

Clemenceau: Let them talk. There's nobody to hear them at the headwaters of the Amazon!

Wilson: This is one case when diplomacy can "proceed frankly and in the public view."

Orlando: But what about the other factions?

Clemenceau (*triumphantly*): Why, *we* are the other factions!

(*The clock strikes five.*)

Lloyd George (*with a start*): Dear me! Six points already. At this rate we'll have nothing to do three days from now—nothing but go home.

Makino (*dreamily*): I *like* Paris, too.

Lloyd George: Just a word about Point Eleven—Belgium, you know. That clause, *without any attempt to limit the sovereignty she enjoys.* Isn't that a bit strong? Of course, we can't permit—

Wilson: That is another matter for the League of Nations. That is what the League of Nations is for.

Clemenceau: And Point Eight—Alsace-Lorraine. I hope

you haven't any foolish ideas about "self-determination" in Alsace-Lorraine?

Wilson: Yes—for all except pro-Germans.

Clemenceau: But the language of the paragraph is open to misinterpretation. It might create a precedent. You know, we intend to annex the Saar Valley, where there *aren't* any Frenchmen. . . .

Wilson: Gentlemen, you seem to have overlooked the essential point—Point Fifteen, if I may be permitted the pun. I have covered it with such luxuriant verbiage that up to this moment no one in the world has discovered it. May I not call attention to the fact that *nowhere in this program have I declared against the principle of annexation? (Frantic enthusiasm.)*

Orlando: And Point Nine—*A readjustment of the frontiers of Italy should be effected along clearly recognized lines of nationality?*

Wilson: You notice that I have not stated *which nationality. . . .*

Lloyd George: I must be going. What's left?

Clemenceau: Only Austria-Hungary, the Balkans, Turkey, and Poland.

Orlando: Give them half an hour tomorrow.

Makino: May I suggest that our American colleague write the statement to the press?

Lloyd George (*to Makino*): And while he's doing it, what do you say to a friendly settlement of the German possessions?

Makino: Charmed.

(*Both take out their dice and while Wilson writes on a piece of paper, they throw.*)

Lloyd George: Pair o' nines! Baby's got to have new socks! What's this for? The Caroline Islands?

Makino: The Carolines! Come seven! Roll 'em down!

Lloyd George (*snapping his finger*): Come on—papa's watching! Choo-choo!

Makino: Come a-running, honey! Oh, you eleven—

Lloyd George: Yours, by Jingo! What'll it be now? Kiau Chao?

Makino: The Marshalls.

Lloyd George: Marshalls it is! Rattle them bones, boy! (*They play.*)

Wilson: It's completed. Shall I read it? (*They assent.*)

Wilson (*reading*): "President Wilson won another moral victory in the Peace Conference today. In spite of ominous predictions, his earnestness and eloquence, supported by the unselfish motives of the United States government in entering the war, completely won over the representatives of the other powers. At present complete harmony reigns among the Delegates."

(*At this moment the door opens and an attendant enters.*)

Attendant: Telegram for Premier Orlando! Very urgent!

Orlando (*opens it and reads slowly*): "Revolution in Italy completely victorious. Rome in the hands of the *Sovietti.*" (*All are thunderstruck.*)

(*Enter attendant.*)

Attendant: Cablegram for President Wilson! Very urgent!

Wilson (*takes it and reads slowly*): "You are impeached for invading Russia without a declaration of war."

(*While they are staring at each other, enter another attendant.*)

Attendant: Telegram for Premier Lloyd George! Very urgent!

Lloyd George (*reads*): "Sylvia Pankhurst* made Premier. Do not hurry home." (*Enter a fourth attendant.*)

Attendant: Cablegram for Baron Makino! Very urgent!

Makino (*reads*): "Infuriated people, unable to get rice, have eaten the Mikado."

---

* British Socialist who opposed World War I and supported the Russian Revolution.—*Ed.*

Clemenceau (*suddenly*): Hark! (*All listen. In the distance can be heard a confused and thunderous roar, which grows nearer, and resolves itself into a mighty chorus singing the "Carmagnole," the people of Paris marching on the Palais d'Orsay.*)

Orlando: Does anyone know when the next train leaves?

Makino: For where? (*General silence.*)

Lloyd George: I feel a hankering to live under a stable government.

Wilson: May I not suggest that there is only one stable government now—at Moscow? . . .

Orlando: Is there a back way out of this place?

Makino: But we'll have to go to work!

Wilson (*cheerfully*): Let us not be prematurely disheartened. Words are words in all languages—and Russians are doubtless human—and I still retain my powers of speech. . . .

(*Exeunt in single file through the window. The clock strikes six.*)

Slow curtain

1919

PLUNGING AHEAD

Thursday, November 8.* Day broke on a city in the wildest excitement and confusion, a whole nation heaving up in long hissing swells of storm. Superficially all was quiet; hundreds of thousands of people retired at a prudent hour, got up early, and went to work. In Petrograd the streetcars were running, the stores and restaurants open, theaters going, an exhibition of paintings advertised ... All the complex routine of common life—humdrum even in wartime—proceeded as usual. Nothing is so astounding as the vitality of the social organism—how it persists, feeding itself, clothing itself, amusing itself, in the face of the worst calamities. ...

The air was full of rumours about Kerensky,** who was said to have raised the Front, and to be leading a great army against the capital. ...

With brakes released the Military Revolutionary Committee whirled, throwing off orders, appeals, decrees, like sparks ... Kornilov was ordered brought to Petrograd. Members of the Peasant Land Committees imprisoned by the Provisional Government were declared free. Capital

---

* Reed arrived in Petrograd (now Leningrad) in September 1917. Between then and November 8, as he reports in *Ten Days That Shook the World,* he studied the background of struggle that made "the Russian Revolution one of the great events of human history, and the rise of the Bolsheviks a phenomenon of world-wide importance."—*Ed.*

** The glossary listed on page 256 will help define and identify some of the terms and names Reed used. They are listed in the order of their appearance in the text.—*Ed.*

punishment in the army was abolished. Government employees were ordered to continue their work, and threatened with severe penalties if they refused. All pillage, disorder, and speculation were forbidden under pain of death. . . .

On the other side, what a storm of proclamations posted up, handbills scattered everywhere, newspapers—screaming and cursing and prophesying evil. Now raged the battle of the printing press—all other weapons being in the hands of the Soviets. . . .

In the high, amphitheatrical Nikolai Hall that afternoon I saw the Duma sitting in *permanence*, tempestuous, grouping around it all the forces of opposition. The old Mayor, Schreider, majestic with his white hair and beard, was describing his visit to Smolny the night before, to protest in the name of the Municipal Self-Government. . . .

News came . . . Kaledin was marching north. The Soviet of Moscow had set up a Military Revolutionary Committee, and was negotiating with the commandant of the city for possession of the arsenal, so that the workers might be armed.

With these facts was mixed an astounding jumble of rumors, distortions, and plain lies. For instance, an intelligent young Cadet drew us aside and told us all about the taking of the Winter Palace.

"The Bolsheviks were led by German and Austrian officers," he affirmed.

"Is that so?" we replied, politely. "How do you know?"

"A friend of mine was there and saw them."

"How could he tell they were German officers?"

"Oh, because they wore German uniforms!"

There were hundreds of such absurd tales, and they were not only solemnly published by the anti-Bolshevik press, but believed by the most unlikely persons. . . .

Smolny was tenser than ever, if that were possible. The same running men in the dark corridors, squads of workers with rifles, leaders with bulging portfolios arguing, explaining, giving orders as they hurried anxiously along, surrounded by friends and lieutenants. Men literally out of themselves, living prodigies of sleeplessness and work-men unshaven, filthy, with burning eyes, who drove upon their fixed purpose full speed on engines of exaltation. So much they had to do, so much! Take over the government, organize the city, keep the garrison loyal, fight the Duma and the Committee for Salvation, keep out the Germans, prepare to do battle with Kerensky, inform the provinces what had happened, propagandize from Archangel to Vladivostok. . . .

The Congress [of Soviets] was to meet at one o'clock, and long since the great meeting hall had filled, but by seven there was yet no sign of the presidium . . . The Bolshevik and Left Social Revolutionary factions were in session in their own rooms. . . .

A little later, as we sat at the press table in the big hall, an anarchist who was writing for the bourgeois papers proposed to me that we go and find out what had become of the presidium. There was nobody in the *Tsik* office, nor in the bureau of the Petrograd Soviet. From room to room we wandered, through vast Smolny. Nobody seemed to have the slightest idea where to find the governing body of the Congress. As we went my companion described his ancient revolutionary activities, his long and pleasant exile in France. . . .

It was just 8:40 when a thundering wave of cheers announced the entrance of the presidium, with Lenin-great Lenin-among them. A short, stocky figure, with a big head set down in his shoulders, bald and bulging. Little eyes, a snubbish nose, wide, generous mouth, and heavy chin; clean-shaven now, but already beginning to bristle with the well-known beard of his past and future. Dressed in shabby clothes, his trousers much too long for him. Loved and revered as perhaps few leaders in history have been. . . .

A delegate of the coal miners of the Don Basin called upon the Congress to take measures against Kaledin, who might cut off coal and food from the capital. Several soldiers just arrived from the Front brought the enthusiastic greetings of their regiments . . . Now Lenin, gripping the edge of the reading stand, letting his little winking eyes travel over the crowd as he stood there waiting, apparently oblivious to the long-rolling ovation, which lasted several minutes. When it finished, he said simply, "We shall now proceed to construct the Socialist order!" Again that overwhelming human roar.

"The first thing is the adoption of practical measures to realize peace ... We shall offer peace to the peoples of all the belligerent countries upon the basis of the Soviet terms—no annexations, no indemnities, and the right of self-determination of peoples. At the same time, according to our promise, we shall publish and repudiate the secret treaties ... The question of War and Peace is so clear that I think that I may, without preamble, read the project of a Proclamation to the Peoples of All the Belligerent Countries. ..."

His great mouth, seeming to smile, opened wide as he spoke; his voice was hoarse—not unpleasantly so, but as if it had hardened that way after years and years of speaking—and went on monotonously, with the effect of being able to go on forever ... For emphasis he bent forward slightly. No gestures. And before him, a thousand simple faces looking up in intent adoration. ...

When the grave thunder of applause had died away, Lenin spoke again:

"We propose to the Congress to ratify this declaration. We address ourselves to the Governments as well as to the peoples, for a declaration which would be addressed only to the peoples of the belligerent countries might delay the conclusion of peace. The conditions of peace, drawn up during the armistice, will be ratified by the Constituent Assembly. In fixing the duration of the armistice at three months, we desire to give to the peoples as long a rest as possible after this bloody extermination, and ample time for them to elect their representatives. This proposal of peace will meet with resistance on the part of the imperialist governments—we don't fool ourselves on that score. ...

"The revolution of November 6 and 7," he ended, "has

opened the era of the Social Revolution . . . The labor movement, in the name of peace and socialism, shall win, and fulfill its destiny. . . ."

There was something quiet and powerful in all this, which stirred the souls of men. It was understandable why people believed when Lenin spoke. . . .

By crowd vote it was quickly decided that only representatives of political factions should be allowed to speak on the motion and that speakers should be limited to fifteen minutes.

First Karelin, for the Left Socialist Revolutionaries. "Our faction had no opportunity to propose amendments to the text of the proclamation; it is a private document of the Bolsheviks. But we will vote for it because we agree with its spirit. . . .

For the Social-Democrats Internationalists Kramarov, long, stoop-shouldered and near-sighted—destined to achieve some notoriety as the Clown of the Opposition. Only a Government composed of all the Socialist parties, he said, could possess the authority to take such important action. If a Socialist coalition were formed, his faction would support the entire program; if not, only part of it. As for the proclamation, the Internationalists were in thorough accord with its main points.

Then one after another, amid rising enthusiasm; Ukrainian Social-Democracy, support; Lithuanian Social-Democracy, support; Populist Socialists, support; Polish Social-Democracy, support; Polish Socialists support—but would prefer a Socialist coalition; Lettish Social-Democracy, support . . . Something was kindled in these men. One spoke of the "coming World Revolution, of which we are the advance guard"; another of "the new age of brotherhood, when all the peoples will become one great family. . . ." An individual member claimed the floor. "There is contradiction here," he said. "First you offer peace without annexations and indemnities, and then you say you will consider all peace offers. To consider means to accept. . . ."

Lenin was on his feet. "We want a just peace, but we are not afraid of a revolutionary war ... Probably the imperialist Governments will not answer our appeal—but we shall not issue an ultimatum to which it will be easy to say no ... If the German proletariat realizes that we are ready to consider all offers of peace, that will perhaps be the last drop which overflows the bowl—revolution will break out in Germany. . . .

"We consent to examine all conditions of peace, but that doesn't mean that we shall accept them ... For some of our terms we shall fight to the end—but possibly others will find it impossible to continue the war ... Above all, we want to finish the war. . . ."

Suddenly, by common impulse, we found ourselves on our feet, mumbling together into the smooth lifting unison of the *Internationale*. A grizzled old soldier was sobbing like a child. The immense sound rolled through the hall, burst windows and doors, and seared into the quiet sky. "The war is ended! The war is ended!" said a young workman near me, his face shining. And when it was over, as we stood there in a kind of awkward hush, someone in the back of the room shouted, "Comrades! Let us remember those who have died for liberty!" So we began to sing the Funeral March, that slow, melancholy and yet triumphant chant, so Russian and so moving. . . .

For this did they lie there, the martyrs of March, in their cold Brotherhood Grave on Mars Field; for this thousands and tens of thousands had died in the prisons, in exile, in Siberian mines. It had not come as they expected it would come, nor as the *intelligentsia* desired it; but it had come—rough, strong, impatient of formulas, contemptuous of sentimentalism; *real*. . . .

MOSCOW

On the evening of November 16 I watched two thousand Red Guards swing down the Zagorodny Prospekt behind a

248

military band playing the *Marseillaise*–and how appropriate it sounded–with blood-red flags over the dark ranks of workmen, to welcome home again their brothers who had defended "Red Petrograd." In the bitter dusk they tramped, men and women, their tall bayonets swaying; through streets faintly lighted and slippery with mud, between silent crowds of bourgeois, contemptuous but fearful. . . .

All were against them–businessmen, speculators, investors, landowners, army officers, politicians, teachers, students, professional men, shopkeepers, clerks. The other Socialist parties hated the Bolsheviks with an implacable hatred. On the side of the Soviets were the rank and file of the workers, the sailors, all the undemoralized soldiers, the landless peasants, and a few–a very few–intellectuals. . . .

From the farthest corners of great Russia, whereupon desperate street fighting burst like a wave, news of Kerensky's defeat came echoing back the immense roar of proletarian victory. Kazan, Saratov, Novgorod, Vinnitza–where the streets had run with blood; Moscow, where the Bolsheviks had turned their artillery against the last stronghold of the bourgeoisie–the Kremlin.

"They are bombarding the Kremlin!" The news passed from mouth to mouth in the streets of Petrograd, almost with a sense of terror. Travelers from "white and shining little mother Moscow" told fearful tales. Thousands killed; the Tverskaya and the Kuznetsky Most in flames; the church of Vasili Blazheny a smoking ruin; Uspensky Cathedral crumbling down; the Spasskaya Gate of the Kremlin tottering; the Duma burned to the ground. . . .

For two days now the Bolsheviks had been in control of the city. The frightened citizens were creeping out of their cellars to seek their dead; the barricades in the streets were being removed. Instead of diminishing, however, the stories of destruction in Moscow continued to grow . . . And it was under the influence of these fearful reports that we decided to go there. . . .

For the past week the Petrograd Military Revolutionary

Committee, aided by the rank and file of the Railway Workers, had seized control of the Nikolai Railroad, and hurled trainload after trainload of sailors and Red Guards southwest ... We were provided with passes from Smolny, without which no one could leave the capital ... When the train backed into the station, a mob of shabby soldiers, all carrying huge sacks of eatables, stormed the doors, smashed the windows, and poured into all the compartments, filling up the aisles and even climbing onto the roof. Three of us managed to wedge our way into a compartment, but almost immediately about twenty soldiers entered ... There was room for only four people; we argued, expostulated, and the conductor joined us—but the soldiers merely laughed. Were they to bother about the comfort of a lot of *boorzhui* (bourgeois)? We produced the passes from Smolny; instantly the soldiers changed their attitude. . . .

About seven o'clock in the evening we drew out of the station, an immense long train drawn by a weak little locomotive burning wood, and stumbled along slowly, with many stops. The soldiers on the roof kicked with their heels and sang whining peasant songs; and in the corridor, so jammed that it was impossible to pass, violent political debates raged all night long. Occasionally the conductor came through, as a matter of habit, looking for tickets. He found very few except ours, and after a half hour of futile wrangling lifted his arms despairingly and withdrew. The atmosphere was stifling, full of smoke and foul odors; if it hadn't been for the broken windows we would doubtless have smothered during the night.

In the morning hours, we looked out upon a snowy world. It was bitter cold. About noon a peasant woman got on with a basketful of bread chunks and a great can of lukewarm coffee substitute. From then on until dark there was nothing but the packed train, jolting and stopping, and occasional stations where a ravenous mob swooped down on the scantily furnished buffet and swept it clean. . . .

The station at Moscow was deserted. Not a cab in sight.

A few blocks down the street, however, we woke up a grotesquely padded *izvostchik* [coachman] asleep upright on the box of his little sleigh. "How much to the center of the town?"

He scratched his head. "The gentlemen won't be able to find a room in any hotel," he said. "But I'll take you around for a hundred rubles . . ." Before the Revolution it cost *two!* We objected, but he simply shrugged his shoulders. "It takes a good deal of courage to drive a sleigh nowadays," he went on. We could not beat him down below fifty . . . As we sped along the silent, snowy half-lighted streets, he recounted his adventures during the six days' fighting. "Driving along, or waiting for a fare on the corner," he said, "all of a sudden *pooff!* a cannon ball exploding here, *pooff!* a cannon ball there, *ratt-ratt!* a machine gun . . . I gallop, the devils shooting all around. I get a nice quiet street and stop, doze a little, *pooff!* another cannon ball, *ratt-ratt* . . . Devils! Devils! Devils! Brrr!"

In the center of the town the snow-piled streets were quiet with the stillness of convalescence. Only a few arc lights were burning, only a few pedestrians hurried along the sidewalks. An icy wind blew from the great plain, cutting to the bone. At the first hotel we entered an office illuminated by two candles.

"Yes, we have some very comfortable rooms, but all the windows are shot out. If the gentleman does not mind a little fresh air. . . ."

Down the Tverskaya the shopwindows were broken, and there were shell holes and torn up paving stones in the street. Hotel after hotel, all full, or the proprietors still so frightened that all they could say was, "No, no, there is no room! There is no room!" On the main streets, where the great banking houses and mercantile houses lay, the Bolshevik artillery had been indiscriminately effective. As one Soviet official told me, "Whenever we didn't know just where the *yunkers* and White Guards were we bombarded their pocketbooks. . . ."

251

At the big Hotel National they finally took us in; for we were foreigners, and the Military Revolutionary Committee had promised to protect the dwellings of foreigners ... On the top floor the manager showed us where shrapnel had shattered several windows. "The animals!" said he, shaking his fist at imaginary Bolsheviks. "But wait! Their time will come; in just a few days now their ridiculous Government will fall, and then we shall make them suffer!"

We dined at a vegetarian restaurant with the enticing name, "I Eat Nobody," and Tolstoy's picture prominent on the walls, and then sallied out into the streets.

The headquarters of the Moscow Soviet was in the palace of the former Governor General, an imposing white building fronting Skobeliev Square. Red Guards stood sentry at the door. At the head of the wide, formal stairway, whose walls were plastered with announcements of committee meetings and addresses of political parties, we passed through a series of lofty anterooms, hung with red-shrouded pictures in gold frames, to the splendid state salon, with its magnificent crystal lusters and gilded cornices. A low-voiced hum of talk, underlaid with the whirring bass of a score of sewing machines, filled the place. Huge bolts of red and black cloth were unrolled, serpentining across the parqueted floor and over tables, at which sat half a hundred women, cutting and sewing streamers and banners for the Funeral of the Revolutionary Dead. The faces of these women were roughened and scarred with life at its most difficult; they worked now sternly, many of them with eyes red from weeping ... The losses of the Red Army had been heavy.

At a desk in one corner was Rogov, an intelligent, bearded man with glasses, wearing the black blouse of a worker. He invited us to march with the Central Executive Committee in the funeral procession next morning. ...

Late in the night we went through the empty streets and under the Iberian Gate to the great Red Square in front of the Kremlin. The church of Vasili Blazheny loomed fantastic, its bright-colored, convoluted and blazoned cupolas vague in the darkness. There was no sign of any damage ... Along one side of the square the dark towers and walls of the Kremlin stood up. On the high walls flickered redly the light of hidden flames; voices reached us across the immense place, and the sound of picks and shovels. We crossed over.

Mountains of dirt and rock were piled high near the base of the wall. Climbing these we looked down into two massive pits, ten or fifteen deep and fifty yards long, where hundreds of soldiers and workers were digging in the light of huge fires.

A young student spoke to us in German. "The Brotherhood Grave," he explained. "Tomorrow we shall bury here five hundred proletarians who died for the Revolution."

He took us down into the pit. In frantic haste swung the picks and shovels, and the earth mountains grew. No one spoke. Overhead the night was thick with stars, and the ancient Imperial Kremlin wall towered up immeasurably. ...

As we left, the workers in the pit, exhausted and running with sweat in spite of the cold, began to climb wearily out. Across the Red Square a dark knot of men came hurrying. They swarmed into the pits, picked up the tools and began digging, digging, without a word. ...

So, all the long night volunteers of the People relieved each other, never halting in their driving speed, and the cold light of the dawn laid bare the great Square, white with snow, and the yawning brown pits of the Brotherhood Grave, quite finished.

We rose before sunrise, and hurried through the dark streets to Skobeliev Square. In all the great city not a human being could be seen; but there was a faint sound of stirring, far and near, like a deep wind coming. In the pale half light a little group of men and women were gathered before the Soviet headquarters, with a sheaf of gold-lettered red banners—the Central Executive Committee of the Moscow Soviet. It grew light. From afar the vague stirring sound deepened and became louder, a steady and tremendous bass. The city was rising. We set out down the Tverskaya, the banners flapping overhead. The little street chapels along our way were locked and dark, as was the Chapel of the Iberian Virgin, which each new tsar used to visit before he went to the Kremlin to crown himself, and which, day or night, was always open and crowded, and brilliant with the candles of the devout gleaming on the gold and silver and jewels of the icons. Now, for the first time since Napoleon was in Moscow, they say, the candles were out. . . .

Also the shops were closed, and the propertied classes stayed at home—but for other reasons. This was the Day of the People, the rumor of whose coming was thunderous as surf. . . .

Already through the Iberian Gate a human river was flowing, and the vast Red Square was spotted with people, thousands of them. I remarked that as the throng passed the Iberian Chapel, where always before the passer-by had crossed himself, they did not seem to notice it. . . .

We forced our way through the dense mass packed near the Kremlin wall, and stood upon one of the dirt mountains. Already several men were there. . . .

Through all the streets to the Red Square the torrents of people poured, thousands upon thousands of them, all with the look of the poor and the toiling. A military band came marching up, playing the *Internationale,* and spontaneously the song caught and spread like wind ripples on a sea, slow and solemn. . . .

A bitter wind swept the Square, lifting the banners. Now from the far quarters of the city the workers of the different factories were arriving, with their dead. They could be seen coming through the Gate, the blare of their banners, and the dull red—like blood—of the coffins they carried. These were crude boxes, made of unplaned wood and daubed with crimson, borne high on the shoulders of rough men who marched with tears streaming down their faces, and followed by women who sobbed and screamed, or walked stiffly, with white, dead faces. Some of the coffins were open, the lid carried behind them; others were covered with gilded or silvered cloth, or had a soldier's hat nailed on the top. There were many wreaths of artificial flowers. . . .

Through an irregular lane that opened and closed again the procession slowly moved toward us. Now through the Gate was flowing an endless stream of banners, all shades of red, with silver and gold lettering, knots of crepe hanging from the top—and some anarchist flags, black with white letters. The band was playing the Revolutionary Funeral March, and against the immense singing of the mass of people, standing uncovered, the paraders sang hoarsely, choked with sobs. . . .

Between the factory workers came companies of soldiers with their coffins, too, and squadrons of cavalry, riding at salute, and artillery batteries, the cannon wound with red and black—forever, it seemed. . . .

Slowly the marchers came with their coffins to the entrance of the grave, and the bearers clambered up with their burdens and went down into the pit. Many of them were women—squat, strong proletarian women. Behind the dead came other women—women young and broken, or old, wrinkled women making noises like hurt animals, who tried to follow their sons and husbands into the Brotherhood Grave, and shrieked when compassionate hands restrained them. The poor love each other so!

All the long day the funeral procession passed, coming in by the Iberian Gate and leaving the Square by way of the Nikolskaya, a river of red banners, bearing words of hope and brotherhood and stupendous prophecies, against a background of fifty thousand people—under the eyes of the world's workers and their descendants forever. . . .

One by one the five hundred coffins were laid in the pits. Dusk fell, and still the banners came drooping and fluttering, the band played the Funeral March, and the huge assemblage chanted. In the leafless branches of the trees above the grave the wreaths were hung, like strange, multicolored blossoms. Two hundred men began to shovel in the dirt. It rained dully down upon the coffins with a thudding sound, audible beneath the singing. . . .

The lights came out. The last banners passed, and the last moaning women, looking back with awful intensity as they went. Slowly from the great Square ebbed the proletarian tide. . . .

I suddenly realized that the devout Russian people no longer needed priests to pray them into heaven. On earth they were building a kingdom more bright than any heaven had to offer, and for which it was a glory to die. . . .

1919

Glossary

Alexander Kerensky, prime minister of the counterrevolutionary provisional government; *Lavr Kornilov,* counterrevolutionary military commander under Kerensky; the city *Duma* or municipal council; *Ataman Kaledin,* military leader of the counterrevolutionary Cossack groups; *Cadets,* the abbreviated name of the bourgeois Constitutional Democrats who formed the first Russian provisional government in 1917; *Smolny Institute,* Bolshevik headquarters, formerly a school for the daughters of the Russian nobility; *Committee for Salvation,* a counterrevolutionary group; *Congress of Soviets,* the representative body of Workers' and Soldiers' Deputies; *Tsik,* initials of the Central Executive Committee of the All-Russian Soviets; *Red Guards,* armed factory workers; *Yunkers,* student officers who formed part of the armed counterrevolutionary forces; *White Guards,* armed counterrevolutionaries led by tsarist officers.

A Hymn to Manhattan

O let some young Timotheus sweep his lyre
Hymning New York. Lo! Every tower and spire
Puts on immortal fire.
This city, which ye scorn
For her rude sprawling limbs, her strength unshorn—
Hands blunt from grasping, Titan-like, at Heaven,
Is a world-wonder, vaulting all the Seven!
Europe? Here's all of Europe in one place;
Beauty unconscious, yes, and even grace.
Rome? Here all that Rome was, and is not;
Here Babylon—and Babylon's forgot.
Golden Byzantium, drunk with pride and sin,
Carthage, that flickered out where we begin . . .
London? A swill of mud in Shakespeare's time;
Ten Troys lie tombed in centuries of grime!
Who'd not have lived in Athens at her prime,
Or helped to raise the mighty walls of Rome?
See, blind men! Walls rise all about you here at home!
Who would not hear once more
That oceanic roar
"Ave! Ave Imperator!"
With which an army its Augustus greets?
Hark! There's an army roaring in the streets!
This spawning filth, these monuments uncouth,
Are but her wild, ungovernable youth.
But the skyscrapers, dwarfing earthly things—
Ah, that is how she sings!
Wake to the vision shining in the sun;
Earth's ancient, conquering races rolled in one,
A world beginning—*and yet nothing done!*   1913

Noon

Swirl and pass of listless eyes,
  Thronging up the breathless street;
Clang and roar of iron wheels
  In the midday heat.

Nervous noon-tide whistles shrill,
  Stabbing through the sullen air;
Hoarse, defiant, like a voice
  Dauntless in despair.

See! Against the blinding sky,
  High above the steel-shod hoofs,
Moving wisps of coloring
  On the factory roofs.

Waving arms and streaming hair,
  Joyous-leaping, hand in hand,
Sweat-shop girls with lifted face
  Dance a saraband.

Not a tap of rhythmic feet,
  Not a shred of melody,
Lilting thinly on the height,
  Flutters down to me.

Whirling dust of city streets,
  Recklessly they laugh on high;
Tiny motes across the sun
  Dancing in the sky!

1913

April

April!
Bird-notes in a gust of rain,
Silver trumpets shivering
Spring's steel armament again—
Hear the world's blood mount and sing
Sweetly on the flowery plain!

April!
Withers all the grass and dies,
Here the flowers dull and fade—
How shall cities know her guise?
See this new-met man and maid
Tremble at each other's eyes!

1913

Deep-Water Song

The bounding deck beneath me,
  The rocking sky o'erhead,
White, flying spume that whips her boom,
  And all her canvas spread.

Her topmast rakes the zenith,
  Where planets shoal and spawn,
And to her stride God opens wide
  The storm-red gates of dawn!

Then walk her down to Rio,
  Roll her 'cross the line;
China Joe's a-tendin' door
  Down to Number Nine.
Deep they lie in every sea,
  Land's End to the Horn—
For every sailorman that dies
  A sailorman is born.

Along the battered sea-wall,
  Our women in the rain
Full wearily have scanned the sea
  That brings us not again.

Oh, I'll come home, my dearie—
  Aye, one day I'll come home,
With heaped-up hold of Spanish gold
  And opals of spun foam.

Then walk her down to Frisco,
Lay her for Hong-Kong;
Reeling down the water-front
Seven hundred strong.
Deep they lie in every sea,
Land's End to the Horn—
For every sailorman that dies
A sailorman is born.

Tall, languid palms that glimmer,
Blossoms beyond belief,
Sea-gods at play in shouting spray
On sun-splashed coral reef.

O falling star at twilight,
O questing sail unfurled,
Through unknown seas I follow these
Down-hill across the world.

Then walk her down to Sydney,
Through to Singapore;
Dutch Marie and Ysobel
Waitin' on the shore.
Deep they lie in every sea,
Land's End to the Horn—
For every sailorman that dies
A sailorman is born.

1913

Winter Night

High hangs the hollow, ringing shield of heaven,
Embossed with stars. The thin air wounds like steel,
Stark and resilient as a Spanish blade.
Sharp snaps the rigid lake's mysterious ice,
And the prim, starchy twigs of naked trees
Crackle metallic in an unfelt wind.
A light-poised Damoclean scimitar
The faintly damascened pale moon. Benumbed
Shrinks the racked earth gripped in the hand of Cold.
O hark! Swift, anvil-ringing iron hoofs
Drum down the boreal interstellar space:
The Blue Knight rides, spurring his snorting stallion
Out of the dark side of the frozen moon—
Eyes crueler than a beryl-sheathed crevasse,
Breath like the chilly fog of polar seas,
Glaciers for armor on his breast and thighs,
A polished Alp for helmet, and for plume
The league-long Northern Lights behind him floating,
Wave on wave of prismatic blazoning,
Glorious up the sky!

The Blue Knight rides
With his moon-shimmering, star-tipped lance at rest,
Drives at the world—Crash! and the brittle globe
Bursts like a crystal goblet—shivering, falling,
Shivers, splinters bristling, tinkling, jarring,
Jingling in fading dissonance down the void—
Jangling down the unplumbed void forever.... 1914

Pygmalion

Pygmalion, Pygmalion, Pygmalion–
A mountain meadow loved Pygmalion.
Where a great shining rock like a fallen shield
Lay heavily in tall grass, he rested once.
Long did it hold the pulsing warmth of his body.
And the apple-tree that shaded him, remembered him;
Grass that was new-born trembled under his feet–
Old withered grass felt green beneath his feet–
And the wide view that sank like sleep after pain
Miles over toppling hills to the wide, still river,
Robed itself in opal, golden and haze for him.

While the sun's shadow stood between light and light
He came, paused and was gone. Though never, never
In the world's old contentment had there passed
Before him any human in this place,
Yet lonely were the rock, the tree, the grass.
Longing of the starved heart for a lover gone,
When all is as before, and yet how empty!

White moved his body, crushing the ferns in the valley,
And his happy singing died along far roads;
But love followed after him–flickered across his sleep,
Breathed pride into his walk, power into his hand,
Sweet restlessness into his quiet thought–
Till he who had needed life now needed more;
And so at last he came to the hills again.

Pygmalion, Pygmalion, Pygmalion—
He said in his pride "Thou art wild, and without life!"
Never feeling the warm dispersed quiet of earth,
Or the slow stupendous heart-beat that hills have.

Pygmalion, Pygmalion, Pygmalion—
He wrenched the shining rock from the meadow's breast,
And out of it shaped the lovely, almost-breathing
Form of his dream of his love of the world's women.
Slim and white was she, whimsical, full of caprice;
Bright sharp in sunlight, languid in shadow of cloud,
Pale in the dawn, and flushed at the end of day.
Staring, he felt of a sudden the quick, fierce urge
Of the will of the grass, and the rock, and the flowering tree;
Knew himself weak and unfulfilled without her—
Knew that he bore his own doom in his breast—
Slave of a stone, unmoving, cold to his touch,
Loving in a stone's way, loving but thrilling never.

In smothering summer silence, pricked with crickets,
Still fell the smiting hammer; happy and loud
Swelled the full-throated song of the adult grass . . .
Full-breasted drooped the tree, heavy with apples . . .
A wind worn lean from leap-frog over the mountains
Spurted the stiff faun-hair of him—whipped desire,
And a bird song "Faint-faint-faint with love-love-love!"

Blind he stood, while the great sun blundered down
Through planets strung like beads on careless orbits;
Blind to the view that sank like sleep after love,
Miles over blazoned hills to the brazen river,
Ceaselessly changing, color and form and line,
Pomp, blaze, pageantry new to the world's delight . . .

Hot moist hands on the glittering flanks, and eager
Hands following the chill hips, the icy breasts—
Lithe, radiant, belly to swelling stone—

"Galatea!"–blast of whispering flame his throat–
"Galatea! Galatea!"–his entrails molten fire–
"Galatea! Galatea! Galatea!"–mouth to mouth . . .

Light shadows of driven clouds on a summer lake–
Ripples on still ponds, winds that ruffle and pass–
Happy young grass rising to drink the rain–
So Galatea under his kisses stirred;
Like a white moth alighted breath on her lips,
Like a blue rent in a storm-sky opened her eyes,
Sweetly the new blood leaped and sang in her veins,
Dumbly, blindly her hands, breast, mouth sought his . . .

Pygmalion, Pygmalion, Pygmalion–
Rock is she still, and her heart is the hill's heart,
Full of all things beside him–full of wind and bees
And the long falling miles and miles of air.
Despair and gnawing are on him, and he knows her
Unattainable who is born of will and hill–
Far-bright as a plunging full-sailed ship that seems
Hull-down to be set immutable in sea. . . .

Hospital Notes*

COMING OUT OF ETHER

Swish-swish-flash by the spokes of the Wheel of Pain;
Dizzily runs the whining rim.
Way down in the cool dark is slow-revolving sleep,
But I hang heavily writhing in hot chains
High in the crimson stillness of my body,
And the swish-swish of the spokes of the Wheel of Pain.

CLINIC

Square white cells, all in a row, with ground-glass windows;
Tubes treasuring sacraments of suffering, rubber pipes,
        apparatus;
Walls maculate with old yellow and brown....

Out of a mass of human flesh, hairy and dull,
Slim shining steel grows, dripping slow pale thick drops,
And regularly, like distant whistles in a fog, groaning....

Young internes, following the great surgeon like chicks a hen,
Crowd in as he pokes, wrenches, and dictates over his
        shoulder,
And hurries on, deaf to the shuddering spirit, rapt in a
        dream of machinery.

1917

* Written while Reed was in Johns Hopkins Hospital where he
had an infected kidney removed.—*Ed.*

Fog

Death comes like this, I know—
Snow-soft and gently cold;
Impalpable battalions of thin mist,
Light-quenching and sound-smothering and slow.

Slack as a wind-spilled sail
The spent world flaps in space—
Day's but a grayer night, and the old sun
Up the blind sky goes heavily and pale.

Out of all circumstance
I drift or seem to drift
In a vague vapor-world that clings and veils
Great trees arow like kneeling elephants.

How vast your voice is grown
That was so silver-soft;
Dim dies the candle-glory of your face—
Though we go hand in hand, I am alone.

Now Love and all the warm
Pageant of livingness
Trouble my quiet like forgotten dreams
Of ancient thunder on the hills of storm.

Aforetime I have kissed
The feet of many gods;
But in this empty place there is no god
Save only I, a naked egoist.

How loud, how terribly
Aflame are lights and sounds!
And yet I know beyond the fog is naught
But lonely bells across gray wastes of sea...

1919

A Letter to Louise*

Rainy rush of bird-song
Apple-blossom smoke
Thin bells water-falling sound
Wind-rust on the silver pond
Furry starring willow-wand
Wan new grasses walking round
Blue bird in the oak
Woven in my word-song

White and slim my lover
Birch-tree in the shade
Mountain pools her fearless eyes
Innocent all-answering
Were I blinded to the Spring
Happy thrill would in me rise
Smiling half afraid
At the nearness of her

All my weak endeavor
Lay I at her feet
Like a moth from oversea
Let my longing lightly rest
On her flower petal breast
Till the red dawn set me free
To be with my sweet
Ever and forever . . .

1919 (Unpublished)

* Louise Bryant, Reed's wife.–*Ed.*

SOURCES OF SELECTIONS

"War in Paterson," *Masses,* June, 1913.

Insurgent Mexico, New York, D. Appleton & Co., 1914.

"The Traders' War," *Masses,* September, 1914.

"With the Allies," *Metropolitan,* December, 1914.

"The Colorado War," *Metropolitan,* July, 1914.

"The Cook and the Captain Bold," *Metropolitan,* November, 1914.

The War in Eastern Europe, New York, Charles Scribner's Sons, 1916.

"Sold Out" (original title "Roosevelt Sold Them Out"), *Masses,* August, 1916.

"This Unpopular War," *Seven Arts,* August, 1917.

"The I.W.W. in Court" (original title "The Social Revolution in Court"), *Liberator,* September, 1918.

"With Gene Debs on the Fourth," *Liberator,* September, 1918.

"The Peace That Passeth Understanding," *Liberator,* March, 1919.

Ten Days That Shook the World, New York, Boni & Liveright, 1919; New York, International Publishers, 1926; New York, Modern Library, 1935.

"A Hymn to Manhattan," *American Magazine,* February, 1913. (Reprinted in *Tamburlaine,* Riverside, Conn., Frederick C. Bursch, 1917.)

"Noon," *Collier's,* July 26, 1913.

"April," *American Magazine,* April, 1913. (Reprinted in *Tamburlaine.*)

"Deep-Water Song," *Century Magazine,* March, 1913. (Reprinted in *Tamburlaine.*)